RAW COURAGE

This Book is Dedicated to Mothers
who Tragically Lost their Sons in Wars

RAW
COURAGE

The Extraordinary and Tragic Story
of Four RAF Brothers in Arms

Norman Franks
and
Simon Muggleton

Grub Street • London

Published by
Grub Street
4 Rainham Close
London
SW11 6SS

Copyright © Grub Street 2011
Copyright text © Norman Franks and Simon Muggleton 2011

British Library Cataloguing in Publication Data
Franks, Norman L. R.
  Raw courage : the extraordinary and tragic story of four
  RAF brothers in arms.
  1. Raw, John. 2. Raw, Peter. 3. Raw, Tony. 4. Raw, Michael.
  5. Great Britain. Royal Air Force—Biography. 6. Air
  pilots, Military—Great Britain—Biography. 7. Air
  pilots, Military—Great Britain—Correspondence. 8. World
  War, 1939-1945—Casualties—Great Britain—Biography.
  9. Brothers—Great Britain—Biography.
  I. Title II. Muggleton, Simon.

ISBN-13: 9781908117137

Cover design by Sarah Driver
Edited by Sophie Campbell
Formatted by Sarah Driver

Printed and bound by MPG Ltd, Cornwall

Grub Street Publishing only uses
FSC (Forest Stewardship Council) paper for its books.

CONTENTS

Acknowledgements   6

Preface by Simon Muggleton   7

Prologue –   The Raw Family   10

Chapter 1   John   19

Chapter 2   Peter   35

Chapter 3   Fighter Pilot   54

Chapter 4   War over France   70

Chapter 5   Rest and Return (1)   88

Chapter 6   Tony   100

Chapter 7   First Tour   113

Chapter 8   Rest and Return (2)   133

Chapter 9   Missing; and Bruce Cole   149

Chapter 10   Michael   161

Chapter 11   Flying   178

Appendices A-V Extracts from Letters, Telegrams   200

Index   222

ACKNOWLEDGEMENTS

Help and valuable assistance has been provided by many people. Martin Smith, who did a wonderful job in finding and preserving the letters, and passing them on. Mr A J Rogers, former headmaster (1995) of Wellington School; Juliet Handley, development officer at Wellington School; the late Roland Beamont CBE DSO* DFC*; Chris Goss; Andy Thomas; Andy Saunders; Graham Day and Anna Gibbs of the Air Historical Branch; Gordon Leith of the RAF Museum; Paul Baillie, researcher; Ealing Library; Wellington School, Squadron Leader Jeff Hesketh FRIN RAF, ex-aircrew, Battle of Britain Memorial Flight; Di Holland, BBMF admin support; Dave Bell, tech support officer, RAF Cranwell; Alycia Bennett, RAF Manning Records at RAF Cranwell; the 609 Squadron Association; Dr Jonathan Oates, archivist, Ealing Public Library; Alfie Windsor, HMS *Conway* Old Comrades Assn; Theresa Thom, librarian, Grays Inn, London; Miss Justine Taylor, archivist, Honourable Artillery Company Museum, City of London; Michael Motum, archivist, Rifles/Somerset Light Infantry Museum, Somerset; Sue Chandler, Richard Epsley, Melanie Oelgeschlager, National Maritime Museum, Greenwich; Rosanna Wilkinson, photographic section, Imperial War Museum, London; Commonwealth War Graves Commission; Judith Harrison, British Library Newspapers; Paloma Kubiak, *Ealing and Acton Gazette*; David Erskine-Hill, Dix Noonen Webb Auctions, London; Edward Raw, barrister, Tanfield Chambers, London; Thibault Williams and Martin Flash, Otters Swimming Club, London; Richard Foster for the photo of HMS *Lysander*; Perry King, Creffield Road Residents Assn, Ealing.

Not forgetting our wives, Heather and Jill, who once more have coped with the mounds of paper around the house!

PREFACE

I always enjoy watching the BBC's Antiques Roadshow, the TV programme where members of the public bring along a variety of treasures to show to the antique experts. The specialists usually ask how the item was acquired, and quite often the owner will explain that either it had been handed down through the generations or occasionally that they purchased the item from a jumble or car boot sale. There are also programmes which raise awareness of the value of antiques or vintage collectables so it is now much more unlikely that anyone can discover a hidden 'gem' in a junk shop, jumble sale, or anywhere else for that matter.

Having said all that, I have been extremely fortunate in acquiring a collection of paperwork and letters in that way from a friend and fellow aviation collector, Andy Saunders, who occasionally organises 'aerojumble sales'. Another aviation contact of his is Martin Smith, who had originally discovered the papers and letters which form the basis of this book when he wandered into a south London bric-a-brac shop during his lunch hour. He discovered, on top of a pile of other bits and pieces, a leather suitcase which contained the documents. After a swift read of some of the contents, Martin quickly realised that the papers gave a vivid insight into the lives of a middle-class family during World War II. The letters were written by four sons, three of whom served in the Royal Air Force during the war, while the fourth, still at school, would later fly with the peacetime RAF. Most were written to their mother, who lived in west London, with her return letters to her sons. Martin passed his find onto Andy, knowing he would be able to take the RAF research further.

Andy called me to let me know about this find, which comprised bundles of private and official letters from and about four pilots. He explained that there were also Air Ministry papers, telegrams, newspaper clippings, and diaries, along with some photographs, mementos and badges.

Andy, who is also an aviation author of several books and articles, being much involved in a number of other projects, including television programmes, and helping to excavate crashed World War II aeroplanes, concluded that I might be able to give more time to this research than he could. When he added that there was a fighter pilot amongst the four sons, I needed no further encouragement.

Amongst the handwritten letters were some with embossed letter headings from such places as the officers' mess at RAF Tangmere, and RAF Manston. To some this might have looked like a typical collection from a house clearance, but to me it looked like a really interesting project to pursue! It took a while to sort through the mountain of documents, etc, but when that was accomplished, I was able to begin reading the correspondence in earnest. The letters ran from 1938 until 1958 and were written between a mother, Mrs Irene Raw, who lived in Ealing, and her three grown-up sons, John, Peter and Anthony. The fourth and youngest son Robert, but known as Michael, was a boarder at Wellington School, in Somerset, and later an RAF pilot after the war. Also included in the pile of letters were some exchanged between Michael (Mike) and another pilot, Squadron Leader Bruce Cole DFC AFC, who turned out to be not only a friend of the family but a godfather to Michael.

Most of the letters were contained in blue envelopes but then I spotted a small white envelope. In black ink on the front of this envelope was written: 'Daddy's Obit – *The Times* 1932.' A cutting inside revealed the tragic news that the head of the Raw family, Commander Frederick Edward Raw, had died of a heart attack on 8 June of that year, whilst gardening at his Ealing home.

From that point, Mrs Raw, had of necessity, become the head of the family, not only of four boys but two daughters too, Beatrice, but known as Trixie, and Patricia, known as Pat. As I continued to read through the letters, more sad and touching news emerged of this family's misfortunes, and it is these events that are conveyed within the pages of this book.

I still wanted to know and learn more about each son, and how each had fared in the RAF, and so corresponded with squadron associations, their old school, the RAF Museum and I also visited the National Archives to check squadron records. I read everything I could find on them. It soon emerged that Anthony had been awarded the Distinguished Flying Cross in May 1942, and the Air Force Cross in December 1943. Peter too had been awarded the DFC in May 1943, while Michael had received the Air Force Cross in January 1955. These awards would have provided Mrs Raw with the possibly unique experience of attending Buckingham Palace on five separate occasions during the reign of three different monarchs, because her husband had also received the Distinguished Service Cross in World War I during his service with the Royal Navy.

In the mid 1990s I attended an auction in West Sussex and whilst there I glanced through the catalogue and to my utter amazement saw that the medals awarded to Commander Raw were also to be auctioned, together with some personal effects. There was no question of which 'lot' I would be bidding for, and was lucky enough to be successful.

That largely was the *status quo* until mid-2010, when I casually mentioned the letters and my early research of the Raw boys, to aviation historian and author, Norman Franks. We had already co-operated in two recently published books, one about a Czech World War II fighter pilot, Stanislaw Fejfar (*A Fighter Pilot's Call to Arms*, Grub Street, 2009) and Air Commodore D'Arcy Greig's own flying story from 1918-29, *My Golden Flying Years*, (Grub Street, 2010). Norman was immediately fascinated and intrigued by the family's story and suggested we try to write a book. It was he who suggested the title. Fortunately, John Davies, publisher of Grub Street, saw merit in the project which allowed Norman and I to press on.

The reader will, I hope, no doubt agree after studying the letters and our joint research, that all members of this family were full of *Raw Courage*.

Simon Muggleton,
East Sussex
April, 2011

Prologue

THE RAW FAMILY

Frederick Edward Raw was born on 26 June 1890, the son of Doctor William Edward St Michael Raw MRC, LRCP, LSA and Mrs Edith Julia Raw. Upon leaving school he began a career with the Merchant Navy, starting on HMS *Conway*, a training ship moored in the Sloyne off Rock Ferry pier, south of Birkenhead, on the River Mersey, in April 1906.

HMS *Conway* had previously been HMS *Nile*, a ninety-two-gun Second Rate Ship of the Line, which had been launched in 1830, and looked very much like a ship from Nelsonian days. Converted to screw propulsion in 1854 she was re-named the *Conway* in 1876 to become a training ship. She remained so until damaged during a refit in 1953 and finally destroyed by fire in 1956.

New boys to the training vessel were known as 'squeakers' and this started a two-year pre-sea training course for the youngsters, after which most went to sea as either apprentices to one of the merchant shipping companies, the Royal Navy as a midshipman (the lowest officer rank), or any of the many empire bodies such as the Bengal Pilot Service or the Chinese Maritime Customs.

From time to time most new boys would be mentioned in the cadet registers or term magazines for either some academic achievement or sporting merit. Young Raw was mentioned in the summer of 1906 for being a member of the 3rd XI cricket team, and also for winning several prize books for proficiency in seamanship, english literature, trigonometry, algebra and mathematics. The following year, during the Easter term, he played rugby for the 1st XV and was awarded colours. That year he excelled at many sporting events, such as the tug-of-war, inter-house cricket, and also received several prizes for academic work.

In 1908 Frederick Raw became captain of the 1st XV rugby team and head boy holding the rank of chief petty officer. He went on to win the Brocklebank

Prize (from the Merchant Navy Brocklebank Line), along with the Dufferin Prize (a naval telescope), the Langton Prize (an aneroid barometer), and the Special Sextant Prize, awarded by the White Star Line for proficiency in use of the sextant, and the Samuelson Prize for Meteorology (a chronometer).

In July of this same year he began his sea-time with the merchant marine, joining Messrs Ismay Imrie and Co (White Star Line) as an apprentice deck officer. He later joined the Royal Naval Reserve, becoming an acting sub-lieutenant on 8 October 1913, and joining an active class destroyer, HMS *Fearless* at Harwich. Acting sub-lieutenant Raw transferred to the Royal Navy on 1 February 1914 (passing his medical three weeks later) and commissioned as a full sub-lieutenant.

By this time he had met his future wife, Irene Barnard, daughter of Mr & Mrs Charles William Barnard of 'Roseleigh', Victoria Avenue, Evesham; Irene was a well known member of the Evesham Amateur Operatic Society, and was prominent in musical and dramatic circles in her Worcestershire town. Irene Barnard's full name was Alice Beatrice Irene, but she was always known by her last forename. She was nineteen years old, born 20 December 1893. Frederick and Irene were married at the Parish Church of All Saints in Evesham, on 11 August 1913, at which time their address is referred to as a maisonette, in Melling Road, Southport, Lancashire.

On 17 March 1914 Sub-lieutenant Raw joined HMS *Lysander*, a destroyer of the Lafrorey Class, originally launched in September 1913 as HMS *Ulysses*. On 24 June 1914 he was promoted to acting lieutenant. Two months later Britain and her empire were at war with Germany, declared on 4 August.

The very next day, *Lysander* was part of a task force that was in action with the SMS *Königen Luise*, a steamer of the Hamburg-America Line now renamed by the German navy, *Hilfstrueminendampfer B*, to be used as an auxiliary minelayer. The German imperial navy fully expected some units of the Royal Navy to head for the English Channel or North Sea via the Thames estuary. On the evening of the 4th, the minelayer, armed with 180 mines, steamed out of Emden cunningly disguised as a Great Eastern Railway ferry (the hull was painted black with a yellow band combined with buff-coloured funnels with black tops) in order to lay mines at the mouth of the Thames. She steamed off without her intended armament of two 88mm guns which had not arrived in time to be taken aboard and mounted.

British fishermen in the area reported that a 'ferry' had been seen dropping large objects over the side and HMS *Amphion*, an action-class scout cruiser, along with a number of destroyers, were sent to investigate. At 10.25 am, the *Hilfstrueminendampfer B* was sighted and challenged by *Amphion* firing the first naval rounds of World War 1. The captain of the minelayer, Kommandeur Biermann, knew the game was up and headed full steam for the nearest friendly port, with the Royal Navy giving chase. By 12.22 Biermann realised it was futile to continue and decided to 'scupper' his vessel, thus becoming the first German naval loss of the war. Out of the 100 German crew aboard, forty-six were rescued by the Royal Navy, who also had to rescue the entire crew of *Amphion*, which had unluckily struck one, and then a second of the mines laid earlier. Therefore naval honours were even on the first day of the war. Some 155 British seamen were lost plus eighteen German survivors the British cruiser had rescued.

Three weeks later, HMS *Lysander* was again in action with the enemy, this time off the Heligoland Bight, attacking some German patrol boats off the north-west German coast. The Royal Navy deployed five battle cruisers, eight light cruisers, thirty-two destroyers and eight submarines, against sixteen German light cruisers, twelve minesweepers and nineteen torpedo boats. In the battle the German navy lost three light cruisers, a destroyer and two torpedo boats with a total of 712 sailors killed. The British only lost one light cruiser, with three destroyers damaged, losing thirty-five men. This was hailed as a great victory and the returning ships were greeted by cheering crowds as they entered port.

HMS *Lysander* was also part of the Third Destroyer Flotilla at the Battle of Dogger Bank on 24 January 1915. Decoded radio intercepts from the German fleet gave the British navy an early warning that they were headed for a rendezvous at Dogger Bank, in the North Sea, in order to carry out a raid. The British ships eventually found the enemy fleet and engaged them, sinking SMS *Blücher*, and chasing the rest back to their home port. Yet again this was regarded as a British naval victory and once more ships returned to cheering crowds upon their return.

Raw's promotion to full lieutenant came in February 1915; obviously his ability during the early action of the war had shone through. However, this was somewhat marred a year later, in February 1916, when *Lysander* was run aground. In the subsequent Court of Enquiry, Raw and his captain, Commander G W Taylor 'incurred the displeasure' of their lordships at the Admiralty, but they survived any serious blot to their careers.

Lysander was part of the 'Harwich Force' that sailed to join the Grand Fleet at the Battle of Jutland on the evening of 31 May/1 June 1916. Jutland is a peninsular situated between the North Sea and the Kattegat Sea, bordering Denmark, Sweden, and a small part of Germany's northern coast. 151 RN ships faced 103 vessels of the Imperial German Navy. Tactically the battle proved indecisive and although the British lost fourteen ships against the loss of eleven German, strategically it was a massive defeat for Germany. Britain maintained an effective blockade of Germany from then on and the German navy never set sail again in such numbers. In December 1920 the *London Gazette* published a notice by the Admiralty offering prize bounty money for all the participants of the Battle of Jutland, although it is not known if Commander Raw had a share.

Raw took a navigation course later in June 1916 and his work gained merit from Commander Taylor, who, after two years under his command, thought Raw had shown, 'great zeal in his navigational duties which he had performed most carefully'.

In February 1917 Raw took command of P50, operating with the Dover Patrol under the aegis of the 6th Destroyer Flotilla. The Dover Patrol had been set up on the eve of WW1, in July 1914, initially with twelve Tribal Class destroyers, to carry out anti-submarine patrols. Its primary function was to prevent German submarines from accessing the English Channel in order to sink any ships of the line or merchant shipping carrying provisions either to England or over to France. Later, larger RN ships were also used. During the war not a single ship sailing to or from France was lost to enemy action due to the vigilance of the patrol.

P-boats had been introduced in 1915 and carried one four-inch gun, one two-pounder, and two torpedo tubes. Generally of over 600 tons they were used for anti-submarine work, and because they sat low in the water, they were not easily seen in mist or at dawn. P-boats sank four submarines in 1917 and that July P50 attacked a submarine in the Channel, for which Raw received a 'Mention in Despatches'. Lieutenant Raw continued to receive good commendations about his work, such as one from a Captain Withers who wrote of him: 'A most promising officer who carries out his duties with zeal and ability.' Consequently Raw was awarded a Distinguished Service Cross, for 'services in the Destroyer and TB Flotilla during period ending 31/12/17'.

The announcement of his DSC appeared in the *London Gazette* on 8 March 1918. Of interest is that the actual recommendation for awards to men of the Dover destroyers, was for Lieutenant Raw to again be 'Mentioned in Despatches', but Vice-Admiral Bacon wanted two names changed, so Raw had his DSC approved, while the other lieutenant, recommended for a DSC, was relegated to a 'Mention'.

Meantime, he and Irene had been blessed with their first son, John Frederick, born on 22 September 1916, at the family home, now situated at 66 Gains Road,

Southsea, Portsmouth. A second son, Peter Edward, was born on 15 June 1919, while son number three entered this world on 9 February 1922, Anthony William. In addition to the three boys, two daughters had also arrived – Lillian Beatrix, but known as Trixie, who was also born in Southsea, and received her education at the Royal Naval College at Twickenham, Middlesex, later to become a member of the St John's Ambulance Service – and Patricia, adopted by Mr and Mrs Raw, known as Pat by the family.

Frederick Raw continued his war service aboard the *Orestes*, a Moon Class destroyer, from 4 April 1918, and then the *Tobago*, an S-type, 905-ton destroyer, in September 1918. At the beginning of 1919, after being given command of patrol craft P68 (a Q-ship) his request to remain in the navy was approved, with further recommendations from Captain Godfrey. Godfrey also noted: 'A most excellent and dependable officer of tact, good sense, initiative, a good seaman, quick and thinks ahead.' However, his request was not immediately granted or approved. In 1919-22 he served with P52, and was known as an able and trustworthy officer.

This book has a great number of letters to and from Mrs Raw by her sons, but only one known letter from Frederick Raw survives and is dated 16 February 1919 while in command of P52. From its introduction, his wife Irene was known at this time as Trixie, the name that was later adopted by the Raw's eldest daughter. The period-piece letter tells of his tortuous journey on a non-too-reliable motor cycle from Evesham, where he had been on leave with his wife and children:

'My darling Trixie,

'I am sorry I have not written earlier today but I have been very busy picking up the threads of my arduous duties and cleaning off the accumulation of correspondence. As we go out tomorrow I had to start in today. Well darling, I started off in fine style yesterday, got to Broadway in a little over ten minutes, started up the big long hill and about 200 yards up my belt broke or rather the bike's. Fortunately a man was walking up and he helped me push it to the top – some hill! When I got up there I put the spare belt on which was rather tight, and that broke about nine miles away from Evesham. The joining clip jumped off into a field and I could not find it. So there I was, six miles from Stow-on-the-Wold, and helpless. I tried lashing the belt together with wire and got on another mile then that broke. Well, after a bit another bike came along and gave me a tow into Moreton [-in-the-Marsh] where I bought another belt and off I went again.

'I got on famously until two-and-a-half miles beyond Farringdon, the petrol pipe started to leak furiously, or rather had leaked, and the tank was nearly empty! I patched it up with a tyre patch and half insulating tape, cadged petrol from a car and got on to Wantage, forty-five-and-a-half miles from Evesham, at 3.30 pm. I did not stop there except to fill right up with petrol, meaning to have tea in Newbury sixteen miles further on. A short while later I came to such a great hill, I had to push the bike up it, with no help from journeying pedestrians. I had done quite a lot of pushing over the mountains and was pretty tired, when at last I got to the top.

'I sat down for a rest and lit my pipe and studied the map. I didn't know what time I sat down but I awoke at 6.50 pm feeling very cold and stiff to see a misty moon looking at me and I wondered where the Dickens I was and why! Then it all came back to me. I was due in Portsmouth at three, or thereabouts, so I started the old bus and rode on to Great Shefford, over fifty miles from Evesham, and finally arrived there about seven.

'Well, I was hungry and cold and saw it would be an all-night job so went into the Swan Hotel, a little country pub, and had four poached eggs on hot toast, soaked in real butter, and some home-made blackberry and damson jam, four cups of tea and two pints of ale, my first real meal since breakfast. This tea cost three-bob and the beer ½d, not bad was it? The old lady had a son in the navy and I told her I was on the way back to my ship, which won her heart. I left there at 8 pm, sixty miles to go with a leaking petrol pipe, and in the dark. I had a very good run to Newbury and went straight on but on the other side I met such a colossal hill that I decided to try for more level country as I did not like pushing the bike for miles of mountains, so I returned to Newbury and went out along the Reading road, which the map showed as level.

'I lost my way in the dark several times as I could not read the sign posts and did not want to stop to look at each one. I took the wrong road out of Winchester and found myself at Allbrook near Eastleigh at 1 am and I again missed the road in Fareham as it did not go as shown on my map. I arrived at Excellent Steps at 3 am – my 'midnight'! Aching all over, sleepy, hungry, drained, battered about, love sick, cold, dirty and fed up. I had a jolly good meal and turned in.

'Well, I must have done 155 miles altogether and the last ninety took seven hours, at night. I didn't think that at all bad, all my troubles came in the first part of the voyage. I must have a good rest before I venture back!

'Well, darling, I must turn in now, as I have to be up early, give my love to the dear little kiddies. I do hope they are all well. Kiss them for me please dear. I miss you very, very much and feel very fed up at coming back. All my love is yours dear always and I long for the time to come when I can see you again.

Ever your loving hubby,
Fred.'

There followed a brief three months on Nelson's old *Victory*, which was a posting to cover a sickness period or a leave of absence, in his case, suffering from pulmonary TB. Fit again in February 1922, that September he took command of HMS *Stormcloud*, another S-type destroyer. By 1 February 1923 his move to the general list was finally approved and he rose to lieutenant-commander and was on HMS *Woolwich*, described as an emergency destroyer. Other ships he commanded were HMS *Scimitar* and HMS *Scotsman*, although he, 'committed an error of judgement whilst going alongside HMS *Scorcher*,' in late 1923, which was duly noted in his records. He was also made an instructor with the Sussex Division of the RNVR at Portsmouth in 1924. Then came another posting to the *Victory*, on to HMS *Saltash*, before returning to the *Victory*, where he remained until 1929. Meantime, son number four had arrived – Robert (but known as Mike), born on 20 April 1928.

A keen interest and hobby of Commander Raw was the study of the kings and queens of England, and his knowledge was such that he was eventually able to lecture on these from time to time. One set of lectures was entitled: 'Evolution not Revolution' and sub-titled: 'In Explanation of the Kings of England.' These covered King Egbert's reign in 827 AD, Henry III and then Henry VIII. In 1926 W Barrell Ltd, of Portsmouth, was arranging for the publication of Raw's genealogical tree, entitled, *The Kings of England*, and the publisher was writing to say he was sending a special cloth-bound edition to the Prince of Wales. The book went on sale during July 1926.

It is obvious that Frederick Raw was far more than just a sailor, and this is further proved as he applied to become a master mariner in 1929. However, as far as the Honourable Company of Master Mariners was concerned, being a lieutenant-commander RN with a certificate of service did not fulfil the conditions of their by-laws governing the qualification for membership. Commander Raw therefore felt obliged to inform the company that his certificate had been issued by the Board of Trade for competency as master, thereby allowing his application to proceed.

As well as history, his interest in the law saw him studying for the legal profession, which he had begun in the early 1920s, and despite his naval career, he had been 'called to the bar' in Grays Inn during 1925, and indeed, the following year he became a barrister at law. Raw later joined the Western Circuit.

In 1928 the family moved to Ealing, residing a short distance from Ealing Common, but three years later moved just north of Ealing Broadway. He officially retired from the Royal Navy on 1 July 1930, with the rank of commander. One of the last comments on his record was from Captain Leverson-Gaser, which ended with the words: 'a nice fellow'. Sadly this new life and career was dramatically cut short in 1932. Working in the garden of his home on 8 June, he collapsed, and died soon afterwards. Reference was made to heart complications, and he was buried in the City of Westminster Cemetery on Uxbridge Road, now known as Hanwell Cemetery. He was only forty-one years of age. It can be assumed that he had some knowledge that his life might be at risk, for he made out a family will in February 1932. He set up a trust fund to look after them all, with a special contingency for Pat. He left a net figure of £21,730.

This meant that his wife Irene had now to bring up her large family on her own. The eldest son John was at Wellington School, joining there in 1929 when he was thirteen. Peter had started there too that same year, while Anthony (Tony) began his studies in 1931. Irene continued living in the family home until she moved to 28 Delamere Road, Ealing in 1947. Her successful, respected and loving husband had tragically died, and she was left with six young, healthy children; the age of the four boys ranging from fifteen, thirteen, ten and four. Her pride as they reached manhood is easily imagined. That three of her boys would be taken from her during gallant service with the Royal Air Force, in a war even now on the distant horizon, added to the tragedy of her life that had started so promisingly.

Irene Raw died in 1957 and is buried alongside her husband. In her last years she still had the love of her fourth son and two daughters, as well as grandchildren. Mercifully she did not have to suffer the heartache of seeing Mike die at the relatively young age of fifty-eight in 1986, following a successful career in the RAF. The Raw men served their country well but at a high price. Their story is

The Raw family, *left to right*: Trixie, Peter, Aunt Agnes, Tony (at rear), Michael in front with unknown girl, Pat, Cousin Agnes Dodds and John.

one worth telling and remembering.

Fortunately all four boys wrote fairly regularly to their mother over the years and these letters were mostly retained, so that we can follow their lives and their fortunes. They provide great insight into young men of that generation who had to face up to the Second World War and were not found wanting, while the youngest brother, mindful of the torch that had been lit and carried by John, Peter and Tony, took it to further fame. That they cared deeply for their mother is all too evident in their letters to her, and her own to them.

Per Ardua ad Astra

Chapter One

JOHN

John Frederick Raw was born at 66 Gains Road, Southsea, Portsmouth, on 22 September 1916, a bright and clear day. World War One was in full swing and his twenty-five-year-old father was serving his country at sea. He had already taken part in some of the greatest sea battles; a task that he had been performing for nearly two years. In France the Battle of the Somme which had begun on 1 July, still raged and almost no progress was being made. Casualties mounted daily and would do so until the battle was called off in November. Further south the French army was bleeding to death, defending their city of Verdun. It was a bleak time to bring a child into the world. Nevertheless, Irene Raw was thankful for a healthy baby, and a son for her husband.

The child grew strong and attended Hillsborough School for Boys, just along their own Creffield Road, Ealing (now a Japanese School), and in September 1929, when he was thirteen, was sent to Wellington School, Somerset. Wellington was an all-boy's school situated in the town of Wellington, surrounded by an area of outstanding natural beauty close to the coast of Devon. It had been founded in 1837 by Benjamin Frost and in those early days was known as Wellington Academy. It was later purchased by Mrs Frost and William Corner, the latter becoming its headmaster. With it came the change of name.

It was and still is a day school, with boarders (and now co-educational), with an excellent record for education and sport. One major advantage was that it was easily accessible by middle-class families from London and the Home Counties by way of Paddington Railway Station.

A combined cadet force was founded in 1901 where students were taught basic military skills such as drill, weapon handling, field craft, map reading and leadership, under the ever-watchful eye of an independent warrant officer. These skills would become invaluable to the four Raw brothers when the time came to serve their country. Other former students saw valuable service in Britain's military, and at least two, John Fraser Drummond and Edward Graham, saw action with the RAF during the Battle of Britain.

John Raw left Wellington in 1934 and the school records the following achievements by him:

House Prefect	'Country Life' Shooting Team
1st XV Colours Rugby March 1934	1933/34
2nd XI Colours Cricket	Cross Country competitor
Captain of the Swimming Team 1934	School OTC
Bisley VIII Shooting Team 1933/34	Certificate 'A'

On 24 October 1935, John enlisted into the HAC (Honourable Artillery Company) but this would appear to be within the area of the army reserve, for he was only with its 1st Company for about a year before requesting release, and then he went into the provisions business, eventually ending up in Northern Ireland. John had already been a cadet sergeant in Wellington's OTC.

As a young man John excelled at sports, in rugby (wing forward), swimming and diving. He played for the 1st Ealing Rugby XV until he left the town to start his working life, in his case in central London and later on a move to Northern Ireland. Once established there, he continued with his love of rugby. Newspaper cuttings bear witness to his sporting success across the water, such as:

> *'But the forward who most impressed was Raw, Corinthians' new breakaway, who is sure of his selection on the Connacht team this season. He has a fine turn of speed, and a grand sense of "spoiling", as well as being a very dangerous man in the loose.'*

He was indeed picked for the Connacht fifteen, and in another article, the reporter was praising a fellow star, J Griffin, in a match between Connacht and Munster at Galway, played in an icy downpour but, added under the sub-heading 'Raw to the Fore':

'He was not alone in his glory, however, for Raw, the young Corinthians forward, even excelled his [earlier] smashing exhibition in Belfast. Other Connacht forwards who shone, allowing for their coating of mud, were [Messrs] Earner and Fitzgerald.

'The Munster pack, though hardly as effective in the loose as the Connacht eight, deserve every credit for the manner in which they curbed the fire-eating qualities of their opponents – but they were bigger and heavier, and they seemed quite at home floundering about in the mud.

'Pressing hard .... was J F Raw who, if the pun may be allowed, was definitely no "Johnny Raw", and his fair hair could be seen in the thick of the battle everywhere.'

Another match between the Corinthians and the University College, Galway, was also reported, Corinthians won by three tries to two. The *Connacht Tribune* reporter wrote:

'Corinthians forwards were magnificent, and it would not be unfair to single out Raw for special mentions. He was undoubtedly the best forward on the field, being always to the fore in the forward rushes, and as well as doing some fine "spoiling" work, he was a continual source of worry to the opposition. It would be a crime to overlook his selection on the Connacht inter-provincial team this year. There are times when he does not push his weight, but these are comparatively few.

'Mr J Raw, who is attached to the Castlebar Bacon Company, has been in the news on many previous occasions in connection with athletic events in the province.'

As referred to in this article, John Raw was working for a bacon company, in County Mayo, and would eventually become an assistant manager at the Belfast office. He had earlier been employed by Messrs Zwanenberg Ltd, of Tooley Street, London, but was transferred to the Castlebar factory, upon promotion. While in Belfast he became a popular member of the Malone Rugby Club. His diving also gained praise in the press, one mention being of his performance at the Blackrock Annual Swimming Gala, Galway. John was reported thus:

'A remarkable array of talent was seen in this competition, for which there were ten entries, and it was noticed that there was a marked improvement in

the diving all round. Some very difficult dives including running swallow,
hand-stand, back-flip and jack-knife, were admirably performed, and a great
attempt at a one-and-a-half somersault was made by J Raw of the Blackrock
Swimming Club.'

John was also the captain of the local water-polo team and then captain of the local
rugby team while holding a place in the Connacht championship senior team.

Until he settled in Belfast with suitable accommodation, he often commuted
to and from Ealing, via Liverpool, where he caught a ferry to Northern Ireland.
He struck up a friendship with a lady called Peggy Bucklebury, who invariably
met him in the town during 1938 and waved him off from the port.

All the Raw children appear close and there are several mentions of some or
all of them spending time together. In March 1938, for instance, brother Peter
travelled to Ireland on a visit to John, spending the week either playing rugby or
watching John play. They had a great time although it rained much of his visit.
Again, in August that year, Peter wrote in his diary that all three [elder] brothers
and Pat, went swimming together.

It was while working for Castlebar Bacon Co, that John met Mona, the sister
of fellow worker, Mr T Dancklefsen. They were to marry in September 1940. In
1939 John was working in Dunmurry, Coleraine, County Antrim, for the Pro-
ducers Bacon Co, Ltd (Collinghem), and an interesting letter to his mother survives, dated 21 February 1939, addressed to 'My Darling Mother':

'Thank you very much for your nice long letter. I'm glad you are feeling
so well; I'm not feeling so bad myself. We had no match last week and
won't have one this week so that will give me time to get rid of all aches
and bruises. I went riding last Saturday and have felt much stiffer than
any game has ever made me.

'It was very funny the other night. I was at the pictures with Mona,
and sitting in the balcony upstairs. Just at the end of a film, there was a
great flash somewhere from the stalls below. Everyone thought the place
was on fire. You should have heard the shouts and seen them rush for
the exits. There were few people upstairs so there was no stampede. I
picked up my coat from under the seat and went and looked over the
balcony to see what was happening. There was no fire, it must have been
a firework or a fuse. The funniest sight of all was to see people streaming

out of the "Ladies", which they had mistaken for an exit.

'More excitement. I was to go over to the Cookstown factory yester-day to have a look round – that's our sister factory. Mr Z. rung up and told me to go. We rung up to tell them I was going but they said, sorry, no visitors. I was dumfounded because I'm not a visitor, I'm more or less connected with each. They've been over to us. So I rang up Mr Shaw, a director of both. He said he would look into it. Later on he rang back to say they had had trouble with their men. Later we heard that plans to blow up the place had been found on one of the men. I'm glad we are a mixture of Protestants and Catholics here, that keeps us safe. The police have raided all the houses round here.

'I'm changing digs tonight. I've got fed up with the old dame I'm with. She reminds me of death warmed up. Besides, it makes me feel independent to "take up my bed and walk" now and again. I'm going in with a lady whose husband has just died. She has bought a big house and is going to take four nice young gentlemen. I'm the first so I picked my room.

Our sausage trade has grown so much that we have to get mince meat in from Cookstown and they vary with the amount of rusk they use. The Suffolk is a 5d sausage and it is hardly fair to judge it with a Palethorpes or Harris. Tell me what you think of the Collis Glen – that is our best.

'I'm going to see the International at Dublin this Saturday. I hope Ireland win.'

At some stage whilst in Ireland, John Raw became interested in flying and joined the Civil Air Guard (CAG). This organisation would whet his appetite and inspire him later to join the RAF. Amongst the memorabilia and letters of the four brothers was a chromed CAG cap badge which had subsequently been made into a tie pin.

During the late 1920s there was a great deal of interest in civil flying, not least because of all the men and women aviators flying to far-flung places of the empire, competing in air races and generally coming across as the playboys (and girls) of the time. Many independent flying clubs were created up and down the country and running these clubs was a costly business.

The RAF in turn had been trying to attract as many recruits as possible, with, of course, the 'carrot' of free flying. With the coming of the CAG this would have a serious monetary effect on the clubs, especially as many of their members could afford to pay to fly. These people could see that flying costs would be much cheaper with the CAG. The clubs wrote to Air Ministry asking for grants to be given for each pilot trained up to an 'A' licence standard. An average pupil needed around thirteen hours of dual instruction plus four hours of solo flying before being able to qualify. Air Ministry came to an arrangement, granting a subsidy, while the charge for flying training would be 5/- per hour. This would generally cost something in the region of £4.5.0d (£4.25). However, clubs that joined the scheme had to agree to operate their CAG section with not less than twelve pupils.

To get all this up and running, the air minister, Sir Kingsley Wood, handed the task to a former WW1 fighter pilot and now an MP, Captain H H Balfour. Harold Balfour had been awarded the MC and Bar, plus the French *Croix de Guerre*, during the war and was now carving a career in politics. Balfour soon got things up and running allowing Sir Kingsley to announce on 22 July 1938 the formation of the Civil Air Guard.

Under the scheme any man or woman between the ages of eighteen and fifty were eligible to learn to fly, provided they pass the medical examination as stipulated under the existing conditions of obtaining an 'A' licence. Membership of the CAG would cost each person 2/6d (12p) a year. The Air Ministry agreed to pay the civil flying clubs grants in aid if they undertook to charge the favourable rates discussed. The organisation would have its own body of commissioners presided over by Lord Londonderry working from Ariel House, Kingsway, London.

This purely civilian body of trained men and women would be of great assistance to the RAF in time of emergency, with the volunteers not undertaking a reserve occupation that would exclude them from flying in any of the three services. All flying kit and a basic uniform would have to be provided by the volunteers themselves. This consisted of a dark blue RAF-style jacket and side forage hats worn with a chrome badge which had a crowned wreath with the enamelled letter CAG in dark blue. A small light blue flag patch, quartered by a dark blue cross with the union jack in the top-left corner, would be worn on the arm of the flying suit. Pilots would wear embroidered white wool wings on a light blue cotton background with the letters CAG picked out in dark blue.

Not only could these volunteers serve as pilots, but they could also be trained for duty as instructors, observers, wireless operators, air gunners, or ferry pilots. Sir Kingsley Wood, when questioned in the House of Commons in 1939, stated that the CAG had enrolled some 5,200 members, of whom 1,400 had already achieved the 'A' licence qualification, with the remainder still training hard.

However, the CAG did not survive the outbreak of WW2. Many of the guards offered themselves for other voluntary service when war was declared, for instance, the Air Transport Auxiliary (ATA), especially older men who would not be eligible for operational flying, or women for the same reason. Others, like John Raw, would immediately volunteer for the Royal Air Force Volunteer Reserve (RAFVR), and hence the Civil Air Guard was disbanded.

Once war came, John soon moved from the Civil Air Guard into the Royal Air Force, enlisting on 15 January 1940. There were so many young men wanting to join the RAF, there was simply no possibility of everyone being immediately awarded jobs and training, so he was sent to 2 Reception Centre at RAF Cardington. Once things settled down, he finally went to 4 ITW (Initial Training Wing) on 18 June 1940. His first letter to his mother with an RAF badge on service-headed paper was dated 23 June, and he noted his address as 'Still don't know'. However, he then became Pilot U/T (946998), 2 Squadron, B Flight [4 ITW], RAF Hydro Hotel, Paignton, Devon, for his pre-flight indoctrination.

'I'm so sorry I couldn't get home for the wedding [Trixie's]. It was all I could do to get away to send a telegram, and as a matter of fact when I got back I was late for a parade. We've done nothing much all week except clean out the latrines, etc. I polished all the brass. We're being posted on Monday, so they are going hell for leather to get us fully equipped. I'll send you a wire as soon as I know where we are, then you can send me all the letters. I hope there's a pile from Mona by now.

'How did the wedding go? Who gave Trixie away – Peter? Was there enough drink? Did it rain? Let me know all about it because I do wish I could have been there.

'We were all inoculated and vaccinated the other day. Quite a lot passed out but it did not affect me at all. My arm just felt as if someone had hit it. I'm sending home my clothes. Will you please wash the pants and vests, the socks and handkerchiefs, and send them back to me? The keys [enclosed] belong to this case, and my big case and my trunk. Will you please look after them for me and see if my pilot's log book is in my wardrobe or anywhere else. I'm not certain if I brought it from Ireland with me. If I did, it might be in the dining-room desk. It's a small blue book.

'How was Peter, were his eyes any better? I suppose he got the goggles all right. It looks as if we'll get very little leave if any. They've cut the course from six months to three. The weather is terrible here; I hope it's better with you.'

The wedding John talks of was that of his sister Trixie to Stan Fenton at St Peter's Church, Ealing. As the eldest son John would have been the one to give her away in the absence of a father. These two had been seeing each other for some time and in June 1940 they became man and wife. Stanley Gilbert David Fenton had also attended Hillsborough School, and later Lindisfarne College. He was an engineer by profession and played cricket for the Ealing Cricket Club as well as the Ealing Rugby Football Club. Patricia Raw was a bridesmaid. The answer to John's question about who had given Trixie away: it had been Mr Douglas Levin Raw, her uncle. Stan's best man was his brother Mr D H Fenton. Their honeymoon was spent in Berkshire, after which they continued to live in Ealing.

Some might say sending home his washing is just typical of a son, but one expects his mother would love to do it. The missing log book was that which he used with the Civil Air Guard, and no doubt he wanted to show his instructors, when he got started, what flying experience he had had thus far.

From June onwards John Raw was heavily involved in his initial training that he had started at RAF Tern Hill, Market Drayton, Shropshire, as a leading aircraftman (LAC). From here he went to 7 EFTS (Elementary Flying Training School) at RAF Desford, Leicester.

In September John and Mona were married in Belfast, but there are no surviving letters of this period, which is a pity.

It is not until he wrote home on 3 October 1940 that we can read his next letter that survives to his mother, again apologising for not writing for some time due to his training. He had moved again, his address was now given as 1 Squadron, 54 Course, RAF Sealand. Sealand was the home of 5 FTS, and John was flying the Miles Master I. There is a nice air-to-air shot of Master N7609, in which John is the pilot. [As seen on page 5 of the photo section.]

'As you can see by the address I've been moved from Desford. I am now on the last lap being trained as a fighter pilot. We are in really fast machines now. This course will take about twelve weeks. The last week at Desford was like the last week at Paignton – nothing but exams. That's why I didn't write, I was very busy swotting. I did OK, and am pleased to say that I was the only one to have "Above the Average" and "no faults to watch" put in my log book. All the rest were "Average". Only seven of us were sent here to be trained as fighters.

'Mona is here with me. We had a devil of a job to get digs for her. She spent the first two days in a hotel in Chester but had to leave after two days as the room was let to someone else. In the meantime we were lucky enough to get a room in a small house, clean but no bath. We thought it would do until we found something else. When I see her in the evening we generally have a good laugh over some of the things that have occurred during the day. We'll tell them some time.

'Last night we found a very nice place, quite near, which she is going to move into on Monday. I feel very relieved. We have one or two [air raid] warnings a day but don't take any notice until they start to drop stuff. How are you doing mummy? We heard that a German plane was brought down over Ealing. So Mona has been trying to ring you up for the last two days. I hope you managed to get through the day.

'Do you think you could send one of the bicycles to me; one that works. Send it by rail to Sealand station, labelled with my name and number. If it is any bother don't worry to send it. If I stop now I'll catch the post.'

Sealand was an advance course on that part of his training. His next letter on 22 October 1940 noted he was now part of 5 Squadron, 54 Course, and in writing to his mother was fully aware of the blitz taking place following the Battle of Britain.

'How are you, still dodging the bombs? With a bit of luck Mona and I will be dodging them with you next weekend. I have been given leave from midday Friday 25th October until mid-day Monday. This of course might be cancelled at any moment so don't be too hopeful. I'll let you know later when to expect us. Is there any chance of Peter being able to get home?

'I have not had your letter yet this week, so this will only be a short note as I want it to catch the post. I'll write a proper letter when I answer yours. Anyhow, there is no news. The weather has been very bad and I've only been able to do about forty minutes flying in over a week.

'Mona is very well and sends you her love. I think she is a wee bit nervous of coming to London. More about the thought of meeting you than of the bombs. Have you decided when you are going to Evesham?'

Obviously, with the increase in night-time bombing, Mrs Raw was thinking of moving to Evesham where she and young Michael would be safer from the air raids whilst staying with her mother. John's letter dated 12 November confirmed that the newly-weds had indeed managed to visit Ealing a couple of weeks earlier.

'I'm still here as you can see. All the other courses have been moved except us and we haven't the foggiest idea when we will. I am in no hurry as Mona is in such nice digs. By the way, you haven't told me how you like her. I know you'll say you do, in any case, so there is no need to ask.

'It was lovely seeing you the other weekend. I hope we will be able to do it again soon. The weather is very bad for flying so I'm just hoping. There is an absolute gale blowing at the moment. Where is Tony now? Has he finished at the ITW yet? He should get forty-eight-hours leave when he does.

'We had a shooting test the other day and I beat the whole lot by getting 118 out of 125. We then had our group commander's flying test. When I came down my examiner said that I'd done very well. A little while later my instructor came up to me and said that he had heard that I'd been doing some great flying. Was I pleased with myself? None of us have been told about commissions yet.

'We've been having a very quiet time here; I haven't heard a bomb since we left London, not even [the firing of] an AA gun. What has it been like at home?

'The results of the exams we took at the EFTS have just come through and I did quite well. I got an average of eighty-two per cent on the seven exams. Otherwise we are just doing lectures and sitting in the crew room waiting for the weather to clear up.'

John's next letter on 23 November confirmed him with 7 Squadron now. He also wrote it on RAF Form 433A, a small sheet used for flying instruction during training flights.

'We finished all the wing exams on Friday. I think I've passed OK. They weren't very hard.

'By the way, I'm a flight leader now. I was made one about a week ago. We haven't moved yet, in fact a new course has just arrived here. We were the only one left for about two weeks. I think we'll stay until we've all got our flying time in. We are meant to do about ninety hours here, and we've only done about twenty-five, owing to the bad weather. We will then be moved to an operational training unit [OTU].

'I had my recognition test (practical) not long ago. I did quite well (my usual luck) in fact I arrived back over Sealand within a quarter-of-a-minute of my estimated time of arrival. We were all interviewed by the flight commander this morning and asked if we wanted to take any specialist courses such as: instructor's in flying, navigation, photography, armament, etc. I told him I'd joined up to be a fighter pilot and that's what I wanted to be. I'd hate to be an instructor, wouldn't you? We still haven't been told anything about commissions yet. They can't keep us in the dark much longer. I'm going to enjoy this life. No more lectures, all flying. Here comes my instructor, so I'll finish this later.'

There was no let-up on writing home. On 24 November he began:

'I've just had a marvellous time 7,000 feet up, singing at the top of my voice, circling around small clouds and beating them up. No one to hear me, I was up for one hour and forty minutes solo.

'How are the air raids now? Are they as bad as ever? Coventry and Liverpool are getting it pretty badly but they miss out us thank goodness.'

John continued this letter on the 25th:

'Twenty-four of us had to go before the CO to be interviewed about commissions. We go before the group commander tomorrow. I don't know how many they are going to select. I do hope I'm one of them. I'll let you know as soon as I know.'

'11 December 1940
'What's all this about me being an uncle? Why wasn't I told all about it? When I told Mona she said that she knew but it was a secret. Please give Trixie and Stanley my love etc, and tell them how pleased I am.

'Peter and Tony are lucky getting leave, don't you think it's about time I got a week or so. All I ever get is a weekend forty-eight-hour pass. I did very well last weekend. I heard I was getting a few days off about three weeks ago, so Mona went over to Belfast last Monday week for two weeks holiday. The idea was that I should go over then we could come back together. Unfortunately I was given Friday 'til Monday morning. I booked a seat on the Irish passenger plane but when I arrived at the airport, the plane didn't go. You know what the weather was like. So I went to Liverpool, but the boat was cancelled too. I was furious by this time as you can imagine so I rang up my CO and asked that if I reported back for duty, could I continue my leave when the weather improved. He said I could.

'I rang Mona and told her but the weather was little better on Saturday morning so I asked if I could start my leave from Sunday morning and again was told yes. I had every intention of going straight to Stranraer and getting the next boat, that was about 10 o'clock. As I left my flight commander's office I saw an Anson land. Something made me think that it might be going to Aldergrove, the aerodrome outside Belfast, so I rushed to the duty pilot's office to find out. The observer came in and asked what the weather was like over the Irish Sea. I asked him if he had room for a passenger. So I was in Belfast within two hours and it only cost me one penny (the tram to Mona's house). I then hitch-hiked from Aldergrove to Belfast. I went to a shop and rang through to Mona, telling her I was in Liverpool and would be coming over that night. I needn't tell you how pleased she was when I walked in a minute or two later. She did the same to her mother when she went over. They hadn't the foggiest idea she was going.

'Well I had a lovely time – two steak and kidney pies, one turkey with a lot of bread sauce and gravy – and breakfast in bed each morning. I only arrived back here midday today (Wednesday) and no one said a word to me.

'I doubt if I'll get any leave for Christmas but if I do we'll come and stay somewhere at Evesham. Give my love to grandma. I've brought some wedding cake from Belfast but I haven't the nerve to send it now it's so late. We'll give it to her when we see her.

'I passed my wings exams OK but we aren't allowed to wear them yet. It's marvellous now, all flying – no lectures at all. They've extended

our course until 6th January, owing to all the bad weather. We've heard
no more about commissions yet.'

On 13 February 1941 John was sent to Bassingbourn, Cambridge and three days
later he was made a temporary sergeant and left 5 SFTS, posted to Sutton Bridge,
Lincolnshire, and 56 OTU, within 81 Group, for fighter pilot training on Hurricanes, and commissioned in the general duties branch of the RAFVR (No.61294).
    John's next surviving letter is dated 7 April 1941, and he gives his address as
RAF Aldergrove, Belfast. His new posting had been to 245 Squadron for flying
duties. The squadron flew Hurricanes.

'We arrived here quite safely, in fact we had no bother at all, but it is a
long tedious journey. We didn't get to Mona's house until 10 o'clock the
next day, Wednesday. I met both the chaps who were posted here with
me on the train to Stranraer so we were able to come here together. In
fact I brought them in my car. I've still got the car here and have managed
to go and see Mona twice so far. Petrol is a bother. As I haven't been able
to get any digs yet for Mona I think I'll give the car back to Theo until
something turns up. I go on the bus to see Mona whenever I can.

'Oh, while I remember, Mona and her mother send you their love.
How is Stanley now? Making good progress I hope. When will he be allowed to return to work? I hope Trixie is keeping OK. I thought she was
looking rather tired when I was home.

'The chaps in my squadron are very nice and we have lovely planes
so I'm quite happy. But there is not much going on. I suppose that is a
good thing really as it gives me more time for training. I practised firing
at a target towed by another plane the other day. I'm glad to say that I
managed to hit it quite a lot, which has given me confidence.

'I spent all day today at a Court Martial. I went in the capacity of an
officer under instruction. It was very interesting. Tony would have loved
it. When the court was closed while the president (judge) was deciding
upon the verdict, I had to stay behind and tell them what I thought the
verdict should be.'

John's time with 245 Squadron was short. The RAF were trying to meet the huge
demand for fighter pilots to be sent to Malta and the Middle East, so John now

moved to the Central Flying School, at Upavon, to attend what he noted as the 22nd War Course. Officially he was a supernumerary preparing for overseas duties with effect from 16 April. He was so close to his dream of becoming a fighter pilot, which tragically he never lived to accomplish. On 20 April he wrote once more to his mother.

'I hope you are quite well and came through the [latest] big blitz none the worse for wear. How did Michael and Pat enjoy it? I've been very worried about Mona being in Belfast, you see it is such a small place compared with London. I've been trying to get through on the 'phone ever since I've been here but they would only accept calls of internal importance.

'I received a telegram from her yesterday morning saying that she was OK. I also managed to get through last night and told her to come over here as soon as possible as I had got digs for us. I left her trying to fix her permit.

'Well here I am learning to be an instructor. That's not so bad, but to add injury to insult, they have put me on twin-engines – yes – Oxfords! Won't Tony laugh. It does seem mad me trying to teach someone to fly a thing that I can hardly fly myself. I only went solo on it yesterday. But still it's good experience, I can fly both types now.

'This course lasts for about six weeks then we are sent away to instruct. I hope to be sent somewhere near Ealing then we can come and see you now and again. I arrived here three days late but I told them that I was delayed while leaving Ireland. No one said anything, so that was that.

'Tell Peter to come and see me when he can. I get next Saturday off, I hope.'

So it now seems that his desire to be a fighter pilot had been put on hold and he had been designated as a flying instructor, while his overseas posting seems also to have been halted. This was no doubt due to his above average ability as a pilot, and while his mother would be happy to know that he was not as yet flying operationally, it must have been frustrating for him. His last letter was dated 29 April 1941.

'Mona tells me that she had a talk with you on the 'phone as she was passing through London. She told me that Michael and Pat seemed to enjoy the raids, especially sleeping in the shelters.

'Mona arrived here safely and we have managed to get quite nice rooms but gosh we are paying for them: £2.15.6d per week. We supply food and coal. They cook and do the rooms for us. Well, it is worth it. I was horribly worried when Mona was in Belfast.

'I managed to get off the Oxfords and back onto Masters, thank goodness. It all turned out for the best as [at least] now I am [also] able to fly a twin-engine machine.

'How is Tony doing? Have you any idea when he will be going to an OTU? What about Peter, has he had any word about his being transferred to the RAF? Wouldn't it be funny if I had to instruct him. I'm rather enjoying this training. Learning to talk and do things at the same time. It's much harder than you would think.

'I'm off to do night flying in about an hour. I've applied to be an instructor at an elementary [flying] school. As they are situated on much nicer spots (I want to go to Reading) and you can do so much more in a Tiger Moth. I should be settled for quite a while then, and we will be able to get a little house instead of all this going from digs to digs.

'Well, cheerio mummy dear. Mona sends her love. Lots of love, John.'

One has to wonder whether his mother received this letter before the shattering telegram telling her of his death, or at the same time, or perhaps shortly afterwards. Whichever it was, his final words illustrating his enthusiasm about his immediate future and hoping to settle long enough for him and Mona to rent a house, convey how very sad it was that his life now came to an abrupt end.

He was obviously being groomed to become an instructor, learning the 'patter' – the talk between pupil and instructor and vice-versa, learning the routine and so on. He was being taught by Flying Officer J E Robins RAFO, a pilot who had completed a short service commission back in the early 1930s, and had passed into the AA2 Class of reservists in September 1932. A married man from Cheshire, he had volunteered his services now that war had come, and was showing pupils and would-be instructors the ropes.

On the evening of 30 April, in fact 11.25 pm that night, John and Flying Officer Robins took off in Master T8678 on a night-flying exercise. No sooner had they gained a little height than the Master was seen, by its navigation lights, to drop a wing and dive straight into the ground at a place called New Zealand

Farm, Littleton Down.. Both men were killed instantly. Who exactly was flying the aeroplane is not known for certain, although Robins was in command. He had quite a number of flying hours on Masters, whereas this was John Raw's first night flight in one. Did Robins give him control, and if so did a problem suddenly occur that did not allow Robins time enough to grab the controls and try to save the situation? There is no way of knowing. Nor is the reason for the crash known for sure, something mechanical perhaps, a snapped cable, a faulty instrument, or simple pilot error? The reason of course is academic. The Raw family had lost their eldest son, a mother her first-born, and Mona a loving husband.

John was buried at Upavon Cemetery, Wilts; obviously his mother had decided he should rest near to the place where he died. His headstone above bears a set of pilot wings with an inscription. John Robins, who was aged thirty, was cremated and his ashes interred nearer to his home, in the Tewkesbury (St Mary) Abbey Churchyard. He was the son of Edward and Bertha Robins and husband to Millicent, of Neston, Cheshire. There is a memorial to him in the south aisle of that church.

In Wellington School's memorial book is written:

> 'A pilot officer in the RAF, after gallant service died in a flying accident in this country. John came to Wellington in 1929 to school house. He became school prefect and his good work as captain of the swimming [team] laid the foundations for the excellent standard the school has reached during recent years. He was a fine forward and played regularly for the 1st XV; a good cricketer too, gaining his XI colours.'

Chapter Two

PETER

Peter Edward Raw was born at 27 Brading Avenue, Southsea, Portsmouth, on 15 June 1919. At the time his father Frederick was commanding PC68. Again the family was blessed with a fine and healthy baby, a brother to John who was now two-years-and-nine-months his senior.

When he was of school age, Peter followed his brother John into Hillsborough School, Ealing, and then, in September 1929, both boys were sent off to Wellington School. Peter was well known here for his swimming ability, boxing, and for 'Fives'. This was a traditional Wellington game played using cricket wicket keepers gloves, and similar to squash, except that one hit the ball against a wall using just gloved hands. He excelled at all sport, and in fact, when he later joined the army, Peter represented the Honourable Artillery Company (HAC) in the 2nd London Rifle Brigade Boxing Championships.

Wellington School also recorded Peter's achievements:

Junior Swimming Cup 1932
Oldway Challenge Cup 1932/33
1st XV Colours December 1936
Swimming Colours July 1936
Bisley VIII Shooting Team 1936
'Country Life' Shooting Team 1936
School Prefect July 1936
Sports Committee and School Librarian
Cricket Captain 1937
1st XI Cricket Colours May 1937

Swimming Captain 1936/37
Captain of Fives 1937
Senior Swimming Challenge Cup 1934/35/36/37 (brother John was runner-up in 1934)
Four lengths Swimming Cup 1934/35/36/37
Senior Fives Cup 1937
Eight lengths Open Record 1936/37
Four lengths Open Record 1936/37
One length Open Record 1937

Two lengths in Flannels Open	School Certificate July 1936
Record 1937	Certificate 'A' Christmas 1936
Sergeant OTC	

Peter was also mentioned for the part he played as Oberon in Shakespeare's A Midsummer Night's Dream, speaking clearly and with understanding of his lines and executing two dances with J D Blake (playing Titania).

Leaving Wellington School in the summer of 1937, Peter was employed by the Ocean Accident Insurance and Guarantee Corporation, at Moorgate, London. He had already taken part 1(a) of the Accident Branch of the Associateship Insurance Exams in March 1937 while still at school.

The following year, no doubt due to the increasing likelihood of war looming on the horizon, Peter, like John, had decided to join the Honourable Artillery Company. Its HQ was not far from his office, based at Armoury House, in the City of London. Just why he and his brother John had decided upon the HAC is not known. Obviously they had no desire to follow in their father's naval footsteps. Peter's enlistment occurred on 31 January 1938 (service no. 6827008), although his initial medical threw up problems with his teeth, having to have two extractions and others filled before acceptance. In his 1938 diary, Peter makes entries constantly about parades and training with the HAC, but he still swam locally and on 28 March he won the 100 yards race at Ealing's Otter Swimming Club. A week later he spent six days sitting his chartered insurance examinations.

In May 1938 Peter mentions Bruce Cole for the first time in his diary, Bruce went swimming at the local baths with Pete, Mike and John. He became a good friend to the Raw family as well as a fellow RAF pilot. He also became a godfather to one of Michael Raw's children. There is also a girl Joyce, whom Peter mentions a couple of times but whether this was an early romance is not known. More HAC parades and more swimming successes help fill his year. There is mention of a trip to Ireland to visit John, where both brothers played rugby but it was a wet week during his stay, as mentioned earlier.

On 23 July Peter helped win the Aldershot Territorial Swimming Championships, and the following day he went swimming with Bruce and Joyce. Another swimming medal comes his way on 20 August, swimming the 100 yards relay against the Penguins Swimming Club at Clacton Pier. He and Bruce made a trip to Ireland in late November. By this time the Raw boys were all aware of the close call the country had had in September 1938 when Neville Chamberlain had brokered a bad deal with Adolf Hitler that had averted war, yet few people believed that a war was really coming.

Like his brothers, Peter was always keen to keep in touch with his mother and letter writing was something of a regular pastime, pre-WW2 especially. This was helped by the fact that there were at least two daily post deliveries at that time. It is fortunate that Mrs Raw kept so many of her sons' letters so that we may have a fascinating insight into their worlds. One of the earliest of Peter's to survive from this period, was dated July 1939, the HAC having gone away on a camp:

'I arrived quite safe and sound after having had a good dinner at Esher at the expense of one of the bloke's parents. On the way down we passed the Queen in her car returning from some function. There were two royal cars and a chap in a small Ford car had managed to get in between them. He looked very pleased with himself as the streets were lined with people waving flags.

'We have had tons of rain, but at this moment the sun is shining. The camp is not so bad but of course rather muddy. There are pools here and there but not in our tent yet although it is a bit slimy. I have found a swimming baths which is quite near. I went in last night but it was very cold. I also visited the aunts last night, turning up with another bloke in a car at about 6.30 pm. I rang the bell but obtained no answer so went into the garden and found Aunt Mabel. She giggled and roared that she thought I was a burglar at first. She then told me Richardson and Aunty Vivian were at church.

'I could see she was at a loss as to what to do with us, so having had an orange and a cake, I said we had to get back but told her we would like to see them all sometime. So I am turning up tonight with this pal of mine. His name is Jackson, of the Otters [Swimming Club].

'Thank Tony very much for his letter and tell him I am surprised that he dared to speak to the female.'

When war was declared on 3 September 1939, Peter had already been within the HAC's Infantry Battalion No. 1 when the company was embodied the day previously, so was on active duty from day one as an officer cadet. When he wrote to his mother on the 6th, he gave his address as, Private P E Raw, 1 Company, HAC

(162 OCTU), Gordon Barracks, Bulford Camp, Salisbury Plain, Wiltshire:

'Dear Old Mum, I have arrived at the above address without mishap and it seemed quite reasonable. At the moment we are billeted in wooden huts and sleeping on the floor. The food is dished up by army cooks and we have to help mucking around with washing up, potato peeling, etc. On Friday we are moving into modern barracks [with] beds and water laid on, and a wireless.

'We had to march from HQ to Waterloo yesterday. It was hot. We were cheered and tons of people saw us off along the route. I saw Dennis but he did not see me. He was taking a movie picture of us marching along. I think I am in it. I was directly behind the band, as I was with three others as "Officer's Escort". I enclose a picture of us marching out of HQ. I am in it [too]. It is rather faint but I am in the middle between two motor cars.'

Five days later (11 September) came another letter from which these extracts have been taken:

'I have just finished lighting my small stove to make some water hot for Guy to shave with. It works but the water is not boiling yet. It is a shame I was unable to get John to fetch some things for me whilst up in town. Amongst other things I want to get are my rugger boots. I have had two games here, one of them today [and had] to play in gym shoes. It was very hot but enjoyable. They seem to be organising plenty of sport here – rugger, gym, and boxing are the ones I am interested in. There is a marvellous gym here. We have to go in it most mornings before breakfast for an hour of exercising.

'Yesterday I went into Salisbury and had a good time. I had a swim in the river and went in a rowing boat. I rounded the outing off with a good tea consisting of cream scones, jam, poached eggs on toast and good service.

'The food here is gradually improving but I am still sleeping on the floor. I am getting used to it and don't think I would sleep in a feather bed now. We have not done much in the way of military work. I have been medically examined – fit of course – and have had plenty of fatigues and fagging. Tomorrow we are being inoculated against typhoid and have been instructed not to drink alcohol twenty-four hours before and after the inoculation. This hits some folk here very hard, but of course, not me.

'I will be here from six to twelve weeks before I am moved to another unit to become an officer. I approached one of the ATS girls today on the subject of mending my tunic. She consented so I suggested I should bring along my "house-wife" [a serviceman's travelling sewing-kit]. I don't think she really knew what I meant by this.'

Mrs Raw was now visiting people in Frome, Somerset, which is where Peter's next letter was sent on 25 September:

'We are doing tons of work. We start at 6.30 am when we get up and finish at 4.30 pm. We have five periods in the morning and three in the after-noon. They are teaching us all about the parts of cars and are also going to teach us to drive cars and motor cycles, which will be very useful.

'The food is simply awful; the meat's tough, the cabbage is sour and fermented and the potatoes are uncooked. There is no bread for lunch and I have only managed to get marmalade or jam for breakfast or supper twice during the last seven days. We only get one cup of tea at tea-time. I have just bought myself a 2lb pot of marmalade.

'We have had two concerts this week, one provided by our band and the other by 1 Company. The latter was easily the best we had, with two of our sergeants on the stage. One was acting as Hitler, the other as his dancing girl. The last mentioned only wore a pair of stuffed braziers and a duck-egg blue pair of pants with a loin cloth. He did an Egyptian dance.

'I heard from Uncle Arthur the other day and he enclosed a cheque for £5, to help me buy my kit when I become an officer. Quite decent of him don't you think? I have told John to tell him he was going into the RAF after Christmas. I bought some shirts, socks and pants as I hear the prices are going up and up. I intend purchasing a pillow and maybe a sheet when I get home.'

When Private Raw wrote next on 8 October 1939, his mother had travelled to Evesham in order to visit her own mother. Peter went to Ealing, on leave.

'I did enjoy my stay at home. I went to the flicks and on Monday morning to the ice rink with Trixie, Tony, Stanley, Denis, Bruce and a fellow from the HAC who I had arranged to meet there. It was good fun as there were few people there.

'I have been moved into the senior platoon now, that means I will probably go to another unit in about five weeks. Terrance has already got a commission and has left us. Funnily enough he has been put into the Royal Fusiliers (City of London Regt). That is the same one as I have my name down for. There seems to be a small probability that I may get a commission in the Indian army. I expect you would like this. If I do, which I hope not, I think I will take it up as a career.

'On Friday night I went into the gym here and did a bit of boxing. I had to have a go with the instructor who was army, British and European Champion for about five years running. He put me through it hot and strong which rather surprised me as instructors are usually rather gentle. I now have a lovely black eye. He explained afterwards that he went hard with me to see what I was made of as he thought it was useless even starting to try and teach a person to box if they hadn't got the right spirit.

'On Saturday I went into Salisbury and saw the picture "The Four Feathers". It was very good and I enjoyed every bit of it. After that I went to a studio and had my photograph taken in uniform. They are rushing [over charging] me 6/- [30p] for six postcard [sizes]. Is that reasonable? I hope to see the results next Thursday. They said the black eye would not come out. I hope it doesn't.'

Few letters survived over the next few months, but Peter eventually received his commission in the rank of second-lieutenant, into the Somerset Light Infantry (SLI), with effect from 12 November 1939. For a period he appears to have been organising concert parties and his address now is Officers' Mess, Sal Wen Hotel, Beach Road, Weston-super-Mare. In May 1940 he wrote to say he would soon be leaving Weston. Meantime he had taken 'his' concert party to entertain 900 RAF personnel. He had damaged his hand and wrist, so this was probably the reason he was organising concerts, although there is no clue to how his injury occurred.

There was now a move to the 2nd Battn. Lucknow Barracks, Tidworth, Wilts, but when he next wrote, on 24 May 1940, it was on YMCA headed notepaper, noting his address as the 6th Battn, SLI, c/o GPO, Ashford, Kent. As the letter conveys, Peter was nearing his twenty-first birthday in June.

'We are billeted in old barns which are full of rats and flees and some are still inhabited by cows, etc. I went back to Chelwood Gate [near Ashdown Forest, Sussex] yesterday to get excess baggage and managed to bring my motor cycle also. We came back in a convoy of seventeen three-ton lorries and I had to run up and down the line to see they didn't get lost. The journey took five hours and it was cold on the motor cycle. I began to doze [at one point] and ran into the back of one of the lorries. I rather smashed up the head lamp but otherwise it was all right.

'Here is a list of things I would like for my twenty-first. I am afraid most of them are much too expensive for one to buy, so I suggest clubbing together:
  - Camp bath and wash basin (folding) (Important).
  - Rubber Mackintosh.
  - Map case with pencils for writing on cellophane.
  - Second hand action camera.
  - Luminous service watch (shock and water proof if possible):
      obtainable motor cycle shop in Bond St, Ealing.
  - Small folding letter writing case.
  - Warm pair of leather gloves.
  - Officer's haversack (large).
  - Tennis Racket.
'It is now 10.30 am and I am on guard duty so I must finish. Lots of love, Peter.'

It seems a pity that someone had to use presents for his birthday to supplement army necessities. One always imagines that men in the armed forces were issued with all they required, but obviously this only covered basic items. We know today, even with forces in Afghanistan among other places, that even non-commissioned soldiers have to purchase items from their own resources.

His next surviving letter is dated 17 November 1940, so a large gap in his life goes unrecorded. However, his address is now 5th Battalion, SLI, c/o the PO at Wakefield, Yorkshire. Once again the weather – bad – features, and so does money and leave. Extracts from this letter read:

'It is bad news about the flooding of your [air raid] shelter. I should think it a simple matter for anyone to stop the leak with a bit of putty or some other such thing. I must say it seems to have been raining like blazes everywhere for the last week or so and this place is no exception.

'I am not quite sure as to the dates of my leave but it is pretty soon. I feel I can hardly afford to have it as this place is bleeding me; I can't stand the pace that cash runs away from me.

'I am going to be gassed tomorrow afternoon so that they can manipulate my wrist for the purpose of un-sticking internal "things" which have become attached to the healing of the fracture. They say the wrist will absolutely be all right after this with a little massage.

'I have been made battalion sports officer which means I have to look after sport for nearly 1,000 men. This is besides my ordinary duties, so I ought to be pretty busy.'

It was about this time that he must have decided to leave the army and transfer to the Royal Air Force. Perhaps he was influenced by what John was doing. In any event, by January 1941 his letters were originating from the Officers' Mess, RAF Montrose, Scotland. However, his service record only shows him as on attachment from the army and he was not released until 1942. One hopes he cancelled some of his Christmas present list before they were bought for him. At least he got his gloves, as he writes on 2 January.

'Thank you ever so much for the lovely gloves, chocs and 15/- you sent me for Christmas. The gloves are ever so nice and warm and if you don't mind, with yours and Grandma's presents I would like to buy myself some black shoes for when I join the RAF.

'I am glad old Mike [brother] did some good work at school last term, it was a pretty good effort getting into the Second XV; he is only thirteen isn't he? As they lost my medical papers I had to go to Edinburgh for 30/31st of December for another medical. We also had one on Boxing Day, when I held the mercury up for two minutes before they told me to stop.'

Another gap in surviving letters brings us to 24 May 1941, the date Peter had been accepted for pilot training and his address was now, D Flight, 1 Squadron, 2 ITW, New Court, Clare College, Cambridge. In many of his letters, he has to ask his poor mother to send items to him, most of which he simply forgets to take with him when he leaves. His letter dated 25 May was no different. His brother John had been killed the month previously and no doubt his letters for the previous week or so would have made reference to this sad loss.

'Here comes the usual scream for the forgotten articles so I will get the worst over first and then tell you the news. I have left my soft army belt on the chair in my bedroom, [and want] my PT shoes, and two films in my brown sports coat pocket. The PT shoes [plimsolls] are white, quite dirty, but quite new. They should be in my bedroom. Could you send everything by return of post as I will have to do PT in shoes until they come?

'Please could you tell Tony to put the two gallons for the two May petrol coupons into "Revolving Albert" and "Waltzing Matilda" (she needs a half pint of oil in the tank), before 31st May as otherwise they will go to waste, and then send the coupon book back to me. I hope he has been in touch with Mr Zwanenberg by now [John's employer].

'I arrived here [Clare College] to find myself in very comfortable quarters. This college has very modern buildings with hot and cold water laid on. I am sharing a sitting room and bedroom with an officer in the London Scottish. I am only waiting for him to put his kilt on and then I will be able to tell you for certain about underpants.

'We have a coal fire, settee, chairs and table in the sitting room. There are baths and the food is good. We are up at 6 am on weekdays and 7 am on Sunday. The course lasts six weeks and we are allowed two weekends off during this period. However I don't think I will be able to take advantage of them for financial reasons.

'I am afraid I must have shaken you up this last leave. I am sorry about it but I am afraid I might have done the same again if I had that leave over again. You see, I rather like Mavis, and I think you are prejudiced against the whole bunch on account of my bringing Agnes to my home that time.

'Well, there is no more news yet but plenty of work to be done. Hard luck about the "Hood" isn't it![1] Tons of love to you, Trixie and Mona. Peter'

---

[1] The battle-cruiser HMS *Hood* was sunk in action with the German battleship, *Bismarck* on 24 May 1941. The *Bismarck* was sunk three days later.

'Revolving Albert' and 'Waltzing Matilda' refers to two motor cycles the boys had. And mentioning Agnes and Mavis brings into the picture for the first time two young ladies, in fact both were daughters of the Van der Beck family. Both girls were born in Rangoon, Burma, but their parents had come to England and settled in Ealing. The girls had been educated at St Gilda's Convent, in Chard, Somerset and then at Winton House School, Ealing. Agnes was the oldest at twenty-one, whilst Mavis was nineteen. It seems that their appearance may have been rather unorthodox, and had caught Mrs Raw off guard. Was it perhaps their nationality? In any event, the sisters were to play a large part in the Raw family.

Things must have returned to normal soon afterwards, for in Peter's next letter dated 3 June 1941, he says that it was nice of her to invite Mavis round for tea. Mavis in turn appears to have a hobby of colouring in black and white photographs, for he states in his return letter:

'I am glad you like the colouring. I thought she made a good job of John in LAC uniform but his face colouring was not so good in the others.

'I hope Revolving Albert is in running order as I intend bringing him back with me. [More importantly] this Scotty does not wear underpants beneath his kilt nor other proper Highland regiments!

'Please give my love to Trixie, Mona and David, and Mavis if you see her.'

By early July Peter, having completed his ground training, had moved, on the 6th, to RAF Sealand, the same place John had been when he was training. The difference of course was that Peter was ensconced in the officers' mess. Sealand was the home of 19 EFTS, and officially Peter remained on attachment. On the 9th he wrote to his mother:

'I arrived here safe and sound with all luggage intact. We couldn't fly yesterday owing to bad weather but I went up today in a Tiger Moth and had excellent fun. When we were in the air the instructor let me take over and I found it much easier than I expected. Of course, he landed it for me. So, now I have done twenty minutes flying, but I will be doing more tomorrow.

'I had a very enjoyable weekend with Tony and the "Becks". We spent most of the time on and in the Thames.

'The quarters here are very comfortable and the messing is terrific. It is just as though you are having each meal at the "Hungaria". There doesn't seem to be a shortage of anything, but we are paying for it dearly (4/- a day). I have a very nice room to myself with a wardrobe, writing desk, dressing table, easy chair, washbasin and a civilian bed – not forgetting a carpet.

'I am doing my best to catch up with my money now but I am afraid my messing and increase in tax are great handicaps. Since I have been here I have only spent 4d.'

A week later and he was able to tell his mother more about 'time in the air'. It also seems that brother Tony was also with the RAF.

'Yes I can land a plane. I landed my "Tiger" last Monday without the help of the instructor, who held his hands above his head. It was rather a bumpy one but I was ever so pleased. Up to date I have done three hours and fifty minutes. The reason I have done so few is because of the thunderstorms. Yesterday we couldn't fly at all and today I could only get twenty minutes in because there was so much wind but in spite of that we had some good fun up at 5,000 feet where the sky was blue. The instructor showed me how to do a slow roll and also how to start the engine by going into a vertical dive. It was great.

'I hope Tony behaved himself over the weekend and was a good son. It was a good effort his landing that plane.

'I went for a lovely swim on Sunday in an open-air water bath on the coast. I was with some other officers and during the proceedings they got talking to some females who they eventually persuaded to come and have a drink after the swim. We were talking about the various parts of England in which we lived and when I said London, one of the ladies said, laughingly, "Do you know someone called John (she didn't know either of my names)?" I said I had a brother called John, and just for curiosity asked her the surname of this fellow. You can imagine my surprise when she said John Raw, and you can imagine her shock when I said he was my brother. There was still further astonishment when I told her he was married last September but was now no longer with us.

'It turned out she was the girl he knew in Liverpool and she used to see him off in the boat when he used to go back via Liverpool to Belfast in 1938. Her name is Peggy Bucklebury. Would you believe it? I remember him telling me about her and showing photographs he had.

'I thought I was going to get a few hours at home next Saturday as I was nearly all set for cadging a seat in a plane that was going to Heston Friday, late afternoon. The damned plane broke its back on rough ground today so it is all off.

'I am so sorry I haven't written earlier but I must say I have some excuse as I have been flying until 9 pm each evening last week and Saturday evening I flew to Manchester and stayed with Uncle Douglas until Sunday evening when I flew back just before dark. I averaged five hours flying each day last week, besides having lectures for half of each day.

'I did enjoy myself at uncles but I can't stand auntie, she hen-pecks him all the time. He did enjoy telling me all about the Home Guard and how the army of today really needed old soldiers. He wants my khaki shirts when I change into blue ones. In the afternoon we went shooting. Uncle has tons of guns and ammunition.

'I am well ahead with my flying as I have completed fifty hours. I have my exams over next week so if I get leave I should be home about the 20th.'

Peter left Sealand on 18 August and after his home leave was sent to 17 EFTS Pool, at Peterborough. On 14 September he was posted again, this time to 8 SFTS, Montrose. There is no surviving letter concerning his first solo flight but obviously he had overcome that barrier and progressed to cross-country flights. Amazing that he is still wearing his army shirts. Perhaps there is no need to issue blue ones in case he writes himself off before he finishes his training! At the top of his letter of 11 September, it shows clearly his address as Officers' Mess, 8 SFTS, RAF Montrose, Angus, Scotland (Service Flying Training School). This meant he was moving on to service aircraft rather than pure training machines. In his letter he writes about Mavis Beck; the relationship is obviously becoming serious.

'I am so glad the Becks came to see you and that my little Mavis [came too]. I hope you don't mind me really liking her, she is not one of my six-monthly affairs so please don't get me wrong. I know she is a blonde but she is good deep down inside, and you will find that out one day.

'Uncle Douglas turned up the night before last and we had a meal at the Central Hotel in Montrose, then had another in the mess. I think he enjoyed that as he was able to air his military knowledge, to everyone who was near, in the anti-room. Anyway, he was so pleased he slipped me 10/- when he left!!!

'I went solo last Monday after four hours on Masters. I was the first to go out of the whole of our fifty-odd course. I like Masters a lot, but I am careful when flying them, especially when I am low.

'We are worked very hard here from 8 am to 5.15 pm, seven days a week, with half-an-hour for lunch. They are now trying to arrange one day a week off which will make things a little better. Thank goodness I have a very nice instructor here. I couldn't ask for a better man. He is a flying officer, married with a wife here.

'Montrose is quite a nice spot, it is very quiet though. The country is stunning from the air. You can see the hills in the distance and there are quite a lot of lakes and some attractive cliffs on the shore.'

One has to wonder if his mother had something against blondes from Peter's remarks in this letter. Not very PC today, of course. One imagines too that his reference to being careful when flying Miles Master trainers is his being mindful of the fact that John was killed in just such an aircraft. This was not, of course, his first solo flight, merely his first on this type.

On 11 October, his letter has the address: Forfar Fever Hospital, Forfar, Angus.

'My Darling Mother, I had better start by explaining my address. Last Tuesday I felt rather itchy and found I had a rash. I was the same on Wednesday morning so I went to our MO. He suspected me of having scarlet fever so I have been bundled here to be under observation. The only thing I have is the rash and the itch otherwise I am as fit as a fiddle, no temperature, no nothing. The MO says it will be at least ten days before he is certain I am infected. I am very worried that I may be kept here too long and so chucked off my course and put on a new one to start again.

'I am allowed to receive letters but not to write them. I have managed to get round one of the nurses and I am hoping she will post this for me. You had better burn this as it may be infectious.'

Mrs Raw obviously did not heed his advice and Peter goes on to write another missive, dated 26 October 1941:

> 'I am now flying the new radial [engined] Masters which are great fun. I do enjoy flying and especially aerobatics but of course I treat them with great respect and don't play around near the ground.
>
> 'There was a dance in the officers' mess last night which was quite a good show. There was a running buffet with lobster, chicken, ham, tongue, cold roast beef and all those nice little things on cheese biscuits, smoked salmon, blancmange, mixed fruits and a host of other things. The whole shoot plus the dance cost 2/6d! You know we are very well fed here and there is tons of food, butter and sugar included. It seems the same throughout Scotland. Last Sunday for lunch we had a choice of hot roast chicken, hot roast pheasant, cold brawn and ham, roast or boiled spuds, greens and carrots. Messing is 2/- a day for food. The P/O who runs the mess has a Rolls-Royce and was manager of a London hotel before he joined up.
>
> 'Tony wrote and told me all about the motor cycle. I replied with various stories he could use, that should get him off with a 10/- fine.
>
> 'The weather is getting quite cold and I may be writing for my skates at any moment. Well, I think the plane I am going up in is just about due down now. Love to all. Mavis is very well and enjoying herself.'

The Miles Master trainer previously had a Rolls-Royce Kestrel XXX engine, but the ones with radial engines (the Mark III) housed a Pratt & Whitney Wasp Junior, in all other respects they were much the same. Once again Peter tries to calm his mother's fears about flying them, especially at low level.

Reading between the lines, it seems brother Tony has had a run-in with the law, and Peter is hoping if Tony uses one of his excuses, it will help reduce the punishment. The other item of interest is that Mavis appears to be in Scotland, and probably living in digs near the aerodrome. Things are getting serious between the couple.

However, from Peter's next letter dated 20 October 1941, it would seem that he was going finally to have to admit to her presence in Scotland to his mother, and he was fearful that she might be far from amused at his antics.

'My Darling Mother, I thought I wouldn't tell you, but now I find I will have to as I wish to send you a little present of shortbread via Mavis, and you would wonder how she got it from me to give to you.

'Well it goes like this: As you know Mavis went on holiday a few weeks ago, she went to Edinburgh which is only about 100 miles from here. I thought this too good to be true, so after negotiating with her mother I managed to get Mavis to come and stay at Montrose with 2/Lt McNeil, his wife and their six-week-old baby. This fellow is doing the same job as me.

'We have had a grand time together. I managed to get days off now and again owing to bad weather and I have also managed to see her every evening. She was my partner at the officers' mess dance I told you about and I may say she knocked all the other females into a cocked hat!

'We spent a very nice evening when we went with an instructor, F/O Smith and his wife to tea and flicks. She seems to occupy a lot of her time during the day bathing and playing with the McNeil's baby.

'Mavis is travelling back all Thursday [30 October] night, and so should be home first thing Friday morning, i.e. about the same time as this letter arrives.'

Brother Tony obviously said something too about Mavis visiting that did not sit well with Mrs Raw. In a letter dated 12 November, Peter said:

'I am so sorry Tony and I upset you over the Mavis and Agnes visits. I am afraid I can only put it down to us being blundering asses with no forethought. Quite honestly, not telling you was intended not to hurt you, rather than the other way around.

'In my case I particularly didn't want you to know how serious I was with Mavis because I have always understood from your attitude that you are under the impression that it is just another of "Peter's affairs", and I thought it best for you to keep on thinking that. As I have made enough muck of things already, I had better let the "cat out of the bag" and tell you that I honestly and seriously intend on marrying Mavis one day. I hope you don't take too poor a view and it doesn't shake you too much, but I know you will understand these things just happen and they can't be helped! That's a big confession but it shows you I am reforming and letting you in on all my little secrets!

'Mavis writes and gives me all the gen on her visits to you and she seems to like them a lot, especially when she is able to see my godson. She tells me he weighs one stone already and will soon be able to turn him into a feather-weight boxer.

'I seem to be missing dear old John more as days roll on, it is like a tooth which has been taken out, thawing out of the cocaine. Anyway, I comfort myself with the thought that he is at least out of it all and in a better place.'

A spot of home leave at the end of November was most welcome and his letter of 1 December 1941 spoke of his return:

'I am again going strong with flying, but just feeling a little homesick. I arrived [back] here without incident last Friday except the train was very late and so I missed my connection at Edinburgh and therefore didn't arrive here until 12.20 pm.

'Since I have been back I have flown, been to the flicks once and last Saturday night I went to dinner with my instructor and his wife. We had partridge for dinner and feeling very comfortable afterwards we sat around the fire and had a good talk.

'You know Mum, you were very kind to me on leave, letting me have breakfast in bed and Mavis round so often. I enjoyed it ever so much and thank you from the bottom of my heart. Please give Mavis my love and thank her for all the little things she did for me whilst I was home.'

At the start of his next letter, 11 December, Peter wrote to say he was trying to get the mess secretary to acquire a chicken and he would send it to her for Christmas. He confided it was not over expensive, especially in Scotland. Four days earlier the Japanese empire had attacked the American's Pacific Fleet base at Pearl Harbor, in the Hawaiian Islands, so these two nations were now also embroiled in what had become a world war. In no time at all the Japanese naval forces had attacked and sunk two of Britain's big warships off the Malayan coast, the battleships *Prince of Wales* and *Repulse* on the 10th. He continued:

'I finished the last of my night flying early this morning and found everything OK. I am even considering putting in for night fighters as there is plenty of leave attached to that branch.

'I am leading a terribly quiet life just now. I have drunk only two glasses of beer since I returned from last leave and I didn't pay for those as I had them when I went to dinner with my instructor.

'I had a good game of rugger last Saturday. It was against the RAF at Arbroath, and we won.

'What do you think about these blasted Japs and our poor ships? We'll certainly have to give them a hiding for what they have done.'

On his mind was the knowledge that the Beck sisters' father was still in Burma, with the Japanese not far away.

His next letter also concerned the chicken, that his mother doesn't seem to want him to send, but it was too late. Peter wished her a happy birthday as well – she was forty-eight. In his letter of 10 January 1942 he is again struggling with understanding his mother's view of the van der Beck sisters. Tony and Agnes are becoming more serious about each other and Peter thinks that sometimes his mother takes opportunities to pick on them, especially Agnes. He also wonders what she really feels about Mavis and his own love affair. He then noted:

'I am so pleased about old Mike, although he is rather letting the side down coming top of his form, it is unheard of in the Raw boys! I came fourth out of fifty-three in our wings examination and averaged for all subjects eighty-six per cent.

'I have been doing some boxing with another of the officers this week. It was good fun and I am feeling pretty fit. I think I will finish here in another month, curse it. I hope it isn't extended beyond that.'

On 19 January he was less hopeful of ending his time in Scotland.

'It now looks as though we will be here for the duration, for snow is falling fast and thick, and since last night it is getting on for six inches [deep]. Having been put off twice, I think we really are going to start flying Hurricanes when the snow clears. This should help us along with our hours and shorten the time before I come home.

'Since I finished my ground subjects, I have been doing tons of read-

ing to help fill in the time and better my education. I am getting a real
old book-worm again. There is one book, or at least two books, that you
really must read. They are: *Rough Passage*, by Gilbert Hackforth and Jones,
and *Random Harvest* by James Hilton.

'No Mum, I don't wear my "wings" or at least get them, until I have
finished all my flying, in spite of the fact that I have passed my ground
subject examination and my wings test in the air.

'I had a very enjoyable game of rugger last Saturday. We played another RAF team at home and won twenty-four to three. I scored a try –
amazing!'

Towards the end of January, Peter was writing to both his mother and to brother
Tony about the latter's intention of marrying Agnes, or Aggie as she was known.
Tony was still only nineteen and although he was getting on well with his flight
training, Peter did not think it was a good idea that he should marry at his age.
Oddly enough, he then went on to make the comment that if he did, perhaps it
should be a joint wedding with himself and Mavis. Peter was also a little put out
that Tony might marry before he did, commenting that: 'It isn't done is it?'

14 February 1942 – St Valentine's Day:
'A week has now passed since my very enjoyable leave and I am glad
to say I have done a reasonable amount of flying in that time. At the moment I am at an aerodrome near Aberdeen flying Hurricanes. We are only
here for two days, so it does not mean a change of address. We start flying
them tomorrow morning and I must say I am looking forward to it.

'I know it makes me feel really good to be engaged to Mavis and I
am so looking forward to having her as my wife. I expect you think I am
a bit of a twerp, but I am afraid I like being a twerp. Tony seems to be in
a blinking hurry to get married. The trouble is I can't really afford it so
soon, but the last thing on earth I want is him getting married before me.
It is bad enough him being a flight lieutenant.'

Obviously Peter and Mavis had become engaged on his last leave, so his mother
must have amended her views on her now future daughter-in-law. Peter had also
received his 'wings', although in a letter dated 22 February he wrote to his mother
that he had lost them from his tunic. He assumed he had taken them off and left

them at home, so asked his mother if she could find them (he may have still been wearing his army tunic whilst training, so had not sewn them on, waiting until he got his RAF tunic).

Peter also commented that he thought it about time Tony was awarded a DFC. Tony had been on operations with Bomber Command for some time now. He also mentioned that he was being very thrifty and cutting down on everything, in order to save up for his future married status. Even so, he asked his mother not to cash a recent cheque for £4.13.0 before his new uniform allowance was credited to his bank account.

On 26 February 1942 he was finally granted an emergency commission as a pilot officer on probation in the general duties branch of the RAFVR – his army 'attachment' at an end.

Chapter Three

FIGHTER PILOT

Peter finally left 8 SFTS at RAF Montrose on 27 February 1942 and moved to RAF Usworth, after another leave, where 55 Operational Training Unit was based. However, in his next surviving letter dated 29 March, he was far more concerned with arrangements for his wedding! However, he starts this missive with a comment about a recent mess fine, presumably following some damage at a party – perhaps one concerning his forthcoming nuptials?

'No, I have not lost 2/6d as yet, there are tons of other ways in which you can be fined, but so far I haven't suffered that way. I think the fines are all put together to help pay for the binge [we will have] at the end of the course.

'Mum, would you be so kind as to organise the bouquets for all parties. I will settle up with you when I get home if you can manage. I think up to 35/- each for the brides and 10/6d each for the bridesmaids should be OK. I am sure you will know better than I which flowers will go, and bring out the beauty in the Van der Becks. If they can look anything like my mother did on her wedding day, I will be quite happy.

'I will be able to get leave for the wedding, I have had that confirmed and if I'm lucky I think it will be seven days. If this is so, it will mean I leave here and then have to return to a place called Annan, seven miles from Gretna Green, as we are due to move the whole station to this place on 28 April. I was speaking to our sports officer's wife who has just been there to look for digs and she says the nearest possibility of getting any is seven miles from the camp, and the nearest real civilization is Carlisle, which is twenty miles away.

'I had a very nice game of rugger yesterday. It was in aid of some charity match for a warship week. Although we lost, it was very energetic and quite heated at times. Our team here is not as good as the one we had at Montrose.

'I have been doing tons of flying and like the Hurricanes very much. We go around with all eight guns loaded and are allowed to have a go at any Germans if we run across them. The Hurricane is known to be one of the safest planes if it is handled the right way. Yesterday I took up an Air Training Corps cadet in a Master and taught him a little flying. He coped quite well and was able to fly straight and level and also to do some turns.

'Mavis tells me she has received some answers to the wedding invitations. Could you tell me who is coming please and if anyone is turning up whom we didn't expect? I enclose a wedding present list. Mavis may have thought of something more to go on it. If you think there is anything on it that shouldn't be or should be, please alter.'

So, things had really moved on apace. From just thinking of marriage, to becoming engaged, now there are firm plans for a joint wedding to the two sisters. What Mrs Raw and the Van der Becks thought about it is unknown, but the girls' mother must have felt some dread at both marrying RAF pilots with a war going on. The wedding date had been fixed for the fast approaching 22 April, so less than a month hence.

6 April 1942

'Many thanks for your letter with all the "gen" in it. Mrs J. very kindly gave me £1.1.0d [a guinea] for my wedding present which of course is very, very much appreciated. What is happening about the cars, will we have to order one or two for our own house, who is organising them to take us away from the church? It is a shame all [the] Evesham [family members] have cried off. If the Zwanenbergs turn up, we can quite easily take them along to the reception.

'It is grand news about old Tony, I do hope he can fix up a permanent job at Heyford, it will be just wizard if he can and he will be so near home. I will try and get home as soon as I can that Tuesday before the wedding. The journey is about six hours so I should be able to get home just before midnight. I am going to have a shot at flying half the way down England. This should be OK if the weather is reasonable.

'That is a good idea of yours about the men-folk going out to lunch. I will fix that and then Tony and I will be able to have a last-minute panic before we take the step. Mavis tells me she and Aggie performed in wedding dresses before all of you. Does she look better than Aggie? I bet she is streaks ahead.

'I expect Mike is home now [half term holidays]. Thank him for his letter and will you send him swimming every day at my expense as he must be fit for the summer term? I am playing rugger this afternoon.

'I now have completed twenty-six hours and thirty minutes flying [on Hurricanes] which is good going. I have been given a week off for my marriage, which is great news.'

Five days later, on the 11th, he wrote to brother Michael:

'My dear Mike, many thanks for your lovely long letter and still more thanks for the kind wishes and beautiful present that Mavis tells me you have given for our wedding. It will be ever so useful. I bet you are longing for the wedding as I know how much you like a binge. You will have to work hard on that day as at the reception you will have to look after the people and see they have everything they want, also at the church you may have to show people to their seats.

'You and Pat must simply do tons of swimming this holiday, as you must win everything as far as swimming goes at your schools, but of course if you lose a race you must never let it upset you and just take it like a good sport. I will certainly lend you my stop watch next term. I will bring it home with me when I come on the 20th. That reminds me, both you and Hitler have your birthdays on that day! I will wish you many happy returns now and give your present when I arrive home. Hitler will have to wait for ours as I will give it to him when I get operational in my fighter plane.

'I have done tons of [flying] hours on Hurricanes here and am doing air firing and dog-fighting at the moment. It is grand fun, especially when you go into a spin in a cloud and don't know whether you are upside down or inside out. Today I have been doing air firing with the camera gun and next week we do it with real ammunition. I have been taking a lot of these ATC boys up for pleasure trips in Masters. If I am stationed near you sometime I will probably be able to take you for a flip and let you fly as well, as I expect you would enjoy that!

'Well Mike, concentrate on your swimming, don't forget to pull straight down, not to wriggle your body, let your feet brush and do plenty of lengths each day, not forgetting sprints. Give my love to Pat and tell her she must look tops as a bridesmaid.'

He wrote to his mother on this same 11 April, telling her too about his Hurricane flying:

'I am now beginning to appreciate them as really marvellous machines instead of being scared to death of them. They are as tough as blazes and it has been known for one to go through a brick building without a scratch. One of our fellows the other day flew into a hangar and he stepped out OK, except for a cut on the nose and a bit of a shaking.

'I missed my game of rugger today as I had to go and do some air firing at an aerodrome near here. It's rather a shame as I think that was the last [match] of the season.'

The wedding when it came, eleven days later, went off splendidly and was re-ported in the local Ealing newspaper on 25 April:

BROTHERS MARRY SISTERS

Two brothers, who are serving in the RAF, were married to two sisters at St Benedict's Church, Ealing, on Wednesday.

Flight Lieutenant Anthony William Raw, son of the late Commander and Mrs Raw of 10 Mount Park Crescent, Ealing married Miss Kathleen Agnes Van der Beck, daughter of Mr & Mrs Van der Beck, of Burma and Ealing. His brother, Pilot Officer Peter Edward Raw, married Miss Mavis Madeleine Van der Beck.

Both brides, who were given away by their mother, wore white satin dresses cut on classical lines with trains. Their head-dresses were of orange blossom and they carried bouquets of pink carnations and white heather. The bridesmaids, Miss Molly Van der Beck and Miss Patricia Raw, wore sky blue moiré taffeta dresses with headdresses of anemones.

The services were conducted by Dom Gregory Murray, and Lieut. G Hawkins RNVR played the organ. Flying Officer A L Searby and Captain the Rev E L Seager each acted as best man.[1]

The reception was held at Sayers restaurant, Ealing, and later the bridal couples left for Berkshire for their honeymoons.

Both bridegrooms were born at Southsea and educated at Wellington School, Somerset. They are members of Ealing rugby football club and the Otter Swimming Club. Flight Lieut. Raw joined the RAF in 1940. His brother joined the Honourable Artillery Company in 1937, and obtained a commission in the Somerset Light Infantry (PA) in 1939. He was transferred to the RAF in May. The brides, who were born in Rangoon, were educated at St. Gilda's Convent, Chard, Somerset and later at Winton House School, Ealing.

There are few surviving letters from Peter after his wedding, but we know he continued his final training over the next few weeks. From 8 FTS Montrose, he had, as we know, advanced to 55 OTU at RAF Usworth in March 1942. An operational training unit, as the title suggests, is generally the final phase of a pilot's preparation for actual combat, from where he would expect a posting to an operational squadron. In the case of his elder brother John, he was posted to be an instructor before such an event took place, and lost his life shortly afterwards.

Peter, who now appears to have acquired the nickname of 'Slosher' Raw, was posted to 609 (West Riding) Squadron on 30 June 1942, along with a pal, Pilot Officer Roy Payne. He and Roy had trained together, meeting at Montrose around Christmas 1941, although being a sergeant pilot, Roy lived in the sergeants' mess while Peter was in the officers' mess. They only really met on the flight lines, but in February 1942 Roy was commissioned and moved into the senior mess. Two other newcomers were Humphrey Gilbert and Humphrey Lestocq (who later became an actor and tv personality).

Their squadron was based at RAF Duxford, Cambridgeshire, where it had been since March 1942. As the number tells us, 609 was an auxiliary squadron, one formed pre-war as part of what became the Royal Auxiliary Air Force. Its part-time airmen generally trained at weekends and in the event of war, would form part of support for the RAF, its members being called for full-time service. 609

[1] F/O A L Searby was reported missing with Coastal Command on 19 August 1942.

had been formed at Yeaden in February 1936 as a bomber unit but changed its role to fighters in December 1938. Its CO at the time Peter arrived, was Squadron Leader P H M Richey DFC & Bar.

Paul Richey was a famous name already, having fought gallantly in the Battle of France in 1940 with 1 Squadron, on Hurricanes. He shot down a number of German aircraft during the *Blitzkrieg* and was awarded the DFC after being badly wounded in action. After a period as a fighter controller, at which time he wrote his famous book *Fighter Pilot*, he was posted to 609 Squadron as a flight commander. Flying operations over France during the summer of 1941 he added to his score and received a Bar to his DFC. His CO at the time was his brother-in-law, Michael Robinson DFC.

Towards the end of his tour with 609, his book was published and the C-in-C of Fighter Command had him posted to Fighter Command HQ as a tactics officer. While so employed, the new Hawker Typhoon fighter started to make its appearance, and Richey approached the C-in-C, Air Chief Marshal Sir Sholto Douglas, and extracted a promise from him that when the first Typhoon Wing was formed, he would be allowed to select the squadrons for it, and to take command of one of them. Therefore, when in June 1942, the first wing was formed at Duxford, Richey had selected his old 609 Squadron to be one of the units, plus 56 and 266 Squadrons. As might be expected, Paul Richey had himself posted as leader of 609.

The squadron had already made a name for itself during the Battle of Britain, flying Spitfires, at first from RAF Drem in Scotland, later at Middle Wallop and Warmwell during the battle. By October it had been credited with 100 enemy aircraft shot down, under the command of Squadron Leader H S Darley DSO. It began converting to the new Typhoon in April 1942, and moved to Duxford, now commanded by another successful fighter pilot, Squadron Leader G K 'Sheep' Gilroy DFC.

Once formed at Duxford the Typhoon Wing was commanded by Wing Commander Denys Gillam DSO DFC AFC, a successful Battle of Britain pilot. However, his first months of command tested him and his pilots sorely, for the Typhoon, built as a replacement for the Hurricane, was pushed into service too soon and still had a number of teething problems to overcome. The Sabre engine was particularly troublesome; carbon monoxide tended to seep into the cockpit, and a weakness in the tail section could cause the whole tail-plane to snap off.

These problems were gradually solved but it took time, but during that time it became only too evident that the Typhoon was not going to be the fighter that the Spitfire was, and so it finally became a low-level ground-attack fighter-bomber, and in this guise it was to excel for the rest of the war.

Although now on a front-line fighter squadron, 609 was virtually non-operational while its pilots and ground personnel converted to the Typhoon. For the pilots the initial problem was that it was a huge aeroplane compared to the Spitfire Vb and twice as heavy. Nor did it look as graceful, with its huge air intake. The cockpit was no longer the sliding hood, but almost like a car door that was pulled open in the same fashion. Once the pilot stepped in, he closed the door behind him. 609 of course suffered the same problems as 56 and 266 Squadrons had earlier found. Apart from the tail-planes falling off etc, engines could easily catch fire, and for unknown reasons, any one of the four 20 mm cannons in the wings might fire off a round or two when on the ground!

Peter Raw arrived on 1 July 1942 along with Roy Payne and Humphrey Gilbert, the latter having once been a make-up artist in Hollywood. Payne and Gilbert, like Peter, were all re-mustered soldiers. For a long time 609 had been the home of a number of Belgian pilots, many of whom had distinguished themselves. With the new influx of British pilots the ratio of British to Belgians was about even.

What was also apparent was that the Typhoon was never going to be a good fighter at height, but the pilots did find it had exceptionally good handling qualities at low level. One of Paul Richey's two flight commanders was Joe Atkinson (who commanded A Flight) and amazingly Joe had managed to remain overlooked as regards a rest, and had been with 609 for an unbroken twenty months! [2]

Peter made his first flight with 609 on 3 July, doing some local flying in a Hurricane I for just over an hour. His first solo on a Typhoon came the next day, a forty-minute trip around the area. More local training flights followed over the next few days but then appears an unusual entry in his log book for 8 July. He was flown from Duxford to Upper Heyford where he and the pilot carried out some practice bombing in a Wellington. Who was the pilot? F/Lt A W Raw DFC – brother Tony. Peter stayed at Upper Heyford overnight and the next day was flown back to Duxford by Sergeant Rastblatt.

Sunday 12 July
'It was great being able to slip over and see you all the other day. I enjoyed my short stay very much. I managed to slip home for an evening

---

[2] Later Sir Alec Atkinson KCB DFC.

and night last Friday. I saw Trixie and David, at least, not the baby as he had been put to bed.

'I came over and looked you up just before 2 pm today, did you see me? I made three or four low runs over the mill. I reckoned you would probably be in the middle of lunch or just finishing.'

On this day, Flying Officer J G Astbury and Pilot Officer Jean de Selys de Longchamps (Belgian), were walking near the dispersal area, where they had a lucky escape. Peter was coming in to land when one of his cannons mysteriously went off, sending 20 mm shells blasting across the spot. In the same letter Peter sent to his mother, he wisely made no reference to his wayward guns. Nor did he make any comment in his log book!

The squadron was now just about operational. A few tentative patrols out over the Channel were undertaken, although permission to fly over the enemy coast was strictly forbidden with the new type. The German Luftwaffe were becoming a nuisance with their hit-and-run sorties along the south coast of England, using Me109 and FW190 fighters, carrying a small bomb load which they dropped indiscriminately. These had started around March 1942. However, the Typhoon with its low-flying capability was starting to be used to counter these intrusions, although to be successful they would really need to be flying low-level standing patrols rather than be scrambled when the enemy was discovered. Once scrambled the Germans had invariably dropped their bombs and were on their way back across the Channel. So standing patrols became the norm for a while, which was far from cosy, operating an aeroplane so near the sea when there is a likelihood of losing a tail, developing engine trouble, and so on, without any height in which to bale out.

On the afternoon of 2 August 1942, Joe Atkinson and Peter were scrambled during an alert, and ordered to orbit base, but nothing developed and after half an hour they were told to 'pancake' – land. A few days later, Peter was patiently waiting while a new tail wheel was fixed to his aircraft when he suddenly noticed another airmen at the other end, carefully removing an oil pipe. Apparently the CO had given permission for bits of this aircraft to be cannibalised.

Another useful bit of training for the new boys was fighter affiliation. Squadron aircraft would be sent off to make mock attacks on a bomber so as to help air gunners to defend their machine, while the attacking fighter pilots could also experience what it was like to attack a bomber. Roy Payne and Peter were given some local flying in a Wellington bomber on the 12th to get the bomber crew's perspective. The pilot was once again brother Tony.

12 August heralded another visit from Tony, and both brothers flew the Wellington around for half an hour.

The Typhoon's first real operational debut came on the day of Operation Jubilee, the combined operations attack on the French Channel port of Dieppe on 19 August 1942. Wing Commander Gillam led the wing on three sweeps along the Channel and did engage in some brief combats, but the appearance of this new fighter confused some RAF pilots, and some Spitfires attacked, shooting down one of the Typhoons of 266 Squadron. Another Typhoon and pilot was lost after a scrap with German bombers. Peter was not involved in these sorties. However, he was involved in some fighter affiliation fights on the 28th. [In early 1944, Denys Gillam would be Peter's wing leader.]

On 29 August Peter had some real excitement, while he was up on a testing flight. Just gone 1 pm, Joe Atkinson and Pilot Officer Johnny Wells were scrambled but despite taking only around four minutes to get off, they were far too late, as group had blocked the scramble, initially due to other fighters being around. However, Peter heard all the excitement over the radio and asked for a vector and having been given a course towards the hostile, spotted a German aircraft some twenty minutes later, somewhere south-east of Braintree, Essex, about two miles away. By this time he had reached around 28,000 feet, so this was not a hit-and-run German, but one flying a reconnaissance mission. No sooner had he seen the enemy machine, now near Southend, than his engine started to cough and bang and he was forced to abandon the chase. It was thought that the hostile aircraft was a high-flying Ju86P, as others had been reported in the area over recent weeks.

Joe Atkinson led a low-level dusk patrol (LFP) on the evening of the 31st, along with Peter, Wells and Pilot Officer R Dopere, but they could only report spotting a loose sea mine bobbing upon the sea. Otherwise not much happened during September, apart from 609 moving from 12 Group, Duxford, to RAF Biggin Hill, Surrey, within 11 Group on the 18th, with Peter flying down in the Magister.

On the 15th Peter had taken part in a fighter sweep from Exeter to Cherbourg and back to Ibsley, but there was nothing to report. On 25 September he took up an ATC cadet in the Magister. The next evening however, he had a moment of panic. He and Pilot Officer R A Hagger were sent off to patrol from North Foreland to St Margaret's Bay, but Hagger's R/T became unserviceable just as it was starting to get dark. The weather wasn't playing ball either and Peter, having called for assistance and a bearing, suddenly realised that his radio still carried the 12 Group radio crystals. Luckily he managed to find and land at RAF Kenley – with the help of the flare path – while Hagger got himself down at Gatwick. Both men remained at these airfields overnight, but Peter was lucky for he was just in time to be invited to a mess party. Four days later he and Paul Richey were out on a late patrol but managed to get home and land at 7.25 pm, when the sky was even darker.

October was another month of little action, although Peter, playing as a forward, got his rugger boots muddy on the 21st, 609 defeating a team from Biggin Hill HQ. This same day Pilot Officer John Boulting was directing a film called 'Between Friends' at Biggin Hill and Peter was included as an extra.

Operational flying consisted almost completely of anti-hit-and-run patrols along the south coast. Occasionally some excitement came, but not for Peter. There was more of the same for him during November; Ramsgate to Dungeness becoming a favourite patrol route. On 13 November Peter and Roy Payne played for the Biggin Hill XV against RAF Kenley, the two pals flying across in the squadron's Tiger Moth. Biggin Hill won with some ease.

The major change in October was the arrival of the new CO, Squadron Leader R P Beamont DFC, who took over from Paul Richey, soon to depart for India. Roly 'Bea' Beamont had flown with 87 Squadron in France and during the Battle of Britain and was therefore an experienced fighter pilot. He was also experienced with the Typhoon for he had earlier been a test pilot with Hawkers, testing both Hurricanes and the new Typhoon. He had then become a supernumerary flight commander with 56 Squadron at Duxford.

The squadron had returned once more to Manston on 2 November. Peter wrote to his mother on the 19th, to Evesham, where she was again visiting her parents.

'The situation here isn't as bad after all, but a little too far from home. We are very comfortable and there are plenty of flicks to see in Margate. Our work is very boring and very safe.'

The next bit of excitement came on 9 December – FW190s were shooting up the barrage balloons and Dover, but Peter saw nothing. By 15 December, with Manston being almost on the coast between Margate and Ramsgate, the squadron kept a couple of pilots on cockpit readiness, for an immediate scramble. A system had been set up with local Royal Observer Corps chaps that if low-flying enemy aircraft were spotted they would fire off coloured rockets. Once seen in the air, the Typhoon section at readiness would fire up and take off immediately.

In mid-afternoon rockets were seen going up near Deal and Peter was sent off; once airborne he reported seeing more rockets being fired near Margate. When he arrived in the area he found a dog-fight in progress between a Westland Whirlwind (whose pilot claimed one enemy aircraft damaged but had his own machine damaged in turn), a Typhoon, and several FW190s. Two other 609 boys had been alerted, Haddon and Amor. As he watched, Peter saw one Typhoon catch fire, rear up in a final attempt to pump lead into the nearest Focke-Wulf from virtually point-blank range, before stalling and falling away.

Other 609 pilots arrived. Johnny Baldwin was on a practice flight and hearing all the excitement, he joined in. The CO, 'Bea' Beamont, who had only just landed after flying on a Rhubarb operation[3], immediately scrambled too – without helmet or parachute!

Peter waded into the fight, managing a head-on squirt at one FW190, then chased another back to France, in company with Baldwin, using all his remaining ammunition although unable to close the range. The pilot of the other Typhoon was Pilot Officer H D F Amor of 609 (in R7689 PR-B), who was killed. Flight Sergeant A 'Babe' Haddon claimed a 190 destroyed east of Ramsgate, the German pilot taking to his parachute. The German unit was 1 Staffel of JG26, and the pilot who shot down Amor, was Unteroffizier Josef Zirngibl. Amor's body was later washed ashore at Margate. The four 190s had earlier made machine-gun strafing attacks between Ebsfleet and Sandwich, firing into buildings and barns, a factory south of Ramsgate, and a lifting crane, while at Ebsfleet they even let fly at herds of sheep and cows, killing ten sheep and five cows.

The Whirlwind pilot, Pilot Officer R L Smith DFM, of 137 Squadron, was flying on a practice flight too, and spotting four FW190s at 1,000 feet over Pegwell Bay, was loath to let an opportunity of attacking them pass. He claimed hits on one 190, but the others set about him and his machine (P6976) was badly shot about.

Thus 609 had suffered its first loss for some time but also claimed its first success in air combat since operations had begun with the Typhoon. That same evening Peter was entered in a boxing contest, and knocked out his opponent

---

[3] Rhubarb sorties were those flown in minimal weather conditions, the object being to fly low over hostile territory and shoot-up anything Germanic and generally cause disquiet to the enemy. Usually flown in pairs or two pairs, low cloud was a condition needed in order to hide quickly if surprised by enemy fighters.

in the first round.

The following day, Polish pilot Sergeant R S Turek claimed another 190 near Boulogne. The outcome of a sortie on the 18th was tragic. Flying Officer 'Moose' Evans, on the last patrol of the day, was warned several times that bandits were in the area south of Dover. Eventually, in a darkening sky, he spotted two aircraft coming from the direction of the French coast, climbed up behind them, and started to close in. Uncertain of the nationality of the two aircraft, and as he had not been told of any 'friendly' aircraft in the area, Evans decided to slip below the two 'bogeys' to try and distinguish markings. He observed they had square wingtips, so assumed they were Me109s.

The aircraft then made a turn back to the south so this convinced Evans they must be Messerschmitts, so he attacked and one of the aircraft caught fire and dived into the sea. Sadly it turned out to have been a clipped-wing Spitfire from 91 Squadron from Lympne. Evans was cleared of any blame but it was unfortunate that the system in place allowed two separate sectors to operate individually, and in ignorance of each other's actions, thus allowing fighters from each to meet up without being told that other RAF aircraft were in the vicinity. This inevitably led to a court of enquiry, Peter attending in support of Evans with Flying Officer Frank Ziegler, the squadron's intelligence officer. Other witnesses were the controllers from Hornchurch, Biggin Hill and Swingate, plus the surviving pilot of 91 Squadron.

At the mention of boxing above, let us reveal another letter to his mother about this time. Although undated it must have been written towards the end of 1942 and after a long leave with his wife.

'Mavis has gone back and I'm feeling pretty browned off after having spent a glorious ten days with her.

'I am getting down to some serious training as I have been asked to box for Fighter Command against the Canadians. The fight may come off in the Albert Hall; anyway it's dated for 10 March, and it will mean I get a night at home. Of course, I'm feeling rather nervous about it as it seems far above my head, but if I am beaten, I've decided to be beaten whilst fit!'

His next dated letter was 21 December 1942. He had finally been able to take his brother Michael up in an aeroplane as he had promised.

'I do hope this Christmas will be as happy a one as possible for you all. Despite the lack of turkeys, etc.

'I took old Mike up for his trip [20 December in a Tiger Moth] as I'm sure you will have heard. I would so like to know what he said to you about it. He flew a bit himself and coped very well, and seemed to enjoy things that scared me to death when I started flying.

'I am feeling a little browned off at the moment, as just when things were warming up here and getting exciting, they have stopped everything we have been doing, except patrols. These, they say, are our proper role and we cannot manage more than one thing at once, so we go back to the old boring days.

'Well Mum, I do so hope this finds you well and happy, and that I will be able to see you again very soon. Tons and tons of love, from Pete.'

One has to wonder at what time of day this letter was written, because far from being boring, Peter was involved in an intensive operation over France on this day. It can only be assumed that, like most men, he had no wish to alarm his mother by telling her what he was really up to.

Shortly before noon, he and his flight commander, Joe Atkinson, took off to seek out German rail transport south of Le Tréport on a miserable day that was just right for a Rhubarb operation. That is to say, low cloud and pretty dismal. The two pilots crossed the French coast and began searching for movement on the railway lines, or indeed, any movement that involved German troops and materiel.

However, the two men became separated near Cayeux in 10/10ths cloud at 2,000 feet. Atkinson searched rail tracks from Gamanches to Hangest-sur-Somme but found nothing. Peter was luckier. Smoke led him to a goods train on the Eu-Aumale section of track and he dived on it, making three low-level cannon attacks on the engine and trucks. When he finally climbed back towards the low cloud the train's locomotive was gushing smoke and steam, and he had seen plenty of strikes on the trucks and a nearby building. As luck would have it both pilots found each other upon re-crossing the coast east of Le Tréport, and flew home together, landing at Manston at 12.42 – less than an hour after taking off. In his log book Peter noted: 'One train immobilized, goods trucks damaged, storage building on fire (Cat B).'

On Christmas Day a dance was put on at Doone House. The do was enlivened somewhat as Humphrey Gilbert and a WAAF came onto the dance floor on a horse, shouting "Tally-Ho!" The next day there were six eventless patrols and a 'comic' rugby match between 609 and the station. 609 won despite being attacked by soot bombs from the men of 841 Squadron of the Fleet Air Arm (Albacores). No doubt Peter, at 6' 2" was a prominent team target.

Christmas interrupted warlike operations but Peter was out again over France on 27 December, in company with a French pilot, Sergent-Chef A C 'Fifi' de Saxce. However, over France the clouds were not as low as over southern England, they were 6-8,000 feet and visibility was 1,000 yards. Peter wisely aborted the mission and returned to base.

Early in the new year of 1943 a bout of influenza laid several of 609's pilots low, including Peter, but he must have made a speedy recovery for on 14 January he and Jean de Selys Longchamps, Joe Atkinson, Flying Officers R A Lallemand (Belgian), and Ziegler the IO, attended a cocktail party at Grosvenor House, in London's Mayfair. Inside, a painting of Air Commodore Harold Peake, the founder of 609 Squadron, and former director of public relations, was being presented to the squadron (who then passed it over to Peake for the duration). Speeches were made by Group Captain Lord Willoughby de Broke MC AFC, Air Commodore of the Royal Auxiliary Air Force, followed by Joe Atkinson, on behalf of 609's CO, who was still under the weather. Others in attendance were Air Marshal A H Peck MC and Lord Sherwood, the parliamentary private secretary to the secretary of state for air, as well as being a former RAuxAF squadron commander. As the squadron diary noted: 'Though the squadron representatives are invited to dinner by Peake, they in fact take advantage of the option to fry other fish.'

While out hunting trains over France, between Le Tréport and Dieppe on 17 January 1943 Peter suddenly saw an aircraft flying towards him north of Aumale. No sooner had he recognised it to be a Ju88 bomber, than it passed below him less than 100 feet away, but then it was gone in the same clouds he might himself have used if he had to. He hadn't even enough time to move his thumb onto the gun button before it was gone.

Slight embarrassment the next day, as Peter, on stand-by for hit-and-run raiders, suddenly spotted 'rockets' over Ramsgate. Aircraft were scrambled but it turned out to be a Fleet Air Arm Albacore torpedo plane on a flare-dropping exercise. Perhaps someone should have made sure this sort of confusion didn't take place, and have the navy boys practice away from such a sensitive area.

Better results came on the 19th, when Peter was on patrol looking out for trains as dusk was approaching. He spotted one near Zarren, and despite some anti-aircraft fire, he made a cannon attack. Then he saw two more at Kortemarck, his cannon shells again producing good spurts of steam from the engine of one of them. Peter was credited with two locos (locomotives) damaged.

For the fourth day in a row, Peter was again in action. 609 sent out Rhubarb sorties, but within a couple of minutes of their departure, 'Cheval' Lallemand and Peter were sent off to fly a standing patrol – radar had picked up something. Heading west towards Dungeness, they spotted rockets being fired off over Dymchurch, then two FW190s were spotted below, flying east, inshore of a convoy, at 9.10 pm.

Lallemand began to dive but both enemy fighters must have seen him and began a climbing turn towards him. Meantime, Peter went for the second 190 that had turned and was heading for France. Suddenly oil spurted over his windscreen and he lost sight of the aircraft. Moments later, his windscreen having cleared somewhat, he saw the 190, or another one, heading towards Dover and being fired upon by the convoy, but lost it again in some haze. Lallemand scored hits on his German that began to leave a trail of flame and smoke and was reported to have gone into the sea. These two 190s were from 8./JG26 flying a weather reconnaissance, and had spotted the small convoy. Leutnant Hans Kümmerling failed to return, but his wingman got home.

This was just the start of a busy day, for a major German attack was made by fighters of JG2 upon London, while others created a diversionary attack on Tunbridge Wells. Twenty-eight Luftwaffe aircraft headed for London, and twelve for the Kent town. Other fighters would carry out a diversionary sweep east of the Thames estuary.

As the raids continued into the afternoon, Joe Atkinson, who had spent the day so far watching other pilots come down with victory after victory, philosophically took off for a stooge around with Peter as his wingman. Twenty-three minutes later they returned, Joe having claimed a 190 destroyed and Peter with a 'damaged'.

The two Typhoon pilots had seen some 190s turning in front of them, some five miles east of Dover, and Swingate Control told them they were friendly aircraft. To the two British pilots, they also looked and behaved as friendly. However, something seemed odd. As they rocked their wings, Joe and Peter could see crosses on a grey background, encircled by a most misleading yellow roundel. These fighters were from 5/JG26 and were on an air-sea-rescue search.

The two Typhoon pilots quickly decided these were hostile fighters and went for them. The 'bogeys' suddenly turned and headed for France, using the usual jinking manoeuvres and cross-over tactics. However, this enabled the two RAF men to close the range more quickly and both opened fire, seeing strikes on two of the fighters. When Peter finished his ammunition he continued to 'shoot' with his cine-camera. Joe Atkinson, after several bursts from 300, closing to 250 yards, saw a flash and his 190 dived into the sea some fifteen miles south-east of Dover. Joe had shot down Feldwebel Alfred Barthel.

The squadron had had a successful day. Johnny Baldwin had shot down one fighter, followed by an attack on another whose pilot collided with one of his comrades, so both went down. All three were Me109s of 6./JG26. Flying Officer Remy Van Lierde (Belgian) also claimed a 190.

More Rhubarb and anti-train missions followed. On 27 January 1943, Peter and Babe Haddon found a train and fired new SAPI [semi armour-piercing/incendiary] ammunition into the engine, which exploded, vomiting black smoke, flame and pieces into the air. Peter's Typhoon was caught in the explosion and when he got home the aircraft was covered in black pieces and the paintwork was scorched. Haddon also attacked some trucks he spotted at Chepy, then went after another train further on from which German soldiers were unloading boxes. These were seen quickly taking cover as Haddon raked the train during three more attacks, leaving the engine spewing steam from its ruptured boiler. Peter was credited with one train destroyed, Haddon one damaged and rolling stock also damaged. There is no mention of German soldiers with soiled undergarments. In his log, Peter wrote: 'One train destroyed (Cat A) – train blew-up, starboard wing of "E" burnt and marked.'

On the penultimate day of January, Peter was sent off to shoot down a barrage balloon that had snapped its mooring cable, and after doing so he reported seeing others down on the sea. Sadly there is no explanation as to why they had become free – but probably it was due to strong wind.

On 4 February, the squadron medical officer, plus Roy Payne and Peter were chosen to play for the Manston XV side against nearby RAF Hawkinge, in the AOC's Cup. Manston won five to three. Soccer and hockey teams were also victorious, so Hawkinge suffered a bad day.

Chapter Four

WAR OVER FRANCE

With better weather in February 1943, 609 Squadron stepped up its operations over enemy-held France. Standing patrols and cockpit readiness continued against the threat of German hit-and-run raids along the south coast of England but Fighter Command was also continuing to harass the enemy's transport systems.

On 7 February, and with some improved serviceability with their Typhoons, 609 began flying Rhubarbs once more with the better weather. Or as the squadron diarist put it – 'in a big way'. Peter took off at 11.51 am in company with Sergeant T D L Leslie and headed south. Crossing the French coast at Bray Dunes at about 2,000 feet amidst low cloud, the two pilots separated to seek out individual targets. Peter turned left and located a solitary engine on the track between Furnes and Dixmude, Belgium and attacked. He observed strikes on the driver's cabin and coal tender and the engine stopped, with masses of steam released from the punctured boiler.

Continuing on he came across a goods train approaching Dixmude from the east. One strafing run stopped it in its tracks and the engine blew up, sending smoke, flames and debris into the grey noon sky, despite some light tracer fire reaching up for the 'Tiffie'. Shortly afterwards Peter found loco number three, another goods train on the Dixmude to Thourout line. Again cannon strikes stopped the engine amidst gushing steam clouds. Suddenly Peter saw telegraph poles directly ahead and quickly pulled back on the stick, causing him to bang his head on the cockpit canopy. He missed the poles but ripped through the telephone wires.

Still flying low he left Thourout behind and headed for Roulers to the south.

He was having quite a day. Train number four came into view, yet another goods train. More strikes and more steam; the engine stopped. Peter turned north-west, back in the direction of Dixmude, found yet another goods train and raked it with gunfire; more steam and another stopped loco. Peter was now heading towards the coast but spotted a barge near a lock on the Canal de Loo. Cannon strike flashes indicated hits, confirmed also by belching smoke. East of Dixmude he came across yet another train, but before he could open fire he was forced to take evasive action as anti-aircraft fire exploded around him and tracer shells whipped past.

Meantime, Sergeant Leslie had not been idle. Several trucks were spotted being loaded at a railway station north of Roulers and he saw hits from his fire. Over Roulers rail yards, he made two dummy runs before finally opening fire on a number of other, covered, trucks, which produced thick smoke. Leslie too was faced with the danger of telegraph poles whilst flying at thirty feet or even less. Forced to pull up violently, he hit some wires, and brought some evidence of this back in his radiator. Reaching 8,000 feet Leslie called it a day and flew home. Peter's record of one train definitely destroyed, and four damaged, plus a damaged barge, was some score.

Another piece on Peter's activities appeared in the *Daily Sketch* newspaper the next day:

TRAIN-BUSTER HIT BY ENGINE DEBRIS

An RAF 'train-buster' shot up five engines in Belgium yesterday and flew so low in attacking one that bits of it flew up and dented his wing.

In strafing another his plane crashed through telegraph wires and he was fired at. The gunners missed him and on the way home he attacked a barge.

Other pilots shot up three more goods engines and three barges in Northern France. One fighter is missing.

On 14 February 609 lost two pilots. Sergeant J G Wiseman and Flight Sergeant Babe Haddon were bounced over the Channel by FW190s of JG2 and shot down. Neither survived.

On the evening of 18 February, four Typhoons, led by Beamont, flew out on an intruder mission, taking Peter, Jean de Selys and a second Belgian, Adjutant A Blanco. Again the aircraft split up after crossing the enemy coast, Peter heading towards Hazebrouck in the darkening sky. Finding a number of trains, he attacked one to the west of the town, seeing strikes and steam. Similar results followed after attacking another loco to the north. Not surprisingly, the sky came alive with bursting AA fire and red tracer shells, but it seemed obvious to him that the fire was more in desperation than actually aimed, for he easily evaded it all. Another barge on a canal received attention before he turned back towards Hazebrouck, but this time the Germans had settled down and the flak seemed heavier and more concentrated, so he turned back north and headed home. His log book entry: 'Two trains immobilised (Cat B), one barge attacked.'

With capture over France or Belgium always a distinct possibility, especially when operating at low level (where the humorists insist they can just as easily be brought down by a well aimed bayonet thrust at the heights they often fly), talks on escape and evasion often occur. Not only talks, but on occasion, pilots were sent off on actual exercises. On 18 February one such exercise was ordered – 'Exercise King-O'. The squadron supplied six of the twenty-five 'volunteer' personnel.

Against them the police and Home Guard turned out in force, but they were a bit miffed to find one of the participants, a navy man, carrying a revolver, which he used to hold one of them up. When they were told all the navy guys were armed, the 'defenders' complained they were not told about this. "It's only a game old boy!" was the response.

All six of 609 manage to get back un-apprehended, except Flying Officer M 'Paddy' Cameron, from Ireland, who was caught by the police (and not for the first time it seems), but he finally turned up after dark, having in the meantime visited some friends in Margate. First home was Flying Officer 'Mony' van Lierde. A veteran escaper in any event – most Belgians had managed some form of escape or other to get to England – he was initially rather irked to have been asked to participate in the first place. He got home by jumping on two successive army trucks, lying on their roofs, and slipping off again without being spotted. (He hotly denied that the second truck actually dropped him outside the airfield!)

All the rest of 609 made it back on foot, except Flying Officer H T Skett, who came back part way on a bus. Peter Raw counted the exercise as part of his training for an upcoming boxing contest, but had a rather sudden encounter with a land girl, who apparently, and for reasons not recorded, ran away blushing!

Squadron Leader Beamont, Johnny Wells, Cameron, Evans, de Selys and Peter Raw took part in an evening Roadstead operation on the evening of 7 March, sweeping off the French coast between the Somme and Boulogne. If any ships had been reported, 609 did not find them. They and their Spitfire escort were subjected to some flak from the forts at Boulogne harbour, but they were not harmed.[1]

The boxing contest referred to above, the same one as mentioned in Peter's previous letter to his mother, duly took place on 10 March. Peter flew a Tiger Moth to Heston that evening for the match – Fighter Command versus an anti-aircraft team, and although he won his bout, the RAF lost by one point overall. One of Peter's fellow pilots wrote in his diary about his boxing:

> 'Peter Raw flew to Heston to box for Fighter Command; won his fight, but the lad who was opposing him was under weight so the fight did not count, but I don't expect the other bloke was comforted by that.'

Newspapers picked up the story too, printing this piece before the event:

THE HEAVY-WEIGHT FIGHTER PILOT

Fighter pilots are not big fellows as a rule. Cockpits are not built for heavy-weights, but Flying Officer Peter Raw is a heavy-weight, and in that class boxes on Wednesday night at an RAF station near London for Fighter Command, South-Eastern area team, against Anti-Aircraft Command. Former Wellington schoolboy, with a fine record on the sport field, Flying Officer Raw, has won a number of heavy-weight competitions at RAF stations. A few weeks ago he shot up and damaged five goods train engines on a sweep over Belgium, and when he came back he said: "Clouds of steam poured out of it as my cannon-fire went home. I was pretty low and went through some telegraph wires. The sudden bump made me bang my head on the cockpit cover." The bump has done him no harm, and he will take the ring against Gunner Kent in the only heavy-weight fight of the dozen bouts to be staged.

Four days later came the squadron's first night intruder sortie of the month; Peter and Remy Van Lierde headed out. Peter had his first attack on a train thwarted by some heavy AA fire near Lille, but then found two more locos heading east, close together south-east of the town. Peter's three attacks immobilised both with a flash and clouds of steam. Two more to add to his growing score of locomotives destroyed

[1] A Roadstead was an attack by fighter and/or light bombers upon shipping off the enemy coast, generally at low level.

or damaged. This effort also received media coverage on 15 March, in the *Daily News*:

LONDONER GOES TRAIN BUSTING WITH RAF AT NIGHT

RAF Fighter Command aircraft were out again during the night, continuing their offensive against enemy communications. Of the four trains attacked, one was in Germany. One of the members of the West Riding of Yorkshire Typhoon squadron that took part first attacked a stationary train near Lille, and then tackled two trains travelling close together south of the city. "I saw my cannon shells hitting the locomotive," he said today. "There was a big flash and clouds of steam."

Searchlight Hunt

The pilot, a twenty-three-year old Londoner, who is a prominent amateur boxer and swimmer, then attacked the engine of the second train. Two searchlights hunted for his Typhoon, but the pilot returned safely to base. Another pilot saw a red glow from a train in the same area and attacked it from behind. Despite AA fire all our aircraft returned safely.

More intruder sorties follow. On 19 March, no less than fourteen were flown but the weather proved uncooperative. Eric Haabjoern (Norwegian), Peter, Les Smith and Roy Payne also tried on the 29th but the skies above the Channel were cloudless with visibility at forty miles, so they were forced to abort. Also on this day two of 609's honourary members turned up on a visit, Air Commodore, the Earl of Harewood, and Air Commodore Peake.

At this time the squadron had a visit from the RAF's official war artist, Captain Cuthbert Orde, who came to Manston to sketch some of the pilots. He was no stranger to 609, having drawn a number of its pilots earlier in the war, and he would come again. On this visit he painted Beamont in oils, and did his more usual charcoal sketches, of Joe Atkinson, Johnny Wells, Moose Evans, Cheval Lallemand, Frank Ziegler and Peter Raw. Orde must have either stayed a few days or completed the drawings at a later date, for the pictures of Atkinson and Lallemand are dated 30 March, while Wells's is dated the 31st, and Evans and Peter's are dated 3 and 5 April respectively.

Orde had himself been a pilot during WW1 after serving with the Army Service Corps. He was active at the start of the war, thus receiving the 1914 Mons Star, when aged twenty-six. He became an observer with the Royal Flying Corps in late 1915, serving in the Middle East. He became a pilot in 1916 and flew at the Central Flying School before taking a post as a test pilot, and later with the Aero Experimental Station, in early 1918. His wife, Lady Eileen Orde was the daughter of the 4th Duke of Wellington.

Peter was out on an E-boat search on 30 March, flying between Dungeness, the Somme estuary, Cap Gris Nez and Dover. The pilots faced 10/10th low cloud and saw nothing. German E-boats – similar to the Royal Navy's MTBs (motor torpedo boats) – were often very active in the Channel at night, hoping to catch any allied shipping trying to slip along the south coast of England, or even looking out for the navy's MTBs out on a similar mission.

More offensive actions occurred in April, although for once 609 found themselves being used as a diversion, but one of them, so the squadron diary records, marked a new epoch – attacks on shipping. Four E-boats, a flak ship and a 200-ton ship were attacked during a battle in which Peter apparently starred.

1 April 1943 marked the twenty-fifth anniversary of the formation of the RAF, and this proved a suitable day to mark the occasion with ideal weather conditions for Rhubarb sorties. At 10.05 am Peter and Les Smith embarked on a successful trip to Belgium, the first for Les Smith, although he had done similar things in Arabia apparently. There he was reputed to have destroyed thirteen aircraft; two in the air and eleven more on the ground. Leslie Ernest Smith had been an 'AC plonk' back in 1935, but after volunteering to be a pilot, he gained his wings and served with 94 Squadron flying Gloster Gladiator biplanes in the defence of Habbaniya, Iraq, in May 1941. He would later be a flight commander with 609 and was decorated with the DFC.

Crossing the hostile coast east of Dunkirk in cloud, they separated at Dixmude, and shortly after this, Peter spotted a train between Courtrai and Deynze. His first attack scored strikes while his second had to be made by firing through a signal box that was shielding his reciprocal approach. Carrying on he attacked another train near Langstaat, then bagged a third between Deynze and Thielt. Down to three cannons, one having jammed, he headed for the airfield at Zwevezele, gave it a good look-over, then headed for the coast, but found a fourth train on the Bruges to Ghent line, and blasted chunks off it. He came out, again in cloud, north-east of Ostend. 'Four trains immobilised (Cat B). W/O Barker lost', went into his log book. Warrant Officer W T Barker had been out too and was brought down by anti-aircraft fire off Dunkirk.

On 4 April fog rolled in some time after Peter had taken off on a patrol at 10.35

am but he just managed to get back down at Manston before visibility was totally obliterated. When it cleared the squadron prepared for Ramrod 46, which required nine Typhoons to provide an escort for eight Whirlwinds of 137 Squadron that were going to attack the railway marshalling yards at Abbeville. It was the first time 609 had been selected for such an operation, and Squadron Leader Beamont put himself down to lead it. Beamont had already led the squadron on a Roadstead sortie earlier that morning but had found no sign of any shipping. Take-off time for the Ramrod was 6.15 pm and they rendezvoused with two Spitfire squadrons from Hornchurch who gave top cover to the seventeen aircraft of the main attacking force.

The aircraft crossed into French territory at Bayeux, with the Whirlwinds at 8,500 feet, and 609 flying 500 feet lower and to the rear. The fighter-bombers went into a dive to 7,000 feet as the marshalling yards appeared ahead, the bombs falling into the target area without opposition. They all turned for home and halfway to the coast, Swingate Control ordered 609 to vector towards a 'special target'. This turned out to be a group of several German R-boats [minesweepers] together with a small flak-ship off Boulogne. Finding these vessels, Beamont manoeuvred his seven remaining pilots (two had continued on with the Whirlwinds) in order to attack from the west so that the setting sun would make it difficult for the ships' gunners to fire on their attackers. Heading in low and fast the Typhoons achieved surprise and in fact no flak came up until Beamont began firing.

However, once it began it quickly became intense, so 'Bea' ordered his men to make just one attacking pass. He and four others went for the last pair of R-boats, while Johnny Wells and Moose Evans opened up on the flak ship. This ship and one R-boat erupted in flames, while a second was damaged. Adjutant Pilot Blanco was hit and part of his rudder was shot away, but he retained control and got home. Control again called to warn them that bandits were heading in, so everyone set course for Manston. Beamont, Paddy Cameron, Blanco, Peter, and Van Lierde were credited with the damage to the R-boats, while Wells and Evans with heavy damage to the flak ship. Peter's machine had been hit too and his engine began to cut out but luckily he reached base and landed safely.

In Edward Lanchbery's biography of Roland Beamont published in 1955, it is recorded:

'Beamont looked round and saw Peter Raw's aircraft a few hundred yards away. It was leaving a trail of black smoke that was ominous indeed. The cliffs of the North Foreland were already in sight, and despatching the remainder to base independently, he turned back to escort Blue One. "Head straight for land, Peter," he advised. "You are leaving a bit of smoke." If he had not known it already, Raw would realize now that his motor was losing its oil. "Yes, Sir," he said cheerfully. "I don't think she'll last long. I'll climb a bit.'"

Beamont followed the other Typhoon up to a thousand feet. At least the pilot was at a sufficient height to bale out if necessary. But Peter Raw's luck was to hold for another year. Crossing the coast he curved straight in to make an immediate landing at base. Somehow, incredibly, he had flown nearly fifty miles with one piston smashed to pieces. Van Lierde's aircraft had been badly shot up, and Beamont's and one other machine had been raked with superficial holes and gashes in wings and cowlings.

The well-known aviation artist Robert Taylor depicted this attack in an oil painting he completed in 1985, entitled, *Typhoon Attack*. In it Peter Raw's aircraft can be plainly seen to the left of Beamont's Typhoon, R7752 – coded PR-G, in the work. Peter was flying DN406, coded PR-F. On this aeroplane's side, by the cockpit, was painted the name 'Mavis', while below it there were the symbols of the trains he had shot up.

Meantime, in his log book Peter recorded: 'Share one R-Boat destroyed and one R-Boat damaged. Observe hits by Whirlwind on target. Tons of flak, engine trouble, landed safely (Sixty pieces taken out of my filter).'

In the 1990s, Simon Muggleton was in touch with Wing Commander Roland Beamont CBE DSO & Bar, DFC & Bar, DL FRAeS, concerning Peter, while they were both flying with 609 Squadron. Bea wrote:

'Peter Raw was in 609 Squadron which I commanded at Manston in 1943. He is the man in that [famous] photo with our squadron mascot, W/Cdr Billy de Goat (we were a part-Belgium squadron!).

'Peter was a quiet giant of a man, much liked in the squadron and a fine, courageous fighter pilot. I knew his wife Mavis in those days but have lost touch with her.

'There is a fine painting by Robert Taylor called *Typhoon Attack* published as a print which shows an action which I led on 4 April 1943 in which Peter's Typhoon was hit by flak which knocked off a complete cylinder head. Peter calmly said he would have to bale out over the Channel but I advised him to stay with it if the engine was still running.

'He got back to Manston (a further twenty miles) and didn't appear at all disturbed by the experience! A great chap.'

In a further letter, Bea explains:

'The shipping attack was Ramrod 46. The intelligence report notes Blanco being hit in the rudder but leaves out Raw's engine. Not unusual in a hurry to get the signal off!

'As I followed Peter back with what looked like a failed engine he was streaming smoke and oil, some of which got onto my windscreen. Then we got warning of "Bandits" over Calais, heading north – luckily for us they did not pursue us – as we had no ammunition left.

'He later joined me at Hawker's, Langley.'

The next afternoon (Peter had already flown a patrol in the morning) the squadron flew eight patrols, both anti-hit-and-run, and convoy escorts. Then quite suddenly, at 8.45 pm, with just half an hour's notice, six pilots who were available, took off under Peter's leadership. Their instructions were to sweep from the Somme estuary to Cap Gris Nez and he was accompanied by Les Smith, Flying Officer E R A Roberts, de Moulin, Blanco and Pilot Officer M L Van Neste. Before they hit the French coast two unidentified aircraft were reported, but these turned out to be Typhoons of 1 Squadron, so after this delay, Peter continued on to reach the French coast south of Boulogne, where they came under AA fire.

With the light beginning to fail, and having seen nothing of interest, Peter began to head for home, but then control gave them a vector against a target to the south. In the gloom Peter requested someone to follow him but only Smithy responded. Changing course they came across four R-boats off Le Touquet but only Peter saw them before they began firing up at the two aircraft. Breaking away, Peter circled before heading in again, dropping to just 100 feet above the water, and holding his fire until the range had closed to 300 yards, where he began firing 'til he was a mere fifty yards from the boats. Intense anti-aircraft fire tried to seek out the onrushing Typhoon but Peter had singled out one of the boats and he could clearly see sparks and flying pieces and as he broke away he got the impression he saw an explosion. Some of his shells zipped over his main target and he saw further strikes on a second boat. Surprisingly un-hit himself, Peter, remaining low, headed towards home. He was later credited with two R-boats, one with Cat II damage, the other Cat III. Again he mentions 'tons of flak' in his log. (Damage to the enemy had been recently changed from Cat A, destroyed, Cat B probably destroyed and Cat C, damaged, to Cat I, Cat II and Cat III.)

The next day he wrote to his mother, yet another typical letter designed to allay any fear or worry she might have. One would have thought he was writing from the highlands of Scotland rather than from 'hellfire corner', which was how Manston and its environs were described.

'Things have been very quiet here just lately, old Jerry seems to have given up his reprisal raids following our bombers' night attacks.

'We have had some very fine weather the last few days and it has been so hot I have been walking about in shirt-sleeves, but today there is a gale blowing and it is damned cold.

'My portrait was drawn yesterday by Captain Orde. It will not be my property as it is being done for Air Commodore Peake, who was the first CO of our squadron, but I think I will be able to get a photographed copy. I think Mavis will be going to see Captain Orde's studio in town, you can go and see it with her if you like.

'Well Mum, I hope to get some time off soon just to pop home for a night, so I hope to be seeing you. I do hope you are keeping well and please give my love to Trixie and David.

'Tons of love to you with a big hug. From Pete.'

More patrols followed, and on 9 April, Peter and Flying Officer H T Skett, flew one at 7.26 pm, which proved interesting. He had reached dispersal with the intention of flying the Tiger Moth to Hornchurch, in order to get the underground train to London. However, radar warned Swingate Control of some activity out to sea, so Peter and Skett were scrambled.

Control vectored them to a spot where they found a black HSL (high speed launch) proceeding north-east at speed, with four other vessels off to the south. Some ten or twelve FW190s were also picked out in a ragged line-abreast formation, with more above. Undaunted, Peter turned to attack the rear-most Focke-

Wulf, but the leading German had the same idea and pulled round and fired at the Typhoon. At this moment the boats joined in with lots of light flak. Both Typhoon pilots decided prudence would be the best course to follow, broke off and headed for home, with four or five 190s giving chase, but they soon broke away too.

Apparently there had been some German fighter-bomber activity in the area and three Luftwaffe aircraft had been shot down, so the boats were obviously engaged in an air-sea-rescue operation. Peter wrote: 'Visibility very bad owing to fog – flew into the middle of twelve FW190s. Made head-on attack and "Beat it". Five on my number two's tail, but out of range – both OK!'

13 June 1943 – Peter was having a few days off with Mavis:

'Mavis and I have been really enjoying ourselves during the last few days. During the course of one day we polished off 4 lbs of strawberries between us. I also had two plates of gooseberries! Most of my spare time has been spent on the beach with Mavis, but we have had a little difficulty with the police as it is supposed to be out of bounds except for organised RAF or army parties.

'The party night last night was one of the better ones as the station commander had taken the trouble to see there were plenty of females by asking some of George Black's show girls and some ENSA girls. I expect Mavis will tell you all about the food when she comes home, but we did have strawberries and cream, and lobster. I'm sorry to make your mouth water.

'You can tell Trixie I now have a brand new plane which is [code marked] 'T' for Trixie. I'm getting very browned off with this place and I only hope I am able to go to Hawkers soon, but not [an] OTU.'

This final reference would refer to the ending of his tour. Most pilots could expect their rest period at either an operational training unit, as instructors, or, if on Typhoons, to be posted to Hawkers at Langley for test flying, or alternatively to Napiers to help test aircraft engines.

Sadly this is the last surviving letter we have on file of Peter's, for almost a year, but his flying with 609 Squadron continued for a while yet. On the late afternoon of 18 April, Beamont led eight Typhoons, including Peter's, as rear cover for Ramrod 64 for an attack on Courtrai. They patrolled from Dunkirk to Ostend, some miles off the coast, as the attacking force went in, but although bandits were reported near

Dunkirk, Ostend and finally Flushing, none were seen, despite wonderful visibility.

Peter was out after trains again over Belgium on the night of 20 April, taking off twenty minutes before midnight. Near Moorseele, he was caught by two searchlights near the airfield there but evaded their beams, picked up the rail line towards Ath, then went on to the Deynze/Ecloo canal. Having found nothing on the rail system he made some attempts at attacking barges, before heading north-west towards Ostend. Still sighting nothing of interest he re-crossed the coast at Blankenberge. Two miles out from Ostend he spotted two ships, each of about 100 tons or so. Again he attempted an attack but could only approach them by flying towards the nearby shore. However, a four-second burst caused strikes and flashes, while some return fire from the ships reached up for him. He was credited with one ship Cat III. His log book entry reads: 'Two 200-ton ships seen one mile off Ostend. One damaged (a little flak from ships, tons from Ostend).'

Two days later the weather clamped somewhat, so Rhubarb operations were suggested. Peter became airborne shortly after 7 am, and headed out with Roy Payne for the Belgian railway system. They crossed the hostile coast in cloud then let down below the cloud some ten miles inland. Passing Ledeghem airfield, they saw a train east of Courtrai, which they left belching smoke and steam. A gun on the train's tender opened up and then some flak from a nearby village joined in. The two pilots separated, Peter attacking a train consisting of cattle trucks east of Lille, but the cattle turned out to be lots of men in uniform who began to disperse either side of the track. Continuing on east, Peter spotted Roy attacking an engine near St Genois, which appeared to blow up. Black smoke and debris, which included the entire cab cover, flew into the air. For a moment it looked as if Payne had been hit by the flying wreckage. Peter made an approach but three of his cannons stopped after a short burst.

Peter was relieved to see Roy nearby and the two joined up, but Payne then went for another train east of Courtrai. The driver attempted to escape by accelerating but the Typhoon quickly overhauled it and the engine was left spurting steam and smoke. Near Roulers, Peter saw some railway trucks, opened up with his lone cannon and left two smoking, but then it was time to head for home. Over the English coast they were welcomed back by some flak from Deal – luckily the gunners missed. With one railway engine destroyed, three damaged, two barges and two rail wagons damaged, it was quite a successful bit of offensive action by the two friends. Peter's log: 'One-and-a-half trains immobilised (Cat II), two barges damaged (Cat III), two trucks damaged. Flak from one train.'

29 April saw Peter involved in two scrambles but neither produced any action. News arrived on 1 May that Joe Atkinson, after one of the longest fighter tours on record, had been awarded the Distinguished Flying Cross, even though, having been found out he had been posted away to 50 OTU at Milfield as chief flying instructor. He had been with 609 Squadron from December 1940 until April 1943 – twenty-eight months. There were in fact two DFC awards to 609 on this date, the second going to Peter Raw. Peter's citation, recorded in the *London Gazette* of 18 May 1943, read:

> *This officer has achieved excellent results in attacks on rail installations in Northern France and Belgium, immobilising seventeen locomotives. Recently he took part in two attacks on enemy shipping, obtaining good results. This officer has displayed great courage and tenacity, pressing home his attacks with vigour.*

Roland Beamont had written up the recommendation for Peter's DFC on 7 April. As was usual, the actual citation differed somewhat from what was written by the person putting it forward. In Peter's case, Bea's words were:

> 'F/O Raw is a pilot of exceptional courage and ability, and is always eager to hunt and engage the enemy. During a period of three months he has attacked and immobilised seventeen locomotives, eleven by day and six by night, during offensive operations over France and Belgium. Recently he has taken part in two attacks on enemy shipping, and in the face of intense flak has severely damaged two and scored hits on two more enemy motor minesweepers. He has also damaged a FW190 raider.'

For any recommendation for an award, it needed the support of the station commander on whose airfield the pilot operated. In this case, Wing Commander D F B Sheen DFC wrote on the 9th:

> 'F/O Raw has displayed the offensive spirit to a very marked degree. He has taken advantage of every opportunity to seek out and attack the enemy. I strongly support the recommendation of his squadron commander.'

Ever upwards, the recommendation now moved on to the sector commander for his support. Group Captain A G Adnams, station commander RAF Hornchurch, wrote on the 12th:

'This officer has achieved excellent results against enemy transportation targets. He recently displayed a particularly high standard of courage and tenacity when he pressed home an attack against a force of enemy mine-sweepers in the face of intense opposition and in failing light. I endorse the recommendation for the award of the DFC.'

This in due course was confirmed and endorsed by the AOC-in-C of Fighter Command, Air Marshal Trafford Leigh-Mallory DSO, on 29 April 1943.

What his mother thought of all this is not known, but obviously her son's 'quiet life' often had moments of amazing disquiet! So now Mrs Raw had two decorated sons, Tony and now Peter, both with DFCs. She must have been very proud.

Rather unkindly there is a note in another pilot's personal diary about Peter's award, saying in jest that: 'Nobody knows quite what it is for, as he has not shot down any Jerries and has only destroyed [sic] seventeen trains – anyway, it's one more gong for the outfit, so we shouldn't worry.'

In fact, to be accurate, squadron records show that Peter claimed eighteen loco-motives, plus another shared destroyed or damaged. In addition he had damaged three R-boats, one 200-ton ship, three canal barges and some rolling stock, plus one FW190 damaged. Most of this was achieved in low-level fighter attacks, often at night, during December 1942 to May 1943, when the weather was often poor.

The record shows:

1942

| 21 Dec | One Loco Cat B | plus rolling stock damaged | R8815 C |

1943

19 Jan	Two Locos Cat B		R8888 Y
20 Jan	One FW190 damaged		R8940 V
27 Jan	One Loco Cat A		DN367 E
7 Feb	One Loco Cat A		DN329 C
	Four Locos Cat B	plus one barge Cat III	DN329 C
18 Feb	Two Locos Cat B	One barge attacked	R8715 J
14 Mar	Two Locos Cat B	another attacked, no result	DN360 A
1 Apr	Four Locos Cat B		DN406 F
4 Apr		One R-boat Cat III shared	DN406 F
5 Apr		One R-boat Cat I	DN329 C

		One R-boat Cat III		DN406 F
20 Apr		One 200-ton ship Cat III		DN406 F
22 Apr	One Loco Cat B			DN406 F
	Half Loco Cat B	Two barges Cat III		DN406 F
	Half Loco Cat B	Two trucks Cat B		DN406 F
16 May		One E-boat Cat II		DN582 P
16 May		One 200-ton ship damaged		DN406 F

It was obviously very difficult to determine if a loco's engine had been written off after an attack, or just damaged slightly and able to be repaired. Therefore, some Cat B/Cat II damage might well have been engines that were indeed written off. Whoever noted the above categories of assessment was somewhat confused.

Looking at the list of Typhoons Peter flew on these particular operations, one can see that pilots did not always have their same aeroplane on each show. On his earlier flights he often flew DN329 'PR-C' and latterly, DN406 'PR-F'. Typhoon 'F' had been the machine flown by Pilot Officer L W F Stark and then taken over by Peter. It is also clear that of the train symbols marked on the side of DN406, only six are attributable to operations in this particular machine.

Once again Peter made the newspapers with his award. The *Middlesex Country Times* for Wednesday, 6 May 1943, gave Peter a long column in its newspaper:

TWENTY LOCOMOTIVES WRECKED

'Flying Officer Peter E Raw has wrecked or damaged nearly twenty locomotives in occupied territory this year, and was in the army for some time before he became a fighter pilot. Born at Ealing, where his home still is – his wife is engaged in war work – he is one of three brothers who joined the Royal Air Force. The elder brother was killed in a flying accident in 1941. The other, Flight Lieut. A W Raw DFC, is in Bomber Command. He and Flying Officer Raw married sisters. After leaving Wellington School, Somerset, with a notable record in swimming, cricket, rugby football, rifle shooting and boxing, Flying Officer Raw went into the insurance business in September 1937. A few months later he joined the Honourable Artillery Company. He was commissioned into the 6th Batt. The Somerset Light Infantry after the outbreak of war, and it was not until France fell that he resolved to follow his brothers into the Royal Air Force.

'F/O Raw does his train-busting as a member of the West Riding of Yorkshire squadron, flying a Typhoon. Early this year he damaged a FW190, but *since then his targets have been chiefly locomotives with occasional attacks on R-Boats off the enemy coast.*

'His best "bag" was when he shot up five trains and a barge in a single sortie over Belgium. Near Roulers he attacked the nearer of two trains and saw strikes on the engine and clouds of steam. "I was down pretty low," he said on reaching base, "and I went through some telegraph wires. I was fired at too, but nothing hit me, so I went on to attack the other engine, and flew through the steam it was giving off. There was no doubt about scoring hits because bits of the engine jumped up and made dents in my wings, but no real damage was done to my aircraft."'

Beamont left 609 Squadron on 5 May, and his place was taken by Squadron Leader Alec Ingle DFC AFC. Bea went on rest and to do some test flying with Hawkers, but would return to operations later in the war, flying the Hawker Tempest.

Peter flew another night intruder mission on the 13th, this time to Chièvres but failed to find any rail activity, nor around Ghent where he went afterwards. Heading back, low on fuel, he did see seven vessels of 600 tons off the Dutch coast, and reported them to HQ.

Three days later, 16 May, Peter was one of a number of pilots who were sent out on night Rhubarb sorties. Leaving Manston at 11.28 pm he headed for Arques where he hoped to attack the ship-lift there. For the first time he was carrying two 250 lb bombs, one under each wing, and sent both down over the target. Heading back he crossed the coast north of Boulogne and spotted three E-boats escorting a 200-ton vessel not far from the harbour mouth. Peter dived straight in, opening up with his cannons on the nearest E-boat from landward. Strikes produced bright flashes followed by a cloud of smoke like an explosion, but by then he was being fired at by the other two motor torpedo boats. He quickly headed north low and fast, landing back at 00.48am.

He was off again at 2.53 am, this time on an intruder sortie to the airfields at Poix and Abbeville. Unhappily he found no activity at the former and only a few aerodrome lights at the latter, so he headed for the Dutch coast where he fully expected to spot some shipping in what could be called 'his happy hunting ground'. Again he saw a 200-ton ship, headed in low, opened up with his 20 mm cannons and obtained a good quota of strikes. For his trouble he was bracketed by heavy flak from ship and shore as he headed north for home. He was credited with two bombs on the ship-lift, with one E-boat and one cargo ship, both Cat III.

Something very different occurred on 19 May. After two morning patrols, the usual day readiness state ended in the afternoon in order to permit the squadron to receive guests. All personnel were assembled to form a hollow square, including Wing Commander William [Billy!] de Goat DFC, the Squadron's famous mascot, to greet the arrival of Air Vice-Marshal H W L Saunders CB MC DFC MM, AOC 11 Group of Fighter Command (later marshal of the RAF Sir Hugh Saunders GCB KBE MC DFC MM) together with Flying Officer Ray Lallemand DFC.

According to the squadron diary, the parade had given the adjutant something of a headache. Having previously given up all attempts at a rehearsal, he suddenly startled everybody by marching off in a most soldierly manner. It was thought he had been coached by Peter, giving him the benefit of his previous army experience.

Peter's tour was now coming to an end. On 23 May he flew to Langley to see his former CO, Bea Beamont, with a view to joining the Hawker test team there. On 3 June radar control reported a blip on their screens at sector HQ that looked like a raid of some thirty-plus bandits. Six aircraft were available on readiness and were scrambled immediately. All were off the ground within six minutes, Peter's take-off being recorded – and noted – as taking just one-and-a-half minutes. However, neither Peter, nor the others were destined to intercept enemy aircraft this day; as the plot faded it was suspected that it had been no more than a thunderstorm.

A couple of days later, Peter and Roy Payne were sent off on a 'jolly', to address workers of the S.U. Carburettor factory. Again the squadron diary made a remark – that the result of their visit probably meant production of carburettors would no doubt treble.

Finally news came that Peter was to leave on 17 June 1943, therefore the squadron held a party on the 16th, at various public houses in the area, in honour of his departure. Back at the officers' mess, among the celebrations was the traditional party trick of hoisting people with blackened feet up to imprint their soles on the ceiling. Peter flew his last sortie with 609 on 15 June, an uneventful shipping strike, patrolling between Cap Gris Nez and Boulogne.

The following day Peter left on his posting to the Hawker Aircraft Company as a test pilot. While with 609 Squadron he had built up a solid reputation as being a highly responsible and fearless pilot, well-liked and possessing a great offensive spirit.

Referring to the squadron's mascot, Billy de Goat, the animal had been 'recruited' originally from the landlady of the Old Jail public house situated near Biggin Hill, by the Belgian pilot Vicky Ortmans in June 1941. The goat was immediately commissioned as a pilot officer and introduced to service life by being fed copious quantities of beer from a baby's bottle and dozens of cigarettes to eat. Further treats would be flowers, top secret maps and various unwanted paperwork. He was promoted to the rank of group captain on 20 October 1943 during a party held at the Hotel Majestic in Folkestone, to celebrate the downing of the 200th enemy aircraft by the squadron (Pilot Officer Lawrence 'Pinkie' Stark DFC was responsible). Billy de Goat also had an honorary DFC – and later the DSO – awarded to him. Following a photograph taken of Peter Raw with Billy on his shoulders, he was given the job of looking after the goat until his posting to Hawkers. Another well-known picture shows Peter on the landing strip trying to cajole Billy into going his way.

Billy also received the attention of the press and the following piece appeared in the *Daily Sketch* of 6 June 1943:

HIGH RANK BUT ACTS THE GOAT

'A wing commander at an RAF station may not sound an oddity, but yesterday I met one who certainly is. Every officer and man on the station salutes him each morning – but when I offered him a cigarette he ate it. He is the mascot of the RAF's Typhoon flying 609 Squadron – a plain lightest brown goat to you and me – but W/C Billy de Goat DSO DFC to every man in the squadron.'

Solemly saluted

'The solemn saluting of Billy every morning is something more than a ritual. It is a superstition of the squadron that unless they salute W/C de Goat when on their way to the briefing, they will have no luck during the day. Billy de Goat joined the squadron as a common or garden AC2. By sterling work he has risen to the rank of W/C, a fact you can see any day from the black and white W/C rings painted on his horns. When the squadron moves Billy flies in his own plane and now has some hundreds of flying hours to his credit. W/C Billy de Goat's dietetic foibles may be peculiar, but as a mascot he is infallible.'

Chapter Five

REST AND RETURN (1)

Officially Peter Raw was on rest, but there was no break from flying. He, like hundreds of other pilots who had finished an operational tour, was still required to serve, either as an instructor, helping to teach others to both fly and to stay alive in combat situation, or as a test pilot.

Test flying wasn't everyone's cup of tea. It took a certain amount of dedication, skill and more than a little guts to test-fly a newly-built aircraft in order to see if the factory workers had put it together correctly. If they found anything that didn't seem right they had to report their findings; this would hopefully allow the aeroplane to be repaired, and then test flown again.

Hawker's airfield at Langley, in Bedfordshire (formally Parlaunt Park Farm), had been acquired pre-war and a factory was completed in 1939 for the express purpose of Hurricane production. In all, over 7,000 Hurricanes were built here during WW2. Now, in 1943, Roly Beamont had arrived once more (he had been a test pilot earlier) and his first job was to try and seek out the reasons for the Typhoon losing its tail, a problem that was still on-going. While commanding 609 he had continually asked to be updated on the progress of this problem, and now he was helping to solve it himself. Soon, however, he would begin to test Hawker's new aircraft, the Tempest.

At Langley Peter Raw had any number of experienced pilots to help him and to fly with. One of these was Hubert Broad who had been a fighter pilot in the Great War, flying with the Royal Naval Air Service. On one occasion, in May 1917, heading back to the front lines over France, he was aware of German aircraft some way behind him, but felt certain they would not catch him before he crossed the lines. Looking back to check, a bullet entered his open mouth and exited under his chin. Although shocked and in some pain, he managed to return to make a forced landing on the British side of the front lines. He had been hit by a long-range shot from the German ace Adolf von Tutschek. After the war he worked for an airline company then became chief test pilot for Welsh Aviation, and then for the De Havilland Company. He also flew in a number of air races in the 1920s. After work with Royal Aircraft Establishment at Farnborough pre-WW2, he joined Hawkers as chief test pilot.

Philip Lucas had been another Hurricane test pilot from 1936. He had earlier been in the RAF, 1926-31. Back in May 1940, while testing the early Typhoon prototype, the aeroplane suffered a failure of the rear fuselage monocoque at the point where it joined the centre fuselage section, just aft of the cockpit. Looking back Lucas could see daylight through a large split that ran down the starboard side. This was one of those occasions where test pilots earn their money. Rather than follow an urge to bale out, Lucas stayed with it and got the machine down. For his courage he was awarded the George Medal.

Others were Frank 'Frankie' Silk DFC, Frank Fox, Bill Humble, New Zealander Harvey Sweetman and Merrick Hymans. Silk and Sweetman were both serving RAF pilots, or in the case of Sweetman, RNZAF, having flown with 486 New Zealand Squadron on Typhoons. Silk had flown in the Battle of Britain with 111 Squadron and later with 91 Squadron as a flight commander and later still as a photographic reconnaissance pilot. Whilst on a photo-recce sortie over the proposed area of the D-Day landings in an unarmed Spitfire, he was attacked by three FW190s but managed to out-fly them and escape. He was awarded the DFC in 1945. Bill Humble was a former Royal Auxiliary pilot, joining Hawkers in 1940, and helping with the Tempest programme. Post WW2 he became Hawker's sales manager after a period as chief test pilot.

Peter spent the next few months testing and flying new Typhoon fighters as they rolled off the production line, and also the newer Hawker Tempest V. It was a constant job, and no doubt Peter preferred this to being sent to be a flight instructor at some flying training school or other. It was all very well imparting one's knowledge and expertise to embryo pilots, but sometimes dangerous being in the hands of the student. Not that aeroplane testing was without its risks. Until that first test flight, there was always the possibility of something not going to plan.

At the end of his 'rest' period, Peter was promoted to flight lieutenant and made a B Flight commander on posting to 183 Squadron, based at his old stamping ground, RAF Manston, Kent, on 17 February 1944. His new commanding officer was Squadron Leader Walter Dring, and 183 was also equipped with the Typhoon. However, Dring was about to leave the squadron and Flight Lieutenant J E Mitchell would be in temporary command. Peter made his first flight with his new squadron on the 24th.

By this time Typhoon squadrons had been grouped together in various wings within the ambit of the RAF's Second Tactical Air Force (2nd TAF) in order to soften up the German defences prior to invasion, after which these mobile wings would gradually move onto the continent behind the British and American armies. 183 became part of 146 Wing, the other squadrons being 257 and 197. The wing was led by the legendary wing leader, Wing Commander D E Gillam DSO DFC & Bar AFC. Denys Gillam had commanded the very first Typhoon Wing back in 1942 and had been operating them ever since. He had been a pre-war airman, receiving an Air Force Cross in 1938 for flying food and supplies to Rathlin Island, off the North Antrim coast after it had been cut off from the mainland for more than three weeks because of severe weather. During the Battle of Britain he had fought with 616 Squadron, and later commanded 312 Czech Squadron. In 1941 he commanded 615 Squadron, flying 'Channel Stop' operations on Hurricane IIs, involving much low-level work against all types of enemy shipping off the French coast or in harbours. He had led a charmed life, surviving many dangerous missions. Aside from the DFC, he would survive the war with no less than three DSOs and a Bar to his DFC.

This was a period when some strange installations were beginning to spring up mushroom-like in the Pas de Calais area; these were soon identified as ski-rocket launch sites for firing off V1 ram-jet flying bombs towards England. 183 were also beginning to start training with rocket projectiles, four beneath each wing of their Typhoon fighters.

It was also a time when Fighter Command was busy in the first preparations for D-Day, the invasion of France, which would eventually take place on 6 June 1944. It meant a prolonged period of ground-attack missions on all sorts of targets, not only the V1 rocket sites – called Noballs – but also German coastal radar installations, transport of every description (rail, road and river) as well as airfields and shipping. Unfortunately, Peter did not live long enough to fly operationally with the new rockets, as 183's first mission using them was 23 April.

However, as mentioned, Peter's first operation was flown on 24 February, in

Typhoon JR385. This was a morning trip to attack a Noball target, which did not get a comment from Peter in his log book except to say there was 'no flak'. Then it was an afternoon sortie, 183 Squadron, with Peter leading, escorting eighteen Mitchell bombers in an attack on Grand Parc. This time, 'little flak'. The next day Peter flew a 'weather reconnaissance' sortie for nearly an hour starting off at 7.35 am. It was going to be a busy day. At 11.10 am there was a squadron scramble, 183 heading out to patrol from Fécamp to Dieppe, providing rear support for Mitchell bombers returning from a raid into France. At 6 pm he led a section off on another scramble, heading for Dieppe where a Mitchell was reported to be in distress, and escorted it back.

On the 28th, in JR385, he flew with the squadron on what was described as a 'flak diversion' mission. A cargo liner of some 5,000 tons had been spotted off the French coast and bomb-carrying Typhoons (known as 'Bombphoons') were going to make an attack, so 183 were on the scene just prior to the bombers and headed in to strafe the vessel, taking the enemy gunners' eyes off the as yet unseen Bombphoons. All the latter could claim was some near misses, and as predicted, 183 soaked up most of the flak but escaped without loss or damage. Peter wrote: 'Draw flak whilst other squadrons dive bomb – shoot up harbour – some light flak. Observed bombing results on ship – three near misses.'

The day's third mission was another escort to Mitchells at 4.40 pm. At first the main group of B25s failed to locate their target but then others found it, and the first group followed in.

Peter flew another weather recco from 7.30 am to 8.30 am on 1 March, with Flying Officer A R Taylor as his wingman. These missions were important to confirm weather conditions, either over the Channel or over the French coast. Naturally all squadrons had access to daily weather reports, but it was always safer to 'see for oneself' in case a sudden call came to head out on an operation. Peter noted that the sortie was flown 'on the deck' off Cherbourg.

The following morning, 183 Squadron went on a dive-bombing sortie, starting off at 10.25 am, led by Wing Commander Denys Gillam. The target, near Fruges, was difficult to locate due to some very good German camouflage, but they dive-bombed it anyway. Peter's wingman reported that his leader's bombs were on target. In the late afternoon they were assigned another dive-bombing mission. By this time it was becoming necessary to have a 'Pathfinder section' in each squadron, whose job it was to locate targets and then direct the main force into the attack once it was identified. Peter led the Pathfinder section on this mission, found the target near Londinières, and led the attack. As they made their run the Typhoon pilots opened up with their 20 mm cannon in order to keep the enemy gunners' heads down. As the Typhoons reformed the target was seen to be covered in great clouds of smoke. Peter led a two-man Pathfinder mission on the 3rd, along with Flying Officer A E Napier, but this time the target was too difficult to find. In fact they later discovered they had bombed the wrong wood!

On the 4th Peter was directed to yet another Noball target. Encountering light flak at the target, Peter was the last to go in, his bombs seen to be on target. The next day an operation had to be scrubbed on the way out due to duff weather off Le Touquet.

Peter had a week off but was back on the flying roster on 11 March after an air test. It was another dive-bombing operation mid-morning to attack targets in the Somme estuary and Abbeville area. Three waves of Typhoons went in, strafing and bombing, again leaving the target area in clouds of smoke. Peter noted: '10/10th cloud over most of France, but dive-bomb gun emplacements through small gap SE of Abbeville. A little flak.'

At 4.30 pm Peter led a section of four on a shipping recco. They planned to be out some time, for each aircraft carried just one 500 lb bomb under one wing, a long- range fuel tank under the other. It lasted two hours and although all they could find was a ship's docking area, they bombed without seeing much in the way of result. His log book records: 'Go to Casquets-Guernsey-Jersey-St Malo-Pt. du Grouin-Granville-Alderney. Drop bombs on Alderney landing ground – lots of light flak.'

Peter flew two more bombing missions, one on the 14th, another the following day, but there was little enough information to write these sorties up in the squadron diary. Nor did he write them into his flying log book!

Tragically, Peter's time with his new squadron was short lived. On 21 March he took his flight on a Ranger operation, a mission led by his old friend, Mony Van Lierde, who was still with 609 Squadron. It was Peter's twentieth operational sortie with 183. The task was a low-level sweep over Holland, in the Twente-Enschede area, but the pilots found thick snow clouds and had to call off the sortie. Whilst making their way back, Peter's section (himself, Flight Lieutenant J E Mitchell and Flying Officer A E Napier) became separated and then found some barges on the Waal. Shooting these up they claimed some damage, and then they found another concentration of barges nearby. As Peter led them into the attack, his aircraft (MN247) appeared to be hit by flak and crashed. However, in a report of the crash written up by local police and with witness testimonies, it appears that he either misjudged or failed to see a ship's loading boom, hit it and went straight in on the other side of the river. A crash at speed and at such a low level would have meant a quick and certain death. Peter Raw's luck had finally run out.

The subsequent police report is very detailed:

MARECHAUSSEE DISTRICT EINDHOVEN
DEPARTMENT BOXMEER, GROUP St ANTHONIS (OPLOO)
SECTION MAASHEES NO.11 (VIERLINGSBEEK)

EXTRACT OF EVIDENCE – concerning the evidence of P van den Hurk and others regarding the crash of an aircraft at Vierlingsbeek on 21 March 1944.

PRO JUSTITIA
On the morning of 22 March 1944, we, Johannes Schrader and Johann Bernhard Fredericks both staffs sergeants [opperwachtmeesters] of the Marechaussee, belonging to the sections of Maashees and Vierlingsbeek respectively, group Oploo, took statements from the following persons with regard to the crash of an aircraft in the municipality of Vierlingsbeek.

Petrus van den Hurk, sixty-one-years old steamboat captain and sailing as such on the steam freighter 'HJ', property of the N.V. Koopvaart-Janssensboten of Venlo, Maaskade No.29, and residing at Lith D36:

'Yesterday, 21 March 1944, about 4 pm, I was moored on the River Meuse at the quay of Afferden, close to the municipality of Bergen in Limburg. At that moment in time, I saw a low flying aircraft coming from the east. It flew from east to west and straight in the direction of our ship. At the same time, I heard firing from machine guns and saw the explosions close by on the quay. I shouted at the men, "Take Cover!" and hid behind the cooling chamber of the engine room flat on the deck. While I took cover, a round passed through the cooling chamber and I felt a shock go through the ship. It appeared that the aircraft had hit the loading boom of the ship and snapped it in two. When I looked in a westerly direction, I noticed that the aircraft had crashed in a field on the other side of the River Meuse. Immediately after, I heard that my first mate, van Teefelen, and the engineer, Jannssen, had been slightly injured.

'I had not noticed any air combat taking place. I did hear people in Afferden talking of several low-flying aircraft but none had observed air combat.

'I found that the port side of the ship had been hit by a round. I cannot estimate the extent of the damage caused, and have nothing to add to my statement.'

Johannes Gerardus van Teefelen, thirty-two-years old, first mate on the aforementioned steam freighter 'HJ', residing at Lith, D36:

'... I did hear at least one or perhaps more aircraft but as I was busy loading and unloading, I didn't pay attention and did not see any aircraft. Suddenly, I heard the captain shout, "Take Cover!" and at the same time I felt a pain in my right thigh and felt it bleed. I looked at my leg and found that I had a deep graze presumably caused by the machine-gun fire of the aircraft. I went to the doctor in Afferden and he stitched the wound. It is remarkable but true; I did not see any aircraft or hear any firing.'

Martinus Jannsen, fifty-one-years old, engineer on the steam freighter 'HJ' residing in Apeltern-Alphen, No.234, stated:

'... I was standing on the boat in front of the helm position when I noticed a low-flying aircraft approaching from the east. It was flying in a westerly direction straight towards our boat. I did not see any other aircraft. I heard machine-gun fire from this aircraft and instantly I let myself drop onto the deck. As I dropped I felt my right hand being hit. I felt pain and noticed a bleeding graze on my hand. I also felt a shock through the ship and saw an aircraft hit the loading boom which snapped, in two.

'Afterwards, I saw the aircraft, a fighter, crash into a field west of the River Meuse. I did not see any other aircraft, neither did I notice any air combat. I cannot say what the nationality of the aircraft was.'

We, reporting officers, established:

A round presumably, bullet, hole in the cooling chamber of the engine room at the aft end and a bullet hole in the starboard side of the cooling chamber (presumably caused by the same round). A round, presumably a bullet, hole in the middle of the deck portside and the wooden loading boom broken in the middle and lying on the deck.

These statements were taken by us aforementioned staff sergeants under oath of office and handed over to our group commander to be sent to the head inspector of civil protection against air raids at The Hague, Maashees, 23 March 1944.

Later another report was written, this by Staff sergeant Fredericks on the subject of the crashed aeroplane and one dead pilot:

I herewith report the following:

'On 21 March 1944, about 5.30 pm, we, Johannes Heinrich Bernard Fredericks and Hendrik van Helden, both staff sergeants of the 'Mareschaussee' at Vierlingsbeek, coming from St Anthonis, were informed verbally by Staff sergeant Johannes Schrader, stationed at Maashees, that an aircraft had crashed at Vortum, municipality of Vierlingsbeek. We proceeded in the direction of the crashed aircraft while Van Helden was to inform the group commander and to report as required. In a field, belonging to J Ebben of Mullem, municipality of Vierlingsbeek, we found a damaged aircraft, presumably English, parts of which were scattered over three fields. The area where the aircraft lay had been cordoned off by Sergeant 1st Class Van Mierlo and Sergeant Pakvis of Group Boxmeer.

'After the group commander had pointed out a body, presumed to be the pilot, covered by a tarpaulin, he declared to have left everything as taken over from a 1st Lieutenant of the Mareschaussee and that nothing had been disturbed.

'I therefore mounted a guard by the aircraft while Schrader proceeded to Vierlingsbeek to make the reports as required by the regulations. At about 10 pm, security was taken over by members of the German army. During the period I stood guard, nothing was done to the site.

'According to reports, the aircraft crashed at about 4 pm having flown against the mast of a ship. It lies at Vortum, municipality of Vierlingsbeek, about one km east of the provincial road between Boxmeer and Vierlingsbeek, and about 500m west of the River Meuse.

'No air-raid warning was given, no members of the German army or the police were killed, communications were not broken nor detours caused or any other disruptions (a separate police report concerning the damage caused is enclosed.) The aircraft was permanently under the guard by Dutch police until the German army took over. The necessary reports have been made.'

Once the squadron had returned to base, it was soon made clear that Peter could not possibly have survived the crash. A telegram was then sent to his wife:

'Regret to inform you that your husband, F/Lt P E Raw DFC is missing as a result of air operations on 21 March 1944. Letter follows. Any further information received will be immediately communicated with you.

'OC 183 Squadron'

This was followed by a letter from Flight Lieutenant Mitchell, who wrote to Peter's wife, advising her that he was missing, although having witnessed his fall, he would have known there was virtually no hope of him surviving:

183 Squadron
RAF Manston, Kent
Ref- 1835/201/1 Air

'Dear Mrs Raw,

'It is with very great regret that I have to write this letter informing you that your husband, F/Lt P E Raw DFC is missing. My squadron and I extend to you our deepest sympathies at this time.

'He had not been with us long, but he had made his place amongst us, and we shall miss him. He was a keen pilot, and led his flight with success on many operations, and earned the respect of both aircrew and ground crew in charge.

'Due to security reasons I cannot give you any particulars about the operation itself, and I am afraid I cannot offer any hope for your husband.

'I well realize the anxiety you will be caused at this time, and should any news come through I will immediately communicate with you. Would you please let me know what you would like to have done with 'Chum', F/Lt Raw's dog.

'If there is anything I can do to help you now or later, please do not hesitate to let me know.

Yours sincerely,
J E Mitchell.
Flight Lieut.'

Top left: Commander Frederick Raw DSC as a barrister at law, prior to his death in 1932.

Top right: Irene Barnard was a well-known member of the Evesham Amateur Operatic Society, seen here in one of her costumes.

Above left: The training ship HMS *Conway*, photographed at the RHYC Regatta, 20 June 1908.

Above right: Miss Irene Barnard, who became Frederick Raw's wife in 1913.

Above left: The family home (as it looks now) at 80 Creffield Road, Ealing, where they moved to in 1928.

Above right: Hillsborough School for Boys, in Creffield Road. Today it is a Japanese school.

Middle right: Illustration depicts the first naval action of WW1 which Commander Raw took part in; HMS *Lysander* can be seen in the foreground with L on the funnel.

Below: The destroyer HMS *Lysander*, in which Frederick Raw went to war in 1914.

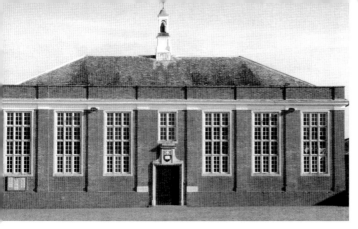

Above left: Wellington School, Somerset.

Above right: The Raw's eldest son John, seen here during a swimming gala in the 1930s.

Left: In 1931 the family moved to 10 Mount Park Crescent, Ealing (as it looks now).

Below: John Raw was also a prominent Connacht rugby player, seen here scooping up the ball before heading for the line in a Leinster v Connacht interprovincial match at Lansdowne Road, Dublin.

Top: John (second from the left, front row). Note the school colours on their shirts.

Left: John Raw in his rugby kit.

Above: John, in his Northern Ireland pass photo.

Above left: Peter Raw in the uniform of the Honourable Artillery Company (HAC).

Above right: Brothers Anthony and Peter Raw in their Wellington School OTC uniforms.

Middle right: The winning team in the Wellington School 'Fives'. Peter front left.

Below: John flying a Master training aeroplane in 1941.

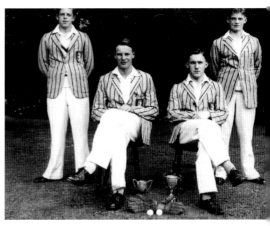

Above left: A squad of the HAC on manoeuvres.

Above right: Peter and Mavis on their wedding day.

Middle left: Miles Master trainers over a snowy countryside, 1942.

Below: Peter soon after gaining his RAF wings.

above left: Posing for the press, Peter seated and his pal Howard Skett trying to look interested.

top right: Peter in his Typhoon PR-C, with his ground crew and two pet dogs.

right: Peter (far right standing) as part of 609's rugby team Manston, November 1942.

below: Members of 609 (West Riding) Squadron at Manston in 1942. Standing: Howard Skett, Erik Haabjoern, Moose Evans, Roland Beamont, M Cameron, Peter Raw, Inkie Stark, Antoni Polek; sitting: West, J S Humphries, Geoff Stevens, Remy van Lierde, André Blanco, Johnnie Wells, Roy Payne and Raymond Lallemand.

Above left: Peter with the famous 609 mascot, W/Cdr William de Goat, and Raymond Lallemand to his left.

Above right: Roy Payne, Peter and W/Cdr de Goat.

Right: Captain Orde's charcoal drawing of Peter, 5 April 1943.

Below: Peter with W/Cdr William de Goat, clearly in a stubborn mood.

Top: Peter's later Typhoon DN406 marked PR-F. The name 'Mavis' still appears by the cockpit while just above the wing-root eighteen train symbols appear in white.

Left: Peter's CO with 609 Squadron was Roland Beamont DSO DFC & Bar. They later flew together testing Typhoons and Tempests at Langley.

Top: School XV 1938. Tony is standing fifth from the left, back row.

Above left: Pilot Officer A W Raw RAFVR, 1941.

Above right: Tony's first tour was flown during night-time operations. Upon his return to ops, this daylight scene would have amazed him. At night, how did they avoid collisions?

Top left: This would be the view seen by Tony during his time flying Hampdens, flak and searchlights into which he and his crew had to fly. The Lancaster was the next aircraft he flew on operations.

Top right: Tony's grave at the Reichswald Forest Military Cemetery, Germany.

Above: The Handley Page Hampden bomber. Tony completed a tour of bombing ops flying the Hampden with 144 Squadron, 1941-42, and received the DFC.

Left: Close family friend Wing Commander Robert Bruce Cole also served with distinction in WW2, being awarded the DFC & Bar, and later the AFC.

Above left: RAF Cranwell, where Michael Raw began his training in 1947.

Above right: Mosquito NF36 of 85 Squadron, West Malling, 1951.

Middle: Cranwell's swimming team, July 1949. Michael, as captain, is in the centre of the front row.

Below: Meteor NF11 WS690 of 85 Squadron, mid-1950s.

Left: Michael after receiving his AFC at Buckingham Palace. His mother is on the left and his wife Maureen on the right.

Middle far left: A stern-looking Michael, this picture appeared on his Norwegian driving licence, 1965.

Left: Mrs Irene Raw's home (as it looks now), 28 Delamere Rd, Ealing, 1947-57.

Below: Meteor NF11 WM145 of 29 Squadron, Tangmere, 1955.

Top: The American Delta Dagger, the type Michael flew while attached to the USAF, 1956.

Middle: Spitfire IIa P7350. A genuine Battle of Britain aeroplane restored to flying condition and flown by Michael.

Above: Hurricane IIc LF363, another WW2 veteran flown by Michael in the Battle of Britain Memorial Flight.

Left: Aircraft of the Battle of Britain Memorial Flight at RAF Coltishall, 1970s.

Below left: Ealing Memorial, with the names of John, Peter and Tony Raw carved on seperate headstones.

Below right: Headstone of Commander Raw and Alice Raw, City of Westminster Cemetery, Hanwell, London.

Bottom: Michael, centre, after his final Spitfire flight with the Battle of Britain Memorial Flight, 29 September, 1976.

OPENING OF THE R.J.MITCHELL HA

7P

40th ANNIVERSARY
OF 1st FLIGHT OF
THE SPITFIRE
SOUTHAMPTON 5th MARCH 1976

FLOWN IN SPITFIRE IIA P7350
Pilot - Sqn. Ldr. R. M. Raw, A.F.C.
Time - 1500 5 March 1976
Overflown Southampton in salute
to R. J. Mitchell's prototype Spitfire
40th ANNIVERSARY

R. J. Mitchell Co
The R. J. Mit
Kingsbri
Southampton, S

To commemorate the first flight of the 'SPITFIRE' from
Southampton (Eastleigh) Airport on the 5th March 1936.
The 'SPITFIRE' was designed by R. J. Mitchell and built
at the   Supermarine Works, Woolston, Southampton

The Civic Centre, Southampton

THE SPITFIRES
OF THE BATTLE OF BRITAIN FLIGHT

Universal Postal Union 1874/1974

RAFA DISPLAY
GOODWOO'D
BRITISH FORCES 1507 POSTAL S
25 AUG 75

First United Kingdom
Aerial Post London

First official airmail Coronation 1911

Flown in Spitfire Mk IIa, P 7350 of the Battle of Britain
Flight on a local flight from RAF Coltishall in preparatio
for the RAFA Display, Goodwood.

Pilot: Sqn.Ldr. R. M. Raw, RAF.
Operations Officer, Battle of Britain Flight

Flight time: 10 minutes.

RAFA GOODWOOD AIR DISPLAY
25 AUG 1975

Top: Another of Michael's deliveries, a first day cover flown on 5 March 1976, and
signed by two WW2 fighter pilots, Douglas Bader and Bob Stanford Tuck.

Above: One of the many post office first day covers, delivered by Peter in a Spitfire, of
the Battle of Britain Memorial Flight, on 25 August 1975.

Left: Michael Raw in later life.

On the 29th another letter was sent, by the Air Ministry's casualty branch situated in Oxford Street, London:

'Madam,

'I am commanded by the Air Council to express to you their great regret on learning that your husband, Flight Lieut P E Raw DFC, RAF is missing and believed to have lost his life as a result of air operations on 21 March 1944, when his Typhoon aircraft was seen to crash south of Nijmegen[1], Holland, at 3.30 am after being hit by anti-aircraft fire.

'Enquiries are being made through the International Red Cross Committee and any further information received will be immediately conveyed to you.

'Should none become available the Council regret that in due course it will be necessary for official purposes, to presume your husband's death and a further letter will be addressed to you.

'The Air Council desire me to convey to you their sympathy in your grave anxiety.

I am Madam,
Your obedient servant,
J A Smith'

In due course, Mr Smith's promised letter was written and dispatched:

Air Ministry (Casualty Branch)
73-77 Oxford Street, London, W1
P414980/P.4.A.2.

20 August 1944

'Madam,

'I am commanded by the Air Council to express their great regret on learning that, in view of information now received from the International Red Cross Committee, your husband, Flight Lieut Peter Edward Raw DFC, Royal Air Force, is believed to have lost his life as the result of the air operations on 21 March. It contains information regarding the place of his burial.

---

[1] The actual crash site was recorded at near Vierlingsbeek. The Germans recovered his body and he was buried in Eindhoven (Woensel) General Cemetery (Grave 14, Plot KK).

'Although there is unhappily little reason to doubt the accuracy of this report, the casualty will still be recorded as 'missing believed killed' until confirmed by further evidence, or until, in absence of such evidence it becomes necessary, owing to lapse of time, to presume for official purposes that death has occurred.

'In absence of confirmatory evidence death would not be presumed until at least six months from the date when your husband was reported missing.

'The Air Council desire me to express their deep sympathy with you in your grave anxiety.

I am, Madam,

Your obedient servant,

J E Gibson.'

With the war still raging on the continent, it was going to take time to find any accurate information for either Peter's wife or mother. Indeed, correspondence carried on for some time, even after the war had ended. Finally, Air Ministry was able to write to Peter's mother in December 1946 with the following information:

'..... details with regard to the resting place of your son, Flight Lieutenant P E Raw DFC, have not yet been received.

'German documents, however, have now been traced, which give the location of the crash as Vierlingsbeek, thirty-five kilometres east-north-east of Eindhoven. A special investigation will be made by the Royal Air Force Missing Research and Enquiry Service as soon as circumstances permit in an endeavour to locate the burial place of your son, and although some time must elapse before the report of the Research Service is received you may be assured that any information obtained will be communicated to you immediately.'

In June 1949, with his mother now residing at 28 Delamere Road, Ealing, Air Ministry were insensitive enough to despatch a letter to her, addressed to her late son Peter. As soon as the error was notified to them, Air Ministry were quick to write and apologise for their gaff, but it was quite a jolt for a still grieving mother.

Some time after the war, Peter's mother was told of a lady in Holland who was

taking care of his grave and made contact with her. She replied from her home in Eindhoven:

'Dear Mrs Raw,

'I was pleased to receive your kind letter. It makes me very happy to take care of the grave of one of the brave soldiers who did help liberate our country. As a mother myself I can understand what it must mean to you that the grave of your son has been discovered.

'Two times yearly I bring flowers to his grave, at the [anniversary] day of liberation of my town in September and the second [each] November.

'Will you be so kind to let me know the date of his birth as I intend to bring flowers on that day [too]. Enclosed you will find a photo of his grave.

'With my best wishes, kindest greetings.

Yours sincerely,
Louise Janssen'

Chapter Six

TONY

Anthony William Raw, Frederick and Irene Raw's third son, was born, like his earlier siblings, in Southport, on 9 February 1922. Like his brothers he too was educated at Wellington School, Somerset, beginning in January 1931 until April 1939, but unlike them his first school had been Ambleside, in Acton, rather then Creffield. According to Mr A J Rogers MA, Wellington's headmaster when Simon Muggleton contacted him in 1995, Tony (as he was always known) excelled in most sports and was also a very competent musician, no doubt a trait passed from his mother. Before he left the school he had been awarded the Crofton Brown music prize.

During his schooling, he decided to study law, while during the latter years he became a member of the school's officer training corps (OTC), for which he passed his Certificate 'A' examination in 1938. He had already passed the School Certificate the previous year. In sport he was in the 1st XV rugby team, awarded his colours in 1938-39, was in the cricket 2nd XI in 1938, gained his swimming colours and had been a participant in the Country Life Shooting Team. He was a house prefect in school house and rose to sergeant in the OTC. The school records his shooting scores in February and March 1939 in competitions as, 64, 78, 72, 65, 63 and 75.

He was also a competent boxer. One of his last fights was for the senior cup, in the light heavy-weight category. His opponent was P F Denny of Willow House and after what was described as a hard fight throughout, Tony was declared the winner, even though he was nearly a stone lighter.

In the first rugby XV in 1938, the school magazine described his efforts as a forward as: 'Raw, A W. Proved one of the few forwards of real value in line-outs. He is inclined to be clumsy in the loose and his pace needs improvement.' Nevertheless he achieved his colours in both 2nd and then 1st teams. He was also a swimmer, as mentioned in a letter to his mother on 19 June 1938. Peter always

opened his letters with 'My Darling Mother', whereas Tony's opening was either
'Dear Mummy', or 'Dear Mother':

'Thank you for your letters, I hope you are feeling better now. So you
have decided to have your tonsils out at last. I hope Peter did well in his
mile swim.

'It has been marvellous all the week, absolutely boiling, but of course,
on Saturday it poured but cleared up in the afternoon and the 1st [team]
played against an eleven from the town and we beat them hollow. Today
the sky is cloudy and dull but it is a sort of musty heat. We had a swimming
practice today. I did two lengths in twenty-nine and seven tenths seconds.
Michael is going off, he did his one length is nineteen-and-a-half seconds,
when he has done it in sixteen at home. He did it in eighteen seconds last
week. If he is not careful he will not be in the swimming team.'

On the same date he wrote to his sister Trixie:

'Dear Trixie, How's life with you? I hear you have been hiking again; it
was somewhere around Denham that I lost my watch when going to Evesham. Did you find it?

'Michael and I are going out to tea with Mrs Clarke this afternoon.
Michael has acquired a name of "Devil" around here. Everyone calls him
devil because they think he has a devilish face.

'I am glad we're all going to Selsey together, it ought to be good fun.
Is Peter coming with us? John is of course.

'Have you been playing much tennis? Something funny happened
the other day. You know Lee Chapman, well, he stays with Michael in
the hols and the other day he put on his clean pyjamas and found they
were a pair of Pritchard's sister's. Talk about looking young in mine. We
all nearly split ourselves.'

When Tony left Wellington in 1939, he could list the following achievements:

Swimming Colours	Certificate 'A' 1938
Country Life Shooting Team	School Prefect
Crofton Brown Music Prize 1937	2nd XI Cricket Team 1938
Junior History Prize 1937	1st XV Colours 1938/39
School Certificate 1937	Form Prize 1938

Tony, like John and Peter, was forced to put his life and career on hold with the
onset of war. Tony had continued his law studies but had also volunteered to join
the Royal Air Force. In due time he was asked to present himself for interview
and medical and having got through those, was accepted for pilot training in June
1940.

Following the usual initial square-bashing, indoctrination etc, firstly as AC2
Raw (1287513) at 1 Receiving Wing at RAF Babbacombe, Torquay, then at Room
4 Majiddo Block, 1 Receiving Centre, RAF Uxbridge, Middlesex. It was then back
to sunny Torquay, and C Flight, 3 Squadron, 5 ITW, RAF Elfordleigh, Torquay.
He did his ab initio training at this initial training wing and by the end of the
year he was sent to 2 EFTS (Elementary Flying Training School) at Staverton Airport (Tiger Moths). On 7 December 1940, AC2 Raw wrote home, from Hut 14
at Staverton Airport, on the Cheltenham Road, Gloucester:

> 'Just a note to let you know I have arrived here. I have only been here a
> few hours so I do not know much. We are in huts on the airport but we
> go to Worcester to fly. The huts are a bit primitive compared with the
> hotels at Torquay. We have to walk to the West Camp (about half a mile)
> to wash in the morning, but the beds are good and warm and the place
> is much better all round than we had at ITW and more freedom.
>
> 'We get one day and sleeping out pass per week so I shall be able to
> come and see you at Evesham. I hope we are allowed to go an hour's
> journey away.'

Once he had completed his flight training, Tony was sent to RAF Cranwell, Lincolnshire and he now gave his address as LAC Raw, Cadet's Mess, 22 Course. 16
February 1941:

> 'Just a note to let you know I have arrived and what it is like. It is a terrific
> place, miles and miles of it. When I arrived with some other chaps all
> togged up as you saw me leave home, they sent us to the wrong place
> twice before they shoved us to the actual college, so we walked miles
> with all our stuff before we came to the right place. Were we annoyed!
>
> 'But I am glad to be here, it is marvellous. I have a room with my
> friend, and we have a basin (hot and cold water), a chest of drawers,
> wardrobe and writing desk, one armchair and one writing chair. A bat-

man cleans our boots and buttons and presses our trousers. We dine in a beautiful dining hall and have excellent food. There is a bathroom outside my door, so I am quite satisfied.

'We have a swimming bath and two cinemas in the camp. I think we work until 7 pm, still, we can't have everything can we? I have not been up in an Oxford yet but I shall tomorrow.[1] I looked over the cockpit today and it looks very complicated. We are told our "wings" exam is to be in eight weeks.

'Has Trixie got settled in her flat yet? I hope so.[2]

'It looks as if I shall more or less stay in camp always as we finish late and Sleaford is six miles away, but I believe we get some weekends off now and again, so I shall be able to come home for a couple of days sometimes, I hope.'

It was one of those strange things now, that while her three older boys were 'away at the war', it was Irene Raw that was in the danger zone, due to the nightly air raids by German bombers. Apparently she was doing some work with the defence forces in fire watching, as referred to in Tony's next latter of 25 February 1941:

'I expect you have been busy lately with one thing and another, and I should think the fire watching must be a bit of a nuisance too. Is Stanley showing signs of getting better yet? Still, never mind mum, the war can't last forever, and if you ask me you are the one who has been in the thick of it more than any of us.

'I had from Saturday afternoon until Sunday night off, so I went as I had promised to see John and Mona. They have very nice digs there, I should say it is one of the best little houses in the town, and they seem very happy.

[1] The Airspeed Oxford II was a three-seat, twin-engined trainer that had entered RAF service in 1937 to become the first advanced monoplane trainer with two engines. It had a maximum speed of 188 mph and a service ceiling of 19,500 feet. The engines were 370 hp Armstrong-Siddeley Cheetah Xs. It proved a long-serving type, the Mark V remaining in service 'til 1954.

[2] The reference to Trixie and her new flat was concerning her recent marriage to Stan Fenton.

'I had an enjoyable time. On Saturday evening we chatted and went and had a drink. Then on Sunday morning John got up early and went to the aerodrome (while I got up at my leisure) and he came in again while I was having breakfast, to fetch me to go and have a flight in a Miles Master. I went with him and met some of his friends (one of which I remembered at the Hydro, Paignton), then we went up, John and I, and flew around the coast, it was marvellous. Then John came down and had to do some formation flying in Hurricanes, so I went up with another chap. John got the afternoon off and as it turned out to be five [o'clock] we went for a walk then I came back in the evening. I enjoyed my little visit very much, it was a change from this place.

'I managed to get in the first college seven-a-side team (they have three teams). We played at Nottingham and the team I was in managed to win the cup; we had to play five games during the afternoon.

'We are getting some comparatively fine weather, strange to relate, so I am getting some flying in. We will start night flying soon. I shall be getting a long weekend soon perhaps in a fortnight, or even sooner. I may get one at anytime so expect me when you see me.

'I am glad to hear Mike is taking some interest in rugger. I enclose £2 towards the pram [Trixie was expecting]. I will try to send some more by instalments. Incidentally, how is that war risk insurance going – has Pete given you any yet? Do you need some more? If so I will rake some up.'

Four days later:

'Thank you so much for the rugger things, everything is all right and I won't have to buy any more. John 'phoned me the other day and I arranged to go to Sutton Bridge tomorrow to see him, but unfortunately yesterday they put my name up to play rugger for the college against another SFTS at Grantham. I can't very well get out of it so I have written to John to tell him I can't get there. In any case, I found out later that I can only get a train that would allow me about an hour there before I came back, so I have suggested to John that we meet somewhere else sometime. He is thirty miles from here.

'They sure do keep us working. We work until seven in the evening and we are also given extra navigation to do in our spare time. I manage to get in a swim on most evenings though.

'I have done some flying this week in these Oxfords. I like them very much, they are much faster and you sit in a glass cabin instead of in the open. We have had a gale for the last two days and it has rather spoilt flying. A barrage balloon [came loose from somewhere] and floated by this morning.

'I nearly came home last weekend. Everybody except ten from each course had the weekend off, and naturally, I happened to be one of the unlucky ten in the draw, and so I had to stay here. Still, it wasn't bad and I had a nice lazy time.

'Our lights keep going out here for some reason or other – I think something has been bombed. I shall have to hurry before they go out again. John tells me that Fred Drury came here and got a commission. I think the chances of getting a commission here are not as ripe as they were. I think only thirty-three (one third) of the course are getting commissions now as opposed to the old seventy-five per cent. It is a pity old Pete is moving, I was hoping to go and see him some time. I am glad to hear that his interview was all right.

'Has Trixie settled down in her new home yet? Or is she still trying to pull down the blackouts??'

12 March 1941:

'John rang me up the other night to say he was having the afternoon off today (Wednesday) but it was no good, we work all day, but I will try to go over and see him on the first possible opportunity. The trouble is it is so out of the way and only about two trains run there and back per day. I will attempt to go this weekend but I doubt whether I shall be able to get there.

'We have been having terrible weather here, so consequently there has not been much flying. I have been solo though – I went after three hours [of dual]. We went to look over an operational squadron of night fighters today, it was very interesting.

'I am glad to hear old Pete is so near to home and has finished the [air raid] shelter. Has he covered the shelter right over with sandbags or earth?

'We certainly do some work here. We had an exam the other day in which I think I have not done too well, worst luck, but it is not an important one. I keep wishing I was on fighters where they don't have to do all this stuff.

'We won our rugger match against the other SFTS at Grantham, and I saw Cribbin there, the boy who was at Hillsborough with us. He was not flying of course, and I did not speak to him as I don't like him. I also saw a friend of Bruce there but I didn't speak to him either.

'I had a letter from Mike the other day, wishing me many happy returns of the day! – adding, "better late than never."[3] Yes, I will help with the pram. When are you getting it and about how much would you like? I think I shall go to bed now.'

Tony's next letter, dated 23 April 1941, came after the news that John, his training finished, had been posted to be an instructor.

'I am grieved to hear of John's plight. I really do feel sorry for him, "but you can't 'elp larfin' can yer?" Isn't it typical RAF to train him on single-engine fighters and then put him instructing on twin-engine machines. I only hope it doesn't happen to me, but I don't think it likely.

'Yes, I believe you did have a terrible air raid last Wednesday. I heard all about it from people who were on leave, it was the worst yet was it not? I am glad to hear you were not worried by it much. Oh, before I forget. Could you let me know as soon as possible the registration number of my war savings certificates as we are buying them here and we have to let them know the number of the card?

'We are having a swimming match next Monday and I hope to get in the team. I am afraid I couldn't let you know about the wings exam before because the results were not out until the day before yesterday. I got through all right and I was twenty-fourth out of about fifty, so it was pretty average (better than I expected). So all I have to do is make sure I don't get suspended from flying. We have started night flying although I have not actually done any yet, I expect I shall tomorrow night or the night after.

'I hope Mike and Pat are keeping well and Trixie is bearing up. Month after next isn't it? I wish I could get home this weekend and see John and Peter but I don't think it is very likely. We have had a big push

---

[3] Tony's birthday was on the 9th of February.

on lately, because they are going to get us out of here to an OTU soon. We have been flying in every spare moment. We had our whole flight changed – instructors and ground staff – and they are very energetic and efficient. They came to ginger us up!'

There is a bit of gap in the surviving letters now, and those missing would have covered the death of brother John. During this period, Tony left RAF Cranwell and moved on to 16 Operational Training Unit (OTU) at RAF Upper Heyford, Oxfordshire. Here Tony moved to the Anson as a training aeroplane.

The Avro Anson was originally designed as a general reconnaissance aircraft, again with two Armstrong-Siddeley Cheetah X engines. It had a similar speed to the Oxford although its service ceiling was only 16,000 feet. In 1934 it had started civil life with Imperial Airways, but later, in 1935, it entered RAF service with Coastal Command. It didn't take long before its worth as a trainer was discovered, and the type was still in service in the late 1950s.

Tony's next letter was dated 21 June 1941, about the time the Germans attacked Russia.

'We have at last started work at this place. I have done a few hours flying and some lectures, as the weather is so fine they are going at it hammer and tongs, so we are getting in as much flying as possible. Consequently we are flying over the weekends and I shall not even be able to get away on Sunday afternoon. I am annoyed but still I am all the more likely to get off next weekend.

'Are you having a heat-wave too? It's terrific here and I can't remember being so hot for years. Matilda [his motor cycle] is in working order again so one of these Sundays or Saturdays you will hear a pop-pop and I will arrive on her.

'You remember my friend Nuirya Khan, well he turned up here today in an Anson; he flew all the way up from Devon for the weekend. He has gone to Oxford to see some friends. We can't see much of him because we are flying all the time.

'We have still heard nothing from our banks although we keep writing. Everyone is getting broke. I am down to my last 10/- [50p] now. If nothing comes from the bank soon I shall have to cash my saving certificates.

'These [Avro] Ansons are very easy machines to fly after the [Airspeed] Oxfords, they just float along like a bus and are rightly named the Queens of the Air. Have you been to see any more Gilbert and Sullivan shows? I hope so.

'I haven't been out much, in fact only about three miles through country lanes on my motor cycle to get a drink at the local. This county is very pretty and it is pleasant riding along the lanes on these fine evenings. One evening I spent four or five hours taking Matilda to bits and putting her back together again. I got in a filthy mess – some people were very amused.'

It is typical of all the Raw boys that he made no mention of a crash he had a few days prior to this letter. On 16 June 1941 he had been slightly injured in a crash flying Avro Anson N9652 at Braile, twelve miles west of Banbury. Yet in his letter he says how easy they are to fly! On the day of the crash, he had been flying under the instruction of Sergeant R D Baxter, in Anson R9652, but they had one engine suddenly cut out and unable to maintain height, he had to make a forced landing. They belly-landed in a field and ran into a ditch. Both men received only minor injuries but the Anson was a write-off with damage beyond repair.

8 July 1941:

'We had a marvellous time this last weekend. I was lucky enough not to be on night flying on Saturday night and on Sunday night when I was supposed to be, it was cancelled. So I was able to be off Saturday afternoon and evening, plus Sunday afternoon and evening, although I had to fly Sunday morning. We spent nearly all our time on the river. The weather was beautiful and we had supper in an Indian restaurant called the Taj Mahal and ate curry. Boy, was I full!

'Peter was looking very well was he not? I expect he is very pleased to start flying. I was going to try and give him a flip in a Hampden but it could not be arranged. Oh, I forgot to tell you I went solo on a Hampden the other day. It was a lucky thing on Sunday morning because I was supposed to be flying and practising night circuits and landings on the aerodrome. I thought of going to Oxford and shooting up Peter but I resisted the temptation. However, Peter said someone had come over very low in a Hampden and swooped about, so he waved to the pilot as he felt sure it was me.

'Well, on Monday morning, myself and five others who were flying on Sunday morning were interrogated by the wing commander to find out who was low flying over Oxford because it had been reported. I was pleased I had not gone over there. The chap was not caught.

'I have just had a nice sleep and a bath and then had some lunch. As I was night flying last night, I have only one-and-a-half hours more night flying to do in this flight, so I hope, with a bit of luck, to get home some time next weekend.

'I went for a little flip over Evesham in a Hampden yesterday afternoon. I circled uncle's house a few times and picked out grandma's house but I did not see anyone. I was rather high up, about 1,500 feet.

'How are Butch and Mrs Butch getting on? Well, I hope. I hope the nurse has learnt to behave herself by now. I am going into Bicester tonight to get Matilda's lights seen to. I hope this beautiful weather keeps up when I get my week's leave in a month's time. I really will bet my week, or more – there is no danger of being called back like Peter was. My wrist is quite better now, it has healed up nicely.

'Well Grandma Raw, Uncle Tony will have to be finishing now.'

This last reference was due to the arrival of Trixie and Stanley's son David in June, who was also referred to as 'Butch'. Readers will recall that Peter had injured his wrist earlier, and we know just as little about Tony's injury as we did Peter's.

There is a gap in Tony's surviving letters, the next being dated 18 August 1941. Having completed his operational training unit work, he had been posted to an operational squadron to fly Hampden bombers. Normally bomber crews got together at OTU and after talking things over amongst themselves, everyone got teamed up. Whether this happened in Tony's case is not known, but he was posted to 61 Squadron, commanded by Wing Commander T C Weir, with effect from 16 August 1941. His four-man crew consisted of himself as pilot, and three sergeants, J R Newcombe (air observer), R F Wardle (wireless operator/air gunner) and F J Sweeney (air gunner). Wing Commander Tom Weir would receive the DFC later that year.

The title air observer was a pre-war classification, but by this stage, the designation was changing to that of navigator. The Hampden carried a crew of four and the air observer flying badge was one much coveted by those who wore them in the early part of WW2. It was a letter 'O' with a single wing attached, and other trades often referred to it as – if the reader will permit – 'the flying arsehole'. As the war progressed the up and coming navigators were known as such and their flying brevet was the letter 'N' with single wing attached.

Their new squadron was based at North Luffingham, near Oakham, Rutland, (Leicestershire) where it had moved in July, having been previously at Hemswell, Lincolnshire. It shared the aerodrome with 144 Squadron, which had also moved there from Hemswell in July.

That first letter from his new home at North Luffingham (dated 18 August) recorded:

'I arrived here after a little bother over transport. I could not get anything to come and fetch me at first so I caught a train to Luffingham. When I got there I put my luggage in a can and told the driver to put it out at the guard room, but I did not see it again; yesterday evening I found it in the sergeant's mess.

'This is a very new place, but quite nice and the countryside is very pretty. I might be able to get home fairly easily. I have not discovered yet. I must make a drive to get back for my motor cycle. I may be able to do so within the next few days but on the other hand I may not.

'It is a pity I shan't be able to see old Peter, as I should have liked to have seen him very much. I have not done anything yet but am expecting to very soon. Naturally I can't tell you when, but we do a very easy trip first to get used to it.

'I miss everybody rather a lot coming to a new station like this, it feels like being a new boy at school. At first I thought I was the only new chap here, but I found one or two more guys gradually and I am delighted to find Tim is coming here with Jock and Rupert.

'The leave is good. We get a week every six weeks and we should get forty-eight hours every fortnight although I think it is a little doubtful. Still I'll wangle my way home somehow.'

Tony was correct in saying to his mother that he and his crew would generally have an easy trip to start their operational tour, often a mine-laying trip. While these were usually easier than a full-blown bombing mission to a German target, they were by no means without danger, and any number of bomber crews failed to return from these types of operations. The aircraft would take a couple of sea mines and 'lay' them in some busy estuary off the hostile coast or near a busy port. From necessity they needed to be dropped from low level and flying low over water at night with only an altimeter to help you judge your height, it did not take much of an error to hit the sea. Often there were flak ships located in these areas too, just waiting to shoot off at low-flying RAF bombers, or shore batteries eager to open up on any aircraft that flew too close to their positions on shore. This operation was coded 'Nectarine 2' and was flown near to the Frisian Islands. In all seventeen Hampdens were mining here and one, from 106 Squadron, failed to return.

According to Tony's records, he flew his first operational sortie on 26 August. While most of the squadron raided Mannheim, seven crews (of a total of seventeen from Bomber Command) went out to drop mines off the Frisian Islands, and Tony was amongst them. The task was noted as successful. Unfortunately there is no record of his flight and one has to wonder if in the event he went with one of the other seven crews 'for experience'.

This too was becoming the norm. There was little sense in training a crew to fly on night operations and then send them out 'dumb, fat and happy' on their first sortie over enemy territory with the risk of losing them all through lack of experience and what today is called 'situation awareness'. Of course, everyone had to start somewhere, but new pilots were now being sent out on their first missions with an experienced crew, so that at least the embryo bomber pilot could gain some idea of what it was all about. His crew waited back at base for their 'driver' to return and thankfully they generally did. Naturally, sometimes the crew that had taken him failed to return, making them spare bods for a while, waiting for an equivalent aircrew member to die, be wounded or go sick, for them to have a chance to getting into a proper crew. Thus Tony's first op, while noted in his diary, is not recorded in squadron records as being part of another crew.

However, Tony's second operation is recorded. This was two days later, 29/30 August, with the target being the dock area at Frankfurt – the facilities on the Oder river that ran south from the Baltic. Take-off time was chalked up as 8.02 pm and Tony, Newcomb, Wardle and Sweeney headed out to Germany. It was to be the first time Frankfurt had been attacked by a force in excess of 100 bombers. In the event bad weather prevented accurate bombing and after failing to find a suitable break in the cloud to see anything like the target area, Tony ordered Newcombe, his navigator, to find and bomb an alternative target, which he did. They landed back at base at 3.12 am in the morning. One aircraft of the squadron failed to return.

Suddenly everything changed. Tony was posted out of 61 Squadron, into 144 Squadron which was across the other side of the same airfield. The posting date was 12 September 1941, but oddly, Tony would fly two more operations before that date, but these would be recorded as 144 Squadron ops. Presumably he was attached to 144 before the official posting became effective. Another strange thing is that he did not transfer with all his crew; only Sergeant Wardle, his WOP/AG, went with him.

It might be that 144 Squadron had suffered losses that made it necessary for someone from 61 to move across, but while 144 did have losses (two crews on 7/8 September) and two more on 11/12, that was all. 61 Squadron had just started to receive the new Avro Manchester bombers, the forerunner to the Lancaster, and some were being tried out on operations. On the night of 2/3 September, one of the first Manchesters on the squadron was lost on a raid to Berlin. That was bad enough, but it had had a crew of senior men aboard, all of whom were killed when brought down by anti-aircraft fire over the German capital. The pilot had been Wing Commander G E Valentine DSO, and with him was Group Captain J F T Barrett DSO & Bar DFC (Luffingham's station commander), who had been awarded his DFC in Iraq in 1922 and followed this by his first DSO for landing in hostile territory to rescue another downed pilot. Flight Lieutenant A B Harrison DSO is noted as a pilot but whether he flew as such on this operation, or perhaps as navigator, is unclear. An officer was in the rear turret and he may have possibly been the squadron or station gunnery officer. These sorts of things did occur from time to time, senior officers deciding to treat an operation, (especially one in a new aircraft and Berlin as a target) as a bit of a jolly. Mostly they got away with it but sometimes, as in this case, they did not.

Anyway, Tony went to his new squadron, and in all probability remained in his same quarters, so at least he didn't have to pack and make a long journey of it. Sergeant Newcombe also left 61, going to 44 Squadron, but he was lost with them just a few days later. The Hampden in which he was navigator had just taken off on a mine-laying trip on 7 September, when the aircraft appeared unable to gain height. It crashed at Branston Hall Farm, near their airfield (RAF Waddington) and the mine they were taking to Kiel Bay exploded. All four men died instantly.

Sergeant Francis John Sweeney, however, who started as an air gunner, was also, like many others a wireless operator/air gunner (WOP/AG), and carried on with other crews of 61 Squadron. In June 1942 he was awarded the Distinguished Flying Medal having completed thirty-six operational sorties.

Chapter Seven

FIRST TOUR

144 Squadron, RAF, was part of 5 Group of Bomber Command, commanded by Air Vice-Marshal J C Slessor. 144 was also equipped with the aircraft Tony had trained on at Upper Heyford, and with 61 Squadron, the Hampden.

The Handley Page Hampden was a twin-engined medium bomber that carried a crew of four, and together with the Vickers Wellington and the Armstrong-Whitworth Whitley, had been the backbone of Bomber Command and bearing the brunt of the RAF's night bombing campaign of Germany, and factories etc. in northern France, since the air war had begun. The Hampden had entered service in August 1938 and was powered by two 1,000 hp Bristol Pegasus XVIII engines. It had a maximum speed of 254 mph at 13,800 feet, cruised at 167 mph and carrying a bomb load of 2,000 lbs, had a range of 1,885 miles, or 1,200 miles with a 4,000 lb load – its maximum. Its service ceiling was around 19,000 feet.

The Hampdens had been operational since day two of the war, 83 Squadron raiding German warships in the Schillig Roads, and already, two Hampden aircrew had been awarded the Victoria Cross. The pilot sat in his own cockpit area, the crew consisting of a navigator, bomb-aimer and an air gunner, who manned upper and lower rear gun positions. In August 1940, aircraft from 144 and 61 Squadrons had raided Berlin, the RAF's first crack at the German capitol.

As mentioned earlier, while still officially on 61 Squadron's books, Tony's next two operations were flown as a 144 Squadron crew. His crew with 144 consisted of Pilot Officer D H Swan (navigator), Sergeant C F Guest (Wop/AG), and Sergeant Wardle in the back. On the night of 7/8 September, the same night as his former navigator would be killed, Tony and his crew were one of seventeen Bomber Command sent out on such mining trips. They were called 'Gardening' ops as the mines they carried were called 'vegetables'. Tonight they would drop their cargo around the Frisian Islands. For Tony it was again the area coded Nectarine 2. They took off almost an hour after midnight and headed across the dark North Sea. At one point they had to alter course around a British convoy, not wanting to risk a 'friendly fire' incident. An hour later they spotted in the gloom a twin-engined bomber flying by in the opposite direction, no doubt another Hampden heading home. The chances of a collision in these circumstances were slight, but no doubt the thought passed through the crew's minds. At 3.20 am they dropped their mine from 600 feet and the rear gunner saw its parachute open and then the 'vegetable' created a splash as it hit the sea.

Then on the night of 11/12 September 1941 Tony and his crew were part of a force of fifty-six RAF bombers that attacked the Heinkel aeroplane factory at Rostock and the adjacent harbour. However, cloud hampered the raid and most of the aircraft bombed the town instead. Of the total of thirty-nine Hampdens on this raid, three did not get back to their bases. One was again from 106 Squadron, whose crew had to abandon their machine over Denmark. The other two Hampdens were from Tony's squadron. One came down just six miles from Luffingham; two of the crew were killed. The other crashed east of Barn Farm, Billesdon, eight miles east of Leicester, and two of the crew were injured.

The naval port of Brest was a target often raided by the RAF. Not only was it a major German port for warships but it was also a sanctuary and base for U-boats. Tony and his crew were scheduled for the raid on this French port on the night of 13/14 September. In total, 147 RAF aircraft took part and their main objective was three capital ships berthed there, the battle-cruisers *Scharnhorst, Gneisenau* and the light-cruiser *Prinz Eugen*. The Germans were quick to spread a smoke screen over the ships and harbour, so that the 120 aircraft that actually bombed, did so more by luck than judgement, but at least no aircraft were lost.

Tony and crew took off at 1.07 am and having reached the port they came in over the estuary at 12,000 feet, then dropped down to 10,000. The smoke screen was coming from the north of the target area but the navigator, Douglas Swan, spotted an area of coastline near the docks and used this as an aiming point allowing him a pin-point approach on the run in to bomb.

On 18 September Tony and crew flew a search and rescue mission, although they did not find what they had been tasked with, but on the night of 20/21 Tony had another chance at Frankfurt. It was an early evening take-off – 7.24 pm – but before they had reached the target the port engine had started to overheat. This forced them to reduce height somewhat, and searchlights probing for them made navigation difficult from about thirty miles inland from the hostile coast.

Eventually Tony managed to keep a reasonable height by using a rich mixture of fuel. Frankfurt was going to frustrate him again because, by using this mix of fuel, it was being used up at a faster rate than was prudent. He and Swan decided to make for an alternative target and spotted Trier aerodrome, coming in to bomb just as the airfield lights were extinguished. As they headed away, Sergeant Wardle, the rear gunner, saw several explosions and a fire start.

The weather was far from perfect, cloud making the flight back a blind one. In fact they saw nothing until they picked up the Feltwell beacon flashing. Sergeant Guest, the wireless operator, called base only to be diverted by them to RAF Scampton and once contact had been made with them, they were diverted again, this time to Middleton St George. There were many problems for returning bombers, and finally they were permitted to land – at RAF Dishforth – with their fuel almost gone. They landed at 2.20 am, almost seven hours after leaving Luffingham. It was a long night indeed, with a far from simple return journey.

Another mine-laying sortie came on 11/12 October, coded as 'Yams', which was carried out in the Elbe and Weser areas. 'Yams' was the code word for operations in the area of the Heligoland Approaches. Twelve Hampdens were involved and none were lost. At least this operation, which started at 12.55 am, went off fairly smoothly, with the mine being dropped from 800 feet at 3.50 am. Wardle again reported it hitting the sea without a problem. They were back at 6.35 am.

Then on the 12/13th, Tony went to the Ruhr Valley for the first time. The Ruhr was where the heart of German industry beat strong and healthily. Many of the towns in this region were sure to have factories or armament works, so this too was a constant place for the RAF bombers to go to. On this night the actual target was a chemical and synthetic rubber factory at Hüls. Cloud over the target meant that bombing was scattered. Indeed, Tony reported 10/10th cloud over the Ruhr.

At 2.15 am Wardle spotted a German night-fighter on the port quarter and Tony took evasive action and lost it. Half an hour later heavy and accurate anti-aircraft fire began to explode about them. With the dense cloud Swan had no chance of finding the target so they decided to bomb a Ruhr gun position they could see. They also bombed a searchlight battery near Essen, again bursts being observed by Swan as they headed away. However, the flak remained constant and a near explosion sent some splinters of shell into the Hampden, one piece injuring Wardle in the hand.

Tony dived out of the flak zone, going down to 500 feet, reducing to 300 feet

as they headed for home. Over the North Sea another night-fighter was observed
on the starboard quarter, forcing Tony to drop to sea level to evade it. Eventually
they found the British coast at Harwich, and turned inland towards Horsham St
Faith's beacon. Because Wardle was wounded, Tony landed there to get him to
the medics quickly.

Of the ninety RAF bombers assigned, seventy-nine were Hampdens, one of
which was lost, along with an Avro Manchester. However the Hampden was from
Tony's 144 Squadron, and its four-man NCO crew did not survive. They fell vic-
tim to a successful German night-fighter pilot, Oberleutnant Helmut Lent, of
4./NGJI. It was his twentieth victory, having brought down his nineteenth, a
Wellington of 40 Squadron, just half an hour earlier.

Tony next wrote home on 21 October 1941, after operating the previous night,
but of course, he wouldn't say anything to his mother about it, even if it was per-
missible. Apparently brother Peter had had a medical scare, as we read earlier:

'It was a shame Pete being suspected of having scarlet fever, I bet it annoyed him. He wrote to me saying he was out now and had not got the
disease at all.

'Sorry I have not been able to get home lately, they have been occupying our time for us pretty methodically. I have been doing rugger and
cross country running in the afternoons. That is their latest idea. It's all
very well but it stops me getting home. I had to operate for two nights in
succession last week, which is rather surprising [11 and 12 October].
Still, they have a new scheme now whereby I hope to get some more
spare time. Anyway, my next leave is only three-and-a-half weeks off now.

'This week has been rather unlucky for me. I left my motor cycle in
a pub yard and some fool stole it. That was all right but then the idiot
had to leave it around and let the police find it, so they found out that it
was not taxed. Now I am in the cart, and of course the police have not
found the bloke that took it.

'Burberry's had the nerve to send me a bill for £14 for a greatcoat,
hat and shirt which I never had from them, so I have written them a very
indignant letter back.

'Well, life goes on much as usual here, nothing ever happens much.
Oh, I had to show a whole lot of ATC cadets from Uppingham School
around the station the other day – it was funny. One of the lads asked

me what happened it you just flew an aeroplane straight down into the ground. I told him I didn't know, having never done it.'

Just like Peter, Tony never mentioned much about the operational flying he was engaged in, and tried to calm any fears his mother might have by saying that 'nothing ever happens around here'. However, on the night of 20/21, he and his crew went to the Bremen ship-building yards. In all a force of 153 RAF bombers, including eighty-two Hampdens, hit the target and left fires burning the area. Five aircraft did not get back; two were Hampdens, one from 106 Squadron based at Coningsby, the other from 50 Squadron, Swinderby. Another 106 aircraft had crashed on landing but the crew escaped unharmed.

Tony had left the ground at 5.37 pm, so another early evening start. With Wardle remaining in the hospital, he had Sergeant W G Carrie as rear gunner. Reaching the target without much trouble, they bombed from 15,000 feet, and saw the bombs explode in the dock area. Heading away they were tasked with dropping propaganda leaflets, landing back at base fifteen minutes before midnight.

On the 24/25th, Frankfurt was on the board again. Going in to the briefing room Tony must have wondered if this time he might actually get there. He no doubt had mixed feelings about the task ahead, for he had a new navigator, Sergeant Harry Cobb who had replaced Swan. Douglas Hurst Swan continued to fly operations with another crew and in April 1942 he received the Distinguished Flying Cross. The reason for the change is not known.

Take-off time was 6.30 pm but the Frankfurt jinx struck again. On the trip out the heating system packed up and the direction finding indicator was discovered to be unreliable. There was no way they were going to locate the marshalling yards at Frankfurt, and then they were plagued by searchlights and intense flak fire. By this time the cold had started to freeze up the instruments so on Bill Cobb's first trip with Tony he had to jettison their bombs. However, as they did so over Germany the trip counted in the squadron records, so it is named as Tony's eleventh operation.

It wasn't a good night for Bomber Command, for of the seventy bombers sent out only eight reported reaching the target area (the marshalling yards) due to the weather. Fifty-seven others bombed different targets, or jettisoned their loads over Germany as Tony had done. Four aircraft failed to return, including one from 144 Squadron. This was not all. One Wellington crew got completely lost and ended up crash-landing in County Clare, Eire!   Another Wimpy came back so badly damaged it was written off, while yet another Wellington, returning with severe damage to its fuel tanks (due to flak), burst into flames after landing and was completely burnt out.

Sortie number twelve came on the night of 1/2 November, which was a return to the docks of Kiel. 134 aircraft took part, and of the thirty-two Hampdens, one was lost [83 Squadron], plus two Whitleys. Once again thick cloud covered the target area, allowing only seventy crews to bomb, and it was later reported that none fell on Kiel itself. Tony and his crew's aircraft suffered severe icing and they were among those who failed to get there. Before he went to briefing, he wrote to his mother:

'I have to answer my summons on Monday and I am horribly afraid they will fine me £5 at least. It is now nearly three weeks since I was home, it is terrible. I miss you all very much and I missed Aggie terribly, in fact, I missed her so much that I wanted her to come and see me, so I asked Mrs Van der Beck if Aggie could come down for the weekend as we were having a party here celebrating the new group captain's (Gus Walker, the international rugger player[1]) arrival here. I found some digs for her in a village nearby and we had a very happy time.

'I have done quite a few raids since I was home last and that reminds me I should be getting another week's leave in a fortnight or so.

'How thrilling, fancy a man dying in the next bed but one to Nanny – was she pleased or horrified? I landed near Croydon in the middle of the night about a week ago, only about fifteen miles from home, but I could not get away as I had just returned from an operational trip; so near yet so far.

'What did Mrs Van der Beck talk about when she met you? I should say a hell of a lot if she talks as much as Agnes. I like people who talk a lot, it keeps life interesting. Well Ma, I have to be running along now...'

This is the first real mention of Agnes Van der Beck, the girl he was to marry in April 1942, with brother Peter marrying her sister Mavis on the same day.

---

[1] Group Captain G A Walker DSO DFC (later Air Chief Marshal Sir Augustus, GCB CBE DSO DFC AFC MA). He played rugby for England in 1939, and captained the RAF team, 1936-39.

In the event the operation on 1/2 November was a dismal failure. Taking off at 5.55 pm they met cloud and ice forcing an abort, returning with their bomb load intact. Tony went back to Kiel on the night of 5/6 November, but this time it was to drop mines in the approaches to the port. Twenty Hampdens did the same, and one, from 83 Squadron, hit the sea and was lost.

On 7 November Tony wrote home, still worrying about not being able to get away and visit. Then he continued:

'I suppose you heard that Tony Hibbel[2] is a prisoner of war did you not? I am pleased because from what I heard about it I had not expected him to survive.

'Things are rather busy nowadays, although we do not seem to do a hell of a lot we are always wanted for something. The last two days I seem to have had no time to spare at all and I only have a few minutes now, so do excuse this, if it is a bit short.

'Very little happened in court. I pleaded guilty and then explained how I could not get the licence because Pete was in quarantine, so they only fined me £3.

'Dear old mum, I am looking forward to seeing your kind face, it seems such a long time since I was home. I don't like being away so long. Give my love to Agnes if you see her. I expect you think she and I are a great joke but I am really very seriously inclined in that direction.

'Well tons of love to you mum darling, I shall see you very soon.'

Two days later, on 9 November, Cuxhaven Bay, and the estuaries for the Weser and Elbe rivers, were the target for Tony's sea mine. Five Hampdens from 144 were involved and while four returned safely, the night ended in tragedy for some of the Raw crew. Hamburg was the main target this night, while Tony headed for

---

[2] Flight Lieutenant A J Hibell ended up in Stalag Luft III, perhaps the most famous RAF prisoner-of-war camp of the war. He had been a Hampden pilot with 455 Squadron RAAF, and had been shot down by night-fighter pilot Oberleutnant Walter Barte of I./NJGI near Winkeldorf on the night of 15/16 September, during a raid on Hamburg. He and his air gunner survived as prisoners, the other two crew members were killed. Although in a squadron mainly manned by Australian personnel, Tony Hibell was one of several British members. It was the first loss of an aircraft with a RAAF bomber squadron in WW2.

the enemy coast. Soon after take-off all the aircraft's lights failed and the only torch they had aboard did not last long and it too became u/s. It became virtually impossible for Harry Cobb to work his navigational skills in total darkness but having turned back, they were eventually able to spot the Linton-on-Ouse beacon.

It was now nearing 1 am in the morning and Tony was having difficulty with one engine. Without lighted instruments it was going to be tough to get down, then the engine quit, so he warned his crew, saying: "Have your parachutes ready."

Tony could now see the aerodrome lights and headed in on one engine and made a successful landing. After he taxied to the dispersal area, he and Cobb discovered the back of the aeroplane was empty. Guest and Carrie had either mistaken Tony's warning or merely decided to bale out anyway. Guest landed safely but the gunner, Bill Carrie, had not. Grabbing his chest-type parachute pack, he would need to clip it to his harness before exiting the aircraft. There were two hooks but he had only managed to clip one on and that alone had not been able to take the strain as the parachute jerked open and had snapped, sending Carrie to his death.

Naturally Tony was devastated by the loss of his air gunner in such a way. The CO sent him off on leave. No blame was attributed to Tony's actions but he had to take time to get over this sad loss of a crew member.

It was at this time that Tony was promoted to acting flight lieutenant. However, while his promotion was welcome, he also became deputy flight commander, which meant more paper work and even less time for any home visits. He also managed a rushed last-minute trip for Agnes to come up again to Luffingham for a weekend visit. With his leave now extended Tony went home, and in fact he did not operate again until 27/28 November. He had a replacement air gunner, Sergeant J Matthews, down the back.

The target that night was listed as Düsseldorf, although bombs appear to have fallen over a large area. Tony and crew are reported as bombing Hohenbudberg, a small town on the west bank of the River Rhine, north-east of Krefeld. It was fairly routine but lots of cloud. With winter came earlier take-offs, and Tony was getting away at 3.15 pm. Once again cloud interfered with the raid and having bombed the target, it was going to be yet another problematical return. Thick cloud over parts of England made for anxious moments until they finally found the Detling beacon. Detling is just north of Maidstone, Kent, well south of the Thames, so cloud had forced them many miles from North Luffingham. However, in cases like this, 'any port in a storm', so Tony landed there, even though the cloud base at Detling aerodrome was at ground level. Detling was not a bomber station but could accommodate a medium bomber landing without trouble.

Unfortunately there is now a large gap in Tony's surviving letters, and after November 1941, the next one is dated Friday, 17 January 1942. By this date, Tony had completed some twenty or more operations. There had been two mine-laying sorties in December, coded 'Jellyfish' on the 13th and 'Yams', on the 14 /15th. ('Yams' has been mentioned earlier, and was the code word for mining in the Heligoland Approaches.) In Tony's case it was the approaches to the important German port of Wilhelmshaven.

'Jellyfish' was the code word for an area near Brest – actually Cap de la Chèvre. While there had been no losses on the Wilhelmshaven operation, the Brest show proved different. Sixteen Hampdens had been sent to Brest, six to bomb the port while the other ten laid mines. In the event, the bombing part was abandoned and only six of the mine-laying aircraft carried out their assignment, due to low cloud. Tony and crew were among those who failed.

It did not help that this was a daylight mission, and two Hampdens were shot down by German fighters. One came from 44 Squadron at Waddington, its pilot being the CO of 44, Wing Commander S T Misselbrook DSO, but the other was a 144 Squadron aircraft. They had been intercepted by single-engine fighters of JG2, with Leutnant Horst Walbeck of the 3rd Staffel claiming one, and Feldwebel Harry Mayer of the 1st Staffel, the other.

So, in the details of the sortie on 13 January to mine Brest's harbour entrance, take-off time was logged as 3.09 pm. Crew members were Sergeant Lamb, rear gunner and Sergeant J F Skingsley was down as beam gunner; so a five-man crew. The additional gunner meant that one rear gunner did not have to man both gun positions, so that against targets that might have more protection than others, any fighter attack could be faced by two gunners.

The mission was flown out via Bridport, Devon, then Start Point and Lizard Point. Tony dropped down to just 50 feet above the sea, not only to keep under the enemy radar, but to ascertain the cloud base, which tonight was around 200 feet. At 4.41 pm the beam gunner reported an enemy aircraft, which the other gunner identified as a Messerschmitt 110 twin-engined fighter. As the cloud base had now risen considerably over the sea – even starting to disappear – Tony decided to abort as control was warning that other hostile aircraft were in the area. He set course back to Start Point and got as far as RAF Polebrook, north of Bedford, where he landed at 8.50 pm, with his port engine out of fuel.

On the 15th Sergeant Matthews was back as rear gunner and there was no beam gunner. Take-off came at 4.43 pm and their actual area to mine was Spiekeroog, an island off the north coast of Germany within the Frisian chain west of the Schillig Roads. It was uneventful and their mine went down from 700 feet at 6.35 pm.

2 January 1942, Tony and crew flew a daylight patrol off the Dutch coast, hoping to discover and bomb targets in the Sylt area, but finding clear skies they were forced to abandon the effort for fear of interception by German fighters. Although recorded as an 'unsuccessful' operation having returned with their bombs, it had been a long night. They had left Luffingham at 11.58 am and did not land until 4.55 pm, so nearly seven hours flying – which in daylight was a new experience for the Raw crew. This sort of operation was something new and called a 'roving patrol'. Twelve Hampdens were sent out on this task, virtually seeking any targets of opportunity, but nothing much happened, just one aircraft bombing an airfield at Leeuwarden. The next day he wrote home:

'How are things going at home? I hope you all had a happy New Year's Eve and had a nice lot to drink. We had a party here which was a bit dead. I played my clarinet at one stage of the evening, much to everyone's amusement.

'That was a lovely leave I just had, thank you mum for making it so happy for me and looking after me at home. You are the best mother in the world. Have you heard from Peter lately? I wonder when he will be getting some leave.

'I went and saw a picture last night with Vivien Leigh and Lawrence Olivier in it. It was called "Twenty One Days", I thought it was rotten. Have you heard from Agnes lately? I wonder if Mavis has started her new job yet, if not she will be registering soon, will she not? They start from 1 Jan, don't they? Give my love to Grandma, Mike and Pat. Tons of love, see you soon.'

On the 5th it was back to Brest and with a new rear gunner, Sergeant Gowland. The German battleships were still there, and an ever-present danger. The RAF and the Royal Navy kept a constant eye on them for any sign of them making a dash into the Atlantic where they could wreak havoc amongst British convoys. So, from time to time, the RAF took time out to bomb the port, just in case they managed to hit something vital.

155 bombers were assigned the task, around half being given the *Scharnhorst* and *Gneisenau* as targets, the rest the general dock areas. Again German smoke screens obliterated any chance of finding an aiming point but some fires were started by the falling bombs. No losses occurred. Take-off came at 3.40 pm in the afternoon, so that their arrival would be in darkness. They left the English coast at Portland Bill, Dorset, heading out over a darkening and cloudy sky. Cloud remained a factor when they reached the target so they had to bomb on dead reckoning, from 11,000 feet, at 5.47 am. Almost an hour later, heading home, Sergeant Gowland spotted a Ju88 night-fighter manoeuvring to make an attack. A call to Tony and he was evading fast and managed to lose the Junkers in cloud. The 88 could still track them on its radar but an attack would be difficult without a visual sighting; no doubt the enemy crew broke off to look for a less alert crew.

Brest was again on the menu for the 8/9th making it three night attacks in five days by Bomber Command to bomb the battleships. Take-off time was 12.47 am. They arrived over Brest at 2.45 am and managed to find a gap in the cloud long enough for them to see the target area and drop their bombs, from 10,500 feet. They returned home in very bad weather, something they were getting sickeningly used to, landing at base at 6.20 for a well-earned egg and bacon breakfast.

Then it was Hamburg, one of the RAF's regular targets, on 14/15 January. Ninety-five RAF bombers targeted the town's airframe factories and the shipyards but only around half were able to bomb successfully, Tony and his crew were one of them. They reached the city at 8.21 pm and with cloud and darkness decided to drop a flare. This allowed them to spot the ground and they were able to bomb from 10,500 feet at 8.25. Bad weather greeted them on their return to England forcing them to divert and land at Woolfox Lodge, a satellite airfield for North Luffingham, situated six miles to the north-west, right alongside the Great North Road (A1). It was about thirty miles from home base. At Woolfox Lodge Tony found his old 61 Squadron, who had moved there the previous October, now fully equipped with Manchester bombers.

Four aircraft failed to return from Hamburg, including two Hampdens of 50 Squadron. A crew from 144 Squadron ran out of fuel on the way home and after clipping a chimney stack at Field Dalling, they crashed just north of the airfield, but the crew survived the experience.

Three days later, on the night of 17/18 January, the target was Bremen. Sergeant Matthews returned, occupying Guest's wireless position, while Sergeant J H H Baness took the rear gunner's spot. Eighty-three aircraft went out, while other bombers were sent on diversionary raids. Two of these were sent to the German air-field at Soesterberg, Holland, to annoy the night fighters. Tony, taking off at 4.20 pm, made it to the Bremen area at 7.30 pm, but found it completely covered with haze and a smoke screen. These were the days long before Oboe-assisted navigators were able to locate the target and aiming points with radar, so crews either bombed blind or tried for an alternate target. In Tony's case they found and bombed the Ger-man airfield near Oldenburg, north-west of the city, at 8.05 pm. Their bombs were seen to explode just to the right of the airfield's flare-path at which time the base's lights were extinguished. Just to add to their troubles, the radio packed up on the way home so navigation became all important to get them back to base safely.

Tony's next letter is dated Friday evening, 17 January 1942, presumably writ-ten prior to this operation, and contained important news:

'… being a flight lieutenant has made things very busy for me and to tell you the truth I am a bit lost at the moment and seem to do nothing but work all the time from morning 'til night. But I will get used to it and have it buttoned up soon. Things are really worse than they should be because I am doing most of the squadron leader's work as he is detached.

'I have been thinking this over for the last month or so mum, and feel I must tell you, I want to get married to Agnes; I can see your face now mum, I expect you will say, "oh, becoming a flight lieutenant has gone to his head" but I can promise you I have been thinking about it for a long time before I ever heard of promotion. This has only made things easier for me, but I know I should have begged your permission sooner or later while still a pilot officer.

'Honestly mum, it is the one thing that will make me really truly happy. I sometimes think that I just can't go on nipping up to London every now and again and then having to leave wondering if I will ever see her again. You may think that sounds absurd but I have been in enough jams now to know how real it is, and I feel I want to take my happiness while I still have a choice.

'I am young, I know, very young, but I have plenty of responsibilities now, worthy of men twice my age and I will show you that I can tackle them. It is not a thing that I am rushing into, I have thought it over for a long while and know my mind perfectly. Agnes and I suit each other perfectly and we would be very, very happy together. I have never been more certain of anything before.

'I can't really see why there should be such a fuss about it, having a wife is a responsibility, a great responsibility I know. I am not forgetting that for one moment, but I am certain that I can manage and will never regret having a wife to look after.

'I think that you will urge me to wait a bit longer, say a year or so, but I feel I just can't wait that long – it seems an age. And anything may have happened by that time. I have talked it over with Agnes and she says that nothing would make her happier but she does not want to urge me on in the least bit. She says she wants me to do just what I feel is right and will not encourage me and yet will not discourage me. She will marry me at any time I wish.

'I have written to Peter and told him all about it but I have not had a reply yet. I don't know what he will have to say. I hope this is not so much of a shock to you mummy, I wanted to get home to talk it out with you, but it is difficult to get home when I want to now. If you refuse me permission I shall be unhappy and I know I shall never be happy until I am married, or the war finishes and lets me lead a normal life, and even if the war were to finish, I would still want to marry her now, however young I was.

'Well, good night mother darling. I am hoping for a favourable answer soon. All my love to you. Tony'

A week later, on the night of 25/26 January, it was back to Brest once more. Sixty-one aircraft took part but again results were not observed. It was obvious that British intelligence was being told that activity above the normal level on and around the battleships made it seem likely they were being prepared for sea. It was imperative that these huge German juggernauts were prevented from getting out into the ocean. Apart from bombing raids, aerial reconnaissance aircraft were always out on surveillance over Brest while British submarines were also on constant watch off the harbour entrance, at all times and in all weathers.

The Raw crew left the ground at 5.40 pm reaching the target at 10.01 pm. Intense anti-aircraft fire and lots of searchlights delayed their bomb run 'til 8.14 pm but they escaped unharmed and headed for England. Weather caused yet another diversion to Woolfox Lodge, where they put down just before midnight.

Tony was sent on a course towards the end of January 1942, at RAF Finningley, in Yorkshire, so at least he got a break from the war. This, with a few days leave, meant that he did not return to the squadron until the second week of February. However, he did write home on 29 January 1942, but says nothing about his proposed wedding. It seems that any reply he had had from his mother and then his further response, has not survived. He does however, mention his childhood friend Bruce Cole who had been wounded:

'I hope Bruce is all right. I had a horrible feeling when I read the first part of your letter that you were going to say he was missing. I was very relieved to see he was just wounded. He will be all right now if he was in hospital in Cairo not long ago, nothing can happen to him there. Yes, Tomahawks are fighters. I am wondering, though, how he was wounded?

'I have quite an easy time on this course. We start at 8 am and finish at 4 pm at the latest. I met several chaps I know here so it is quite good fun. This course may go on until Tuesday so I may not come on leave until Wednesday or Thursday. This is not a bad place. I went into Doncaster the other night and had a good time.

'I had to do a trip before I came here so I arrived a day late and got a bit behind but I am catching up now.

'I am sorry to hear you fell off your bike, you should not ride in this slippery weather because you never know when you may skid. I hope you have not done anything serious.'

Robert Bruce Cole was born in India, and as an RAF fighter pilot he had been flying P40s in the North African desert with 250 Squadron. He was shot down in a fight with JG27 on 5 December 1941. Despite the news of being wounded, it was not serious enough for him to be returned to England, and he was soon back in action once more and awarded the DFC. When he did return to England he became a Tempest pilot. We shall read more of him later.

Tony's next sortie was 12 February 1942 and once again the targets were the *Scharnhorst*, the *Gneisenau* and the *Prinz Eugen*, although not in the port of Brest this time. These dangerous capital ships, as half expected, had managed to break out of the port and were making a bold dash along the English Channel, headed for the North Sea. In doing so they hoped to reach Norway and the protection of the fjords.

Operation Fuller was the British plan devised for just such an eventuality, although nobody really thought their would-be route to Norway or the Baltic would be the narrow English Channel. If they did head to sea, it was thought far more likely they would make an attacking foray into the Atlantic and then head for northern ports of safety between Iceland and the north of Scotland. Their daring plan worked. Taking advantage of some bad weather, and with some superb planning by German naval and Luftwaffe personnel, the three ships had exited Brest and steamed round into the Channel to make, what was later called, their 'Channel Dash'. So great was the surprise that they were not spotted until mid-morning of the 12th, when they had almost reached Boulogne.

Most of Bomber Command had been stood-down because of the weather, so when Operation Fuller was finally set in motion, there were frantic calls to all commands to get underway. Everyone had been issued with sealed orders should such an operation be called for, although some remained under lock and key in intelligence officers' or COs' safes. British coastal guns, RAF fighters, bombers and torpedo planes were alerted, and of course, the famous formation of twelve Fleet Air Arm Swordfish aircraft at RAF Manston. They were sent out on what became a suicide mission, and its gallant leader, Commander Eugene Esmonde, was awarded a posthumous Victoria Cross.

Bomber Command sent off Wellingtons, Hampdens, Manchesters, Short Stirlings, Handley Page Halifaxes, Bristol Blenheims and Douglas Bostons – all to virtually no avail. In fact it was the largest daylight force of bombers so far. 144 Squadron, and Tony, were among the sixty-four Hampden crews. Of these, 49 Squadron lost no less than four aircraft, 50 Squadron another, 420 and 455 Canadian Squadrons were missing three, while 144 Squadron lost two. 144 Squadron lost its commanding officer, Wing Commander G F Simond, in one, while the other missing aircraft was piloted by Sergeant E I Nightingale, who had just been awarded the DFM. He was almost at the end of his tour, having already completed twenty-three operations. During the attack on Brest on 5 January (the mission in which Tony had encountered the Ju88), Ernest Nightingale lost his port propeller over the target but got home safely. On this day Nightingale's Hampden was hit by ship's anti-aircraft fire and in trying to get his crippled bomber home he crashed attempting to make an emergency landing at Norwich. Nightingale was killed but his crew survived. One of Wing Commander Simond's crew had been Sergeant John Baness, who had flown with Tony on the Bremen raid of 17 January.

Tony and crew, which also included a beam gunner again – Sergeant Thomas

– took off at 2.40 pm and just over an hour later, in miserable weather, the gunners spotted a Me110 fighter just twenty or thirty yards away. The Messerschmitt pilot attacked and opened fire but by skilful evasive flying, Tony side-slipped the shell fire and deftly nipped into some cloud as his rear gunner fired back. At 4.10pm some light flak began exploding near to their Hampden and immediately the rear gunner called out to say he could see the battleships. Tony zipped back into the cloud, headed towards the sighting location, and dropped out again but poor visibility made it impossible to make a bomb run. Circling in cloud he came back once again, this time his navigator could clearly see one of the big ships ahead and directed Tony towards it. Their bombs went down at 4.35 pm, and as they started to climb back into the cloud again, the rear gunner reported two bombs straddling the ship. It had been an exciting day, and they landed back at 6.55 pm.

It had also been a frustrating day for the bomber crews, not to mention the torpedo boys. During this afternoon Bomber Command had despatched 242 aircraft in three waves, mainly equipped with Hampden, Wellington and Blenheim aircraft. Due to weather and low cloud, only about thirty-nine of these had actually located the convoy and made some sort of attack, with no obvious results. Sixteen had failed to return while flak and fighters had damaged another twenty or so. Fighter Command had lost twenty aircraft and most of the pilots flying them. All six Swordfish of the Fleet Air Arm were shot down. Coastal Command put up Beauforts and Hudsons almost piece-meal. Again they achieved no hits on the enemy and three Beauforts and two Hudsons were lost, with others damaged by the intense AA defences. Tony had been involved in a particularly nasty and dangerous operation this day.

It was in Tony's letter of 15 February that he made one of his rare references to his war flying, by mentioning this operation to his mother. As stated earlier he had just returned to North Luffingham after a long leave at the end of January and the start of February, and the letter opens with him giving thanks to his mother for such a wonderful time. It seems it was also something of a family get-together. He then continued:

'The day I arrived back I was down to operate and got prepared to go in the middle of the night, but just as we were setting off it was cancelled. I suppose you have read all this flap about the [German] battleships. Well, we suddenly got the news through and were off like a bomb in daylight. I passed over them three times, very low down, and, oh boy! did they throw some stuff at us. I dropped my bombs the third time; we are not sure whether we hit them or not but one of the bombs was seen very near.

'I was on ops again last night but had to turn back because of technical failure,[3] so my time is now 150 [operational] hours, so seven or eight more trips should see me through now. [At this stage a pilot had to fly approximately 200 operational hours for a tour of ops, or around twenty-five missions, whichever came first.]

'I have been saving like mad since I came back and am continuing to do so for the rest of the month. I am not touching any drinks at all and only go out very seldom to the pictures, so my campaign is going quite well. Agnes may come down to see me next weekend I hope. I heard from Mike for my birthday, good show what!'

What was he saving for? His approaching wedding of course.

It was back to mine-laying on the night of 16/17 February, another Nectarine sortie to the Frisian Islands. On the 17/18th there was another 'roving commission', with three Hampdens going out to the French coast. Tony's operation is marked in the squadron diary as 'successful – north-west of [the island] of Juist'. Their 'vegetable' went down at 7.35 pm and they were home by 10 pm.

On the night of 22/23 February 1942, the port of Wilhelmshaven was the target for thirty-one Wellingtons and nineteen Hampdens. The aiming point was a floating dock that might be used to repair any damage to the battleships *Scharnhorst* or *Gneisenau*. Once again cloud was the main obstacle and bombs were dropped over an estimated position. Perhaps it is of significance that a local diary made no reference to this raid. Fortunately there were no Bomber Command losses this night. This date also saw the appointment of Air Marshal Sir Arthur Harris as C-in-C of RAF Bomber Command.

Another mine-laying trip on 24/25th saw Tony and crew tasked to place their mine near Heligoland. They encountered heavy rain so diverted to another area, off Ameland, one of the Wadden Islands to the north of Holland. They placed their mine there at 9.40 pm and were home by midnight, having been airborne

[3] The target had been Mannheim, on 14/15 February, from which poor old 49 Squadron lost another two of their Hampdens. Tony had taken off at 5.15 pm but was forced to abandon the trip when the aircraft's heating and intercom failed.

since 6.15 that afternoon. Forty-two Hampdens and nine Manchesters took part and two Hampdens failed to return, both from Tony's squadron. There were no survivors. One crew was captained by Flight Sergeant [!] Lord Dundas the son of the 2nd Marquess of Zetland, holding the title of Lord Dundas of Orkney. Ober-leutnant Egmont Prinz zu Lippe-Weissenfeld of 5./NJG2 made claims for two Hampdens north of Terschelling this night, his sixteenth and seventeenth victories of an eventual fifty-one night kills.

Tony's next mission on the night of 26/27 February was to Kiel, in order to bomb the *Gneisenau*, but proved unsuccessful, having to return early due to tech-nical trouble – the heating packed up yet again. However, his final three opera-tions that were flown in early March, were all successful – and comparatively comfortable. On Monday 2 March, Tony wrote to his mother:

'My Darling Mother. Thank you so much for the chocolates and for your letter. Those chocolates were jolly nice, how did you get them?

'It's a pity that I cannot get home while Pete is there but he may stay quite a while if he is pending posting, then I might be able to see him next Monday when I hope with a bit of luck to go on leave. I hope Pete is posted somewhere nearer to home next time.

'It seems from Agnes's letter that Pete is doing great planning for the wedding, good show! I also hear that the girls are going to try to wear white if possible, great news too! The idea of having the reception in Say-ers is a good one I think. I should rather like to have Tim as my best man, what do you think? By the way, I suppose you do have two best men at a double wedding don't you?

'Yes, my time has gone up quite a bit. I have 178 [operational] hours now, so that leaves only four trips to do, so I will be finished pretty soon now. We have been working very hard lately; I did seven trips in two weeks.

'Have you heard any more from those income tax people yet? Those people seem to need shaking up every so often to keep them awake.

'We went and had a run around with a rugger ball this evening to get in trim for a game on Wednesday. Boy did I find how unfit I am, I ache all over. It stays light for a nice long time in the evenings now doesn't it? I like it like that.'

The Renault factory at Billancourt, France, just west from the centre of Paris, was the first of the March operations, flown on the night of 3/4 March. Air Ministry had asked Bomber Command to try and knock out this factory which was known to be producing war materials for the German war effort. The factory's main product was around 18,000 trucks a year. A large force of bombers went there, 235 in all, in three waves, and precision was necessary to prevent civilian casualties in the surrounding area. The force met almost no anti-aircraft defences and only one Wellington failed to reach home. An estimated 300 bombs fell on the factory, destroying forty per cent of it and production came to a standstill for four weeks and it took several more months for repairs to be completed. Unhappily there were a lot of civilian casualties. Many people and workers lived close-by and many did not bother to heed the warning sirens, as these often sounded when aircraft were flying too and from Germany. In all 367 civilians died, with a further 347 injured, many housed in blocks of flats close to the works.

The Raw crew set off at 6.00 pm crossing the French coast south of Dieppe, and reaching Paris two hours later. On the approach the target was in full view, having been clearly illuminated by flares. Tony circled the target area, gradually losing height, not a difficult task with so little flak. To make certain of hitting the works, Tony had reduced height to just 1,800 feet and their bombs went down at 9.10 pm. If this recorded time is accurate, then they had circled the works, along with other aircraft, for over an hour. As he curved away, he and the crew could clearly see bombs bursting and many fires burning. Bad weather made a diversion to RAF Cottesmore necessary, and Tony set his bomber down ten minutes into the new day.

Overall it was a successful raid – and for more than one reason. With 235 aircraft making the attack it was the largest RAF effort against a single target thus far in the war. Well over 400 tons of bombs rained down, helped by the first concentrated use of target flares. This and the fact that the operation was led by several experienced crews was really the forerunner of the Pathfinder tactic that was on its way within Bomber Command.

On 10/11 March Tony and his crew went to Essen, the third successive night Bomber Command had gone there. 126 aircraft in all headed out, including forty-three Hampdens. Four aircraft were lost, including two Hampdens, but neither one came from 144. Other bombers crashed on getting back. Unexpected cloud caused poor bombing, but Tony was noted as having a successful raid. They had departed base at 7.10 pm that night. At 9 pm an enemy fighter was sighted astern and Tony put the Hampden into some violent evasive action. Having lost the potential danger, the target was reached at 9.50 but then they were caught by a searchlight. Tony dived to 6,000 feet to lose the frightening glare and levelling out, headed across the target at this height and the bombs were sent down into an already burning target at 9.58 pm. They were back home at half-past midnight.

Tony had started his tour with a mine-laying trip and he completed it with another, off Heligoland, on the 12/13th, again a task noted as successful. Twenty-six Hampdens were on this show and there were no losses. They had set off at 2 am on the 13th and made a successful drop at 5.45 am. They reached base at 7.50 that morning but low cloud prevented a quick landing, and in fact, Tony had to circle for nearly forty minutes before it was clear enough for him to make his final approach.

Upon his return he was told his tour was finished. According to records he had completed thirty operational sorties, although depending on the count it may have been only twenty-six. Nevertheless he had survived and for a while now he could expect to live fairly free from the constant thought of death. It is difficult to make a total of his operational flying hours but it must have been approximately the 200 generally required.

He remained on squadron strength for several days, followed by a spot of well-deserved post-operational leave. Officially he was posted to 16 Operational Training Unit at Upper Heyford, on 31 March 1942.

Chapter Eight

REST AND RETURN (2)

Having completed a Bomber Command tour of operations, which at times meant having flown 200 operational flying hours, or approximately thirty missions, a crew were rested. It was not always so clear-cut, for with long, deep penetration sorties, 200 hours could be accomplished some time before the magic figure of thirty. Then again, later in the war when there were far more short-range ops into northern France, it could take up to thirty-five missions to reach the 200-hour mark. However a good CO might decide that a particular pilot or crew had had a pretty gruelling tour and end their tour before either figure was reached. In this he might well be counselled by the station doctor.

As all aircrew were, strictly speaking, 'volunteers', having completed a tour there was no obligation for any of them volunteering for a second tour. Many did of course, and some even elected to carry on their first tour up to forty to forty-five missions, at the end of which they were deemed to have completed two tours. This also made sense because the crew were by that time highly skilled and on the ball, but by the same token, many made the decision to say enough was enough. Why risk death or captivity when they thought they were on borrowed time anyway?

Tony Raw and his crew decided that completing a tour was enough for the moment, and at this stage of the war, there was less pressure for maximum efforts, where every crew and aircraft were wanted in the air, so they could happily take a break and decide later on if they wanted to return to operations.

While this post-tour period was noted as being 'on rest', it generally meant a posting to Training Command, in order to pass on their knowledge to the next generation of bomber crews. Many would argue this was far from a rest, risking their lives by taking novices into the air and trying to explain the mysteries of survival, when in reality it was not so much a mystery as luck. There were as many crews lost on their first mission as on their last. Skill and experience helped but it could not divert an anti-aircraft shell or an experienced German night-fighter crew.

Before any serious posting came about, there was the matter of the double wedding of him and Agnes, together with Peter and Mavis. As recorded in Chapter Two, this happened on 22 April 1942.

Meantime, things had been put in motion for an award for Tony. Decorations are a strange area and a book on the subject of how they were awarded would be very interesting. Some people seem to get awards at the drop of a hat whilst others are ignored or passed over. In general terms, it was often the norm for a pilot of a bomber crew to be awarded the DFC, if an officer, or a DFM if non-commissioned, but it was not mandatory. As authors we have both known of airmen not being rewarded for completing a bomber tour, and it does seem a pity that when a crew does survive one, in the main it is only the pilot who is rewarded, with perhaps one other member, if he is lucky. There was never any suggestion that every crew member be given an award, and of course, with no posthumous awards allowed (except for a Victoria Cross) even men who had almost completed a spectacular tour had no recompense for their work.

However, in Tony's case, the CO of 144 Squadron wrote up Tony for an award and this was forwarded to the station commander of North Luffingham, Group Captain Gus Walker. The recommendation noted:

Total hours flown on operations, 191 hours, thirty-five minutes.
Number of sorties carried out, thirty.
Recognition for which recommended, DFC.
Appointment held, pilot.

Particulars of Meritorious Service

For continuous gallantry and devotion to duty during raids into enemy territory.

Flight Lieutenant Raw has completed thirty sorties, always showing great determination and courage. A large number of these sorties were carried out in adverse weather conditions, in spite of this Flight Lieutenant Raw had always used his utmost endeavours to locate and attack his target.

In his capacity of deputy flight commander the example he has set has inspired the other crews to greater efforts.

Date: 26 March 1942.

G A Walker
Group Captain
Commanding RAF Station, North Luffingham.

Remarks by Air Officer Commanding
RECOMMENDED

Date: 3 April, 1942

J C Slessor
Air Vice-Marshal
Commanding 5 Group, RAF

BRIEF DETAILS OF ALL SORTIES CARRIED OUT
1941

August	26	(G) Nectarine 2	Task successful
	29	Dunkirk	Task successful
September	7	(G) Nectarine	Task successful
	11	Rostock	Task unsuccessful
	13	Brest	Task successful
	18	Search	Task unsuccessful
	20	Trier 'drome	Task successful
October	11	(G) Yams	Task successful
	12	Ruhr	Task successful 10/10th cloud
	21	Bremen	Task successful
	24	Bombs jett. in Germany	Task unsuccessful
November	1	Kiel	Task unsuccessful (icing)
	5	Kiel [mining]	Task successful
	9	Cuxhaven [mining]	Task successful
	27	Hohenbudberg	Task successful
December	13	Jellyfish [mining]	Task unsuccessful (No cloud cover)
	15	(G) Yams	Task successful

1942

January	2	Mole A	Task unsuccessful (No cloud cover)
	5	Brest	Task successful
	9	Brest Docks	Task successful
	14	Hamburg	Task successful
	17	'Drome N.W. of Bremen	Task successful
	25	Brest	Task successful
February	12	Battle-cruiser at sea	Task successful
	14	Mannheim	Task unsuccessful (Technical trouble)
	16	(G) Nectarine	Task successful
	18	N.W. of Juist	Task successful
	22	Wilhelmshaven	Task successful
	24	(G) Off Ameland	Task successful
	26	Kiel	Task unsuccessful (Technical trouble)
March	3	Billancourt	Task successful
	10	Essen	Task successful
	12	(G) Heligoland	Task successful

The award was duly made and his name appeared in the *London Gazette* dated 26 May 1942. If space allowed, the actual recommendation was printed in the *Gazette* too but if time or space precluded this, then only the name appeared. In Tony's case, only his name appeared, but the actual recommendation in the records is as follows:

> *'Flight Lieutenant Raw has completed many successful raids and despite adverse weather has shown great perseverance in locating and attacking his targets. He has displayed gallantry and devotion to duty during raids into enemy territory and has set an example which has inspired other crews to greater efforts.'*

There was another pilot of 144 Squadron, whose DFC was promulgated in the same issue of the *London Gazette* as Tony's. He was Acting Flight Lieutenant Robert S Radley, who had also completed thirty trips with a total of 186 operational hours. According to his citation, he must have been deputy flight commander of the other flight.

Now at RAF Upper Heyford, Tony and Mavis had set up home at, 'The Mill', Middle Barton, near Oxford, which they appeared to be sharing with another couple. On 7 May 1942 Tony wrote to his mother:

'Well how are things going now that it has all settled down again? I have been meaning to write for quite a while now, but what with one thing and another, getting settled in here, I have had to keep postponing it.

'We are well settled in now and extremely happy, it is lovely here and very comfortable. Agnes is marvellous in the house and she and Joyce really look after Bob and I like kings. We have a piano and also an organ in the house, which has tons of stops and things, and makes you sound as if you can play beautifully as we do not lack music. We have a wireless but it is not as good as Agnes's so we are waiting to get that, hers has a gramophone too.

'I am writing this on my knee in the garden. It is a beautifully sunny day. They have just called me for supper, so I will finish this afterwards.

'Of course, directly I got back here I was put on night duties (very annoying) and was only able to get home during the daytime, still it is over now and everything is running smoothly. When things have properly calmed down and we are quite old hands at running the place you must come and stay with us as we suggested before.

'What do I owe you for various things at and after the wedding, let me know? We have just been out to try and shoot rabbits but the land owner came along and took the number of our car so we sheered off again!'

By the end of the month Tony was selling his motor cycle and asking his mother if the person who was showing an interest in its purchase had agreed a price. He wanted £16 for it but would take £15. He no longer needed it because he was about to buy a car for when he was on night flying – at a cost of £25 – but he didn't want to get it if he couldn't sell the bike. Tony had other reasons to be feeling a bit low too:

'I am feeling rather depressed at the moment because I have not been able to see Agnes since last Wednesday and I sure do feel it after having been with her all the time for about a month. Last Wednesday we were told we had to live-in [the officers' mess] until further notice and were not allowed out of camp, Lord knows why! Then yesterday I asked if it would be all right to go on my forty-eight-hour pass and they said yes. So Bob and I went home to find Agnes and Joyce had gone to Oxford. We hung around for two hours then the 'phone rang and we were told to return to camp.'

Tony also mentioned in the letter that he had received several telegrams (presumably about his DFC), including ones from Peter, Trixie and Stan, and 144 Squadron. Had he not been on rest, he would no doubt have been on Bomber Command's first 1,000-bomber raid, where a real maximum effort had been mounted against Cologne on the night of 30/31 May.

Regrettably there is another long gap in Tony's surviving letters to his mother. He had continued instructing for the summer but was then posted to another unit on 27 July 1942. This was to 30 OTU at Hixon, Staffordshire, part of 93 Group, which had just been formed in July 1942, and whose main equipment was Vickers Wellington bombers. When he wrote home on 8 August, his new address was 11 The Crescent, Walton, Near Stafford:

'I am sorry I have not written before, but with this sudden change of abode I have been in a bit of a flap.

'We have settled down in this place now, it is very nice and we have two good rooms and the kitchen is very modern, but the lady who owns the place is unbearable and we just do not get on with her. She interferes with everything, you just would not believe anyone could be like it. I have just had twelve rounds with her this evening and at the moment we are looking around for another place, either a furnished flat or a cottage. We are going out to look around this evening if it stops raining. It is so hopeless around here, everywhere is full up. I have to pay 45/- [£2.50p] a week here plus electricity and gas. It is far too much but it's such a nice place and accommodation is so hard to find here that I took it but we are getting out as soon as we can.

'I don't mind Hixon, it is quite a good place. It looks as if I shall get more of a rest here than at Upper Heyford. We are only just starting and had our first pupils in the other day. So far we have done nothing and for the next fortnight we shall continue to do nothing.'

The couple obviously found another place to reside, for his letters now had the address as Heather House, Milford, Near Stafford. In mid-September Tony managed to get some leave and visited Ealing. Returning from that leave was a bit of a trial, as he told his mother:

'At about 1.30 in the morning we got a puncture and after taking the whole wheel off and finding the pump would not work, we were helped by a lorry driver and finally got the puncture mended, put the wheel back on and resumed our journey.

'After about five minutes the tyre went down again and I got out and blew it up. About an hour later it had gone down again and I then had to mend four punctures. We finally arrived here at 8 am after about nine hours on the road.

'We are having a mess party on the 11th [October] so will you tell Pete if you see him? Tell him I have invited Mavis, F/Lt Atkinson and himself. Could you let me know Pete's 'phone number so that I can give him a ring sometime.

'Things have been going quite well since I have been back. We went to a Home Guard dance the other night and had a lot of fun. Have you heard from Mike since he went back to school?'

It is difficult to remember that Tony was still only twenty years of age, but in a letter dated 14 February 1943, he thanks the family for all the lovely presents and telegrams he received for his twenty-first. He was now living at The Crown Inn, Tetbury, Gloucestershire.

Tony was on another course at the end of February, to early March. He also managed to visit his brother Mike and they all went and had a look round the old school. By April Tony and Agnes had moved again, this time to Holly Bank Farm, Scropton, near Derby, while still at RAF Hixon, although he had attended 3 FIS (Flying Instructors School) between 2 February and 17 March.

10 April 1943:

'My Darling Mother, I am pleased to say we are settled down in a really nice place at last. This is a wizard farm and the people are awfully decent. Mrs Simpson does all our catering for us and we have a good lot of eggs and about a quart of milk every evening. It is quite a big farm with bulls, cows, sheep, ducks and hens. I like wandering around and looking at them.

'I work in definite shifts now. It is not bad but it works out that I almost never get an evening off. It goes like this. First day I work in the morning 'til 1 pm, afternoon off, and all night from 9 pm. Second day, work in afternoon from 1 pm until 9 pm, and on again next morning at 8 am. I do know where I am although I have to work pretty hard nevertheless. I get more leave, once every five weeks. Incidentally, my next starts on 6 May – tell Pete will you please.

'I had to go and make a speech yesterday evening at a picture house in Rugby, for the Wings for Victory Week. It went off all right but just as I thought it was all over and breathing a sigh of relief, I was whipped off to a dance to do it again.

'When does Mike go back, before the 6th? I expect I shall just miss him, what a shame. Have you heard from Pat lately?'

Sister Pat had joined the Women's Auxiliary Air Force and was an ACW2, starting at RAF Wilmslow, Cheshire. Tony was posted to 27 OTU, as an instructor on 30 April and promoted to squadron leader at RAF Litchfield.

There is hardly any talk of flying in Tony's letters, but he does mention one occasion in July 1943 when he had a trying time:

'I was held up at Church Stanton for two days recently. The weather was terrible. The hill we were on was in cloud most of the time, and it was pouring with rain. I was a shocking sight, as I had been soaked through in the clothes I stood up in about four times and was unshaven.

'If I had got away when Peter did I would have been all right but they could not start my engines, and when eventually they did start, then I took off quickly but had to land even quicker as the cloud had all gone down into the valley below. So there I was – stuck for two days. I could not leave the place very well until late in the evening because I had to stand by to get off immediately if the weather improved.

'However, I attempted to get to Wellington [school] on the second night, trying to hitch-hike in the rain, but I gave it up when I got to the Merry Harriers, foot sore and soaked once again. I did not manage to see Mike again. I got up at dawn the next morning because I thought the weather had changed but still we had to wait until about 10 am. Boy, was I pleased to leave.'

By the autumn Tony was writing from the Officers' Mess, RAF Church Broughton, near Derby. Tony Raw had, meantime, been decorated once again. This time he was given the Air Force Cross for his services to Training Command. The recommendation (which was approved and notified on 31 December 1943) states:

> *'Flight Lieutenant A W Raw, 30 OTU (total instructional hours 346)*
> *This officer was posted for duty as a screened instructor and has shown exceptional ability as a pilot. He was selected as one of the four most outstanding pilot instructors within the group for duties as an instructor at 93 Group Screened Pilots' School. He has shown unflagging zeal and has set a fine example to both instructors and pupils alike.'*

So 1943 ended. Tony had been doing a lot of instructing and had been off operations for some twenty-one months. However, now came the time to return to operational flying should he choose to do so, although his training work was very important in the overall scheme of things.

In early 1944 he volunteered to go back to the real war but was retained as an instructor for the present. With his experience and his knowledge, men such as him could be of invaluable service with the Pathfinder Force, where he was posted. The Pathfinders were experienced crews who were expected to lead raids onto a hostile target, their task being to locate it accurately, and once having done so, they would mark it with various illuminations. Once the accuracy of these coloured markers was ascertained, the main force bombers would be told where – on what coloured markers – to bomb.

It was no easy task. They were the first aircraft over a target, which would remain blacked out to try and avoid being seen by the in-coming raiders; expert navigators and bomb aimers had to fly around to make positive identification and once they had done so they would need to head in to drop the markers. Once they began to fall, the ground defences, flak gunners and searchlight crews, would immediately open up. In addition, German night-fighter aircraft would be directed to areas where their ground controllers suspected the RAF's target would be, they would then give the order to attack. Night fighters that carried radar would attempt to pick up the heavy bombers on their screens, while single-seat fighter pilots would be watching intently for the black silhouettes of the bombers as they crossed the now burning and lit-up target area. Meanwhile, Tony waited patiently for the call to return to active duty. It was the nature of Tony

Raw that he saw further operational flying as his duty to king and country despite there being no need to volunteer again.

In the spring of 1944 Tony was posted to RAF Ossington, near Newark, Nottinghamshire. This was the home of 82 OTU, again a part of Bomber Command's 93 Group. Tony was now a family man, for Agnes had given birth to a daughter, whom they named Paula. It was a sad time with Peter having been reported missing in March. Tony wrote to his mother on 3 April 1944:

> 'We are quite settled down again here. Agnes arrived with Paula yesterday. I was very glad to have them with me. They made the last part of the journey by lorry and trap!
>
> 'Bruce rang me today and is probably coming to spend tomorrow with me if the weather is good enough for him to fly down. I hope he can make it. How is Mike getting on? I hear he went to watch a game of rugger the other day, where was that?
>
> 'I have a prospective buyer for my trumpet, he called while I was away. I have not seen him yet but I am hoping to do some more business with him soon.
>
> 'Keep your chin up mum and be a good girl until I come home.'

It's amazing how, despite the war etc, losing a dear brother, it is the little, almost mundane things that people still had to deal with; life carried on.

Bruce Cole was now based at RAF Milfield, Northumberland, converting to Tempest V fighters, and had not managed to visit Tony and Agnes as yet or to add his condolences, due to bad weather preventing him from flying.

However, Peter's widow Mavis had managed a visit. According to Tony she seemed to be as happy as could be expected under the circumstances. She had been contacted by the Air Ministry about Pete's kit that had been sent somewhere or other. It hadn't helped.

Back in London, Mrs Raw and the other family members in and around Ealing were now being plagued by the German V1 flying bombs. Everyone had previously thought that any real attempts at bombing London had long past. Tony wrote on 12 July:

> 'I am glad that Trixie and the kids have managed to find a place for evacuation. I suppose she will be there for the rest of the war now, or until

we have captured the Buzzy bomb projectors anyway. I hear that you haven't been bothered quite so much over the last few nights by the Buzzers. I suppose it was the one dropped on Sanders that blew the windows in and the tiles down, or have you had one nearer than that?

'I think you ought to take a holiday or leave town anyway. Why do you not go to Evesham – there is no need for you to stay in town.'

By this time Peter's wife Mavis had given birth to a daughter, Maureen. Mavis and the baby visited Agnes and Tony towards the end of July, Tony remarking to his mother:

'Mavis arrived yesterday with little Maureen, she certainly is a big baby now, a wonderful improvement. My little Paula can stand perfectly without holding [on to] anything now.'

In August 1944 Tony had been hoping to get some leave but he wrote home:

'At the moment the position of my leave is rather in doubt so I think you had better hold your fire. The two other squadron leaders are indisposed, one has been in hospital for quite a while and the other has had a motor cycle accident so I shall very probably have my leave postponed.

'I went in for a swimming contest yesterday but unfortunately came up against a bloke who just beat me by a touch in every race. However, I got second prize in the 100 yards and the fifty yards, and [helped win] the relay. The prizes were saving certificates which I have given over to Paula.

'I am in charge of the band here now and I do quite a bit of practising. I did not play in the contest, our band came third. Agnes and I went to Lincoln for the night to see the contest. Mavis looked after the babies for us. I saw Bruce the other evening, he flew down and listened to one of our rhythm club sessions.

'Paula will soon be walking, and can stand with ease now. I should think the war should be over soon now. I hope I shall see you soon.'

One cannot tell why he thought the war would soon be over, and in any event, he was about to return to active duty. His next letter to his mother is dated 15 August 1944, his address given as Officers' Mess, RAF Warboys, Huntingdon.

'As you will see by my address I have moved. This place is not too bad; it is a bit scattered. I am still on training. The position here is quite convenient for London. Agnes is still at the farm but she is going to try and find somewhere down here.

'We took some photographs of Paula the other day, I will enclose them for you to see but please send them back. I hope I will be able to wangle something to see Mike. Tons of love to you and all at Evesham.'

It was not long before Tony was on the move again. This time it was to RAF Upwood, near Ramsey, Huntingdon, the home of 156 Squadron. He had completed a conversion course onto four-engined Avro Lancaster bombers, and had been posted to 156 from 82 OTU. The posting date was 13 August, but clearly he had arrived a few days later. Tony wrote from Upwood on the 30th, which was to be his last letter home.

'My Dearest Mother, I received a letter from you which was forwarded from Ossington, it was written about a month ago. As you will see I have moved to another aerodrome, although it is only across the road from the other place, about four miles away.

'It looks as if I shall not be getting my leave for another fortnight, somewhere about 20 September I think. I am still not sure though, if it will happen. I wonder if Mike could go back to school a bit late. When do the results of his school certificate come out?

'Bruce flew down to town the other day and gave Pat a bit of a fright – at 10 Mount Park I think. I whistled down the next evening to see Mike (it is quite easy to get to town from here), but I arrived late and had to catch an early train back, so I stayed in town with Bruce. Keep it under your hat because I had just come back from seeing Agnes and she would take a dim view of it.

'I 'phoned Trixie from Ossington the other day. She is moving into the digs next door to hers as the woman she is with is going into hospital. She is hoping to live near Stan soon. The trunk call system is terrible here. I have not been able to get through since I have been here.

'Well I hope all is well at Evesham. Hope to be able to see you soon. Maybe the war will finish before my leave but I doubt it – the doodle-bugs might though. Tons of love to all at Evesham. Tony'

Again he makes reference to the war ending. One supposes he must have been encouraged by the advances made by the allied armies following the Normandy invasion and break out from Caen. Perhaps subconsciously he was boosting his courage knowing that he was about to return to operational flying, with all the dangers that entailed, and was indulging a bit of wishful thinking.

Tony's new squadron's motto was 'We Light the Way' and as this suggests, it was a Pathfinder unit. The Pathfinder Force had been formed in August 1942 due to the fact that a high percentage of bombs dropped were missing targets by a long distance. To a degree this was due to human error coupled with a crew's desire to drop their bomb load and 'get the hell out of here'. The urge to drop must have been compelling with all the flak and searchlights about them, and the knowledge that they were most vulnerable on the run-in, when the bomb-aimer would be asking for a steady approach to his aiming point. This period gave the ground gunners valuable seconds to aim at a steady target, and the radar operator in a night fighter might easily be closing in at that very moment. It was so easy to let the bombs go and dive away towards home.

Obviously a better method was needed, and marking a target was the way to go. But the marking must of course be accurate, which is why these specialist squadrons had been formed into 8 Group of Bomber Command. By definition too, the Pathfinder crews had to be experienced men, and have that extra bit of courage to linger over a target, to make sure the markers had fallen in the right place.

This had led to the creation of the job of master bomber, or master of ceremonies. Again these were highly experienced crews, whose pilot had to have the nerve to stay over the target for a long period, not only to check the fall of the markers, but then to radio the main force bombers to confirm which markers to drop. The marking flares did not last forever, and so the MC would later have to call in other Pathfinder aircraft to re-mark, and again go through the routine of confirming the correct aiming points.

It was into this field of operations that Squadron Leader A W Raw DFC AFC now moved, as a flight commander. 156 had been one of the original four squadrons that formed the PFF and it remained one for the rest of the war. It was commanded by Wing Commander D B Falconer DFC AFC, who like Tony, had won his DFC back in 1941. He had been with 49 Squadron, operating with Hampdens. Not only that, but Wing Commander Falconer's AFC appeared in the same list of periodic awards for the Air Force Cross, as Tony's, Falconer having received his for work with 14 OTU at RAF Cottesmore, Leicestershire.

By definition Tony's new crew were also experienced men. His navigator was Flight Lieutenant Charles William Reeves, aged twenty-one, from Bulwark, Chepstow, Monmouthshire, and he had a wife Lillian in Manchester. He had been with 156 Squadron for some time and had been notified of the award of the DFC, although it would not be recorded in the *London Gazette* until 15 September 1944.

His flight engineer was Pilot Officer Alfred Brooks, aged twenty-three, from Harwood, Lancashire, also married – to Marion. The wireless operator was twenty-eight-year-old Flight Lieutenant Alexander Millar, who had a wife Elsie in Cheltenham, Gloucester.

The two air gunners, who would man the mid-upper and rear turrets, were Flight Sergeant Norman Warwick, thirty, another married man (wife Norah) who lived in Wetheral, Cumberland, and Pilot Officer Raymond Haines Leonard RAAF, aged twenty-two, from Berri, South Australia.

Specialist navigator and bomb aimer was Acting Squadron Leader Geoffrey Alan Ritchie Undrell, aged twenty-four, whose wife Alice Marguerite lived in East Sheen, Surrey. His DFC would appear in the *London Gazette* on 17 August 1945, but, significantly, 'with effect from' 10 September 1944. Alex Millar would also receive a posthumous 'Mention in Despatches' after 10 September.

They did not have long to prepare for operations, for their names were down for a raid on Eindhoven on 3 September. In fact this was a daylight mission, something new to Tony. No fewer than 675 aircraft carried out raids on six German airfields in southern Holland, all being recorded as successful, with just one Halifax bomber lost. 156 Squadron had provided nine Lancasters for this raid, and also the master and deputy master bombers.

Three days later, it was another daylight trip, this time to Emden, in fact the first time Bomber Command had attacked this target since June 1942 – and the last. 105 Halifaxes and seventy-six Lancasters from 6 and 8 Groups got the task and they were escorted by RAF Spitfires on the way out, and American P51 Mustangs on the return. The bombing was accurate and the town was left in flames. Only one Lancaster failed to return and that was skippered by the deputy master bomber, whose machine received a direct hit by anti-aircraft fire. 156 Squadron's contribution was eleven aircraft, with two pilots being the master bomber and the deputy master bomber.

Tony's third raid was to Gelsenkirchen on the 11th, in fact, a synthetic oil plant at Nordstern, one of three such plants. 379 aircraft were involved in yet another daylight op, 205 Halifaxes, 154 Lancasters and twenty Mosquitoes. 156 put up thirteen Lancasters. The first two targets were clearly visible and bombed successfully, but the Gelsenkirchen plant was partially obscured by a smoke screen that hindered the bombing. Spitfires, Tempests and Mustangs gave escort, but two Lancasters from the PFF over Gelsenkirchen were lost, and so were five Halifax bombers. These, it was noted, were caused by flak or by 'friendly' bombs. Tony's Lancaster (ND534) was one of the two Lancs lost. There were no survivors from Tony's aircraft, and only two survived from the other loss, a bomber of 35 Squadron. 156 Squadron had ten of its returning bombers sporting flak damage, from a target that was 'strongly defended'.

Was it friendly bombs that killed Tony and his crew? It seems as if Tony's mother was later told it was, for in her diary for 17 August 1945 she wrote: *'Heard that my darling Tony was killed through one of our own bombs dropping on his plane. What a waste!'*

Another incredible factor to this story again involves Peter Raw's old CO, Roland Beamont. Martin Smith (who originally found the Raw letters) wrote to the wing commander in August 1992 regarding Peter, and quite a coincidence occurred. Beamont wrote back to him:

'My log book shows that I led my Tempest wing to escort Lancasters bombing Gelsenkirchen on 11 September 1944. We saw two of them explode in heavy flak over the target – a terrible sight which I have just been writing about in my latest book. Of course, I did not know who was in them, but they had no chance. The bomber boys were very courageous, as indeed was Peter.'

The book in question was *Tempest Over Europe* (Airlife, 1994). Beamont wrote:

'The bomber force was making its run into the Gelsenkirchen target exactly on time and had already been ranged by the formidable 88-mm flak defences of the Ruhr. The bombers flew on relentlessly into this enormous barrage, and as I turned the wing slowly to starboard to take up position about one mile south of the Lancasters and 500 feet above their level to give ourselves tactical advantage against any Luftwaffe attack, it seemed that the barrage was creeping towards us and individual shell bursts were getting uncomfortably close.

'Then it happened. An enormous flash and a mushrooming cloud of black smoke showed amongst the nearest Lancasters on our port side as one of them took a direct hit. In an instant a ball of flame rolled downwards from the formation and small black objects streaming smoke fell until lost to sight.

'The bombers flew on unflinching through the storm of shell-fire, and then another massive flash as another bomber's bomb-load exploded leaving nothing but smoke and a fireball with a hail of falling debris.'

It is almost beyond imagination how Tony's mother must have grieved terribly, now having lost her third son to this awful war. She did in fact write on the envelope of Tony's last letter to her: 'The last letter from my darling Tony.'

The Raw family is left with three names carved on separate white CWG headstones all together on the Ealing Memorial, but these sad tablets, like millions of others, are more than cold monuments to the fallen. These were men, ordinary men with lives, but heroes. Blood ran through their veins. All made the ultimate sacrifice. Many families lost multiple members but Mrs Irene Raw was hit hardest, losing three loving sons.

Each Raw boy would have known the dangers. Volunteering for active duty took bravery, but in some ways it was an adventure, tinged with thrills and the unknown. For Peter and Tony it took the courage to continue, raid after raid, mission after mission, knowing full well that the next one could be his last. All three were married, and Tony and Peter both had children, and all three knew the importance of, and had experienced and had grown up surrounded by, a loving family.

What were their last thoughts in those final seconds? Fear, shock, the inevitability of it all? John, Peter and Tony would, perhaps, have visualised a final flash of the faces of loved ones – then terrible oblivion. Wars often take the best and they certainly did here.

Chapter Nine

MISSING; AND BRUCE COLE

Mrs Irene Raw had twice received that knock on her front door, to find a post boy holding a telegram that had shattered her world. On this occasion it is thought she was still at her own mother's house in Evesham, so that inexplicably, the telegram was sent to 10 Mount Park Crescent, Ealing, addressed to Mr P E Raw. Peter had, of course, been dead for six months, and had been a flight lieutenant. Clearly RAF next of kin records had not kept up with either time or events. It must have irked the family that someone had not twigged this, and it must have seemed that Peter's death had all but been forgotten by the RAF. Added to this the RAF couldn't even get Tony's name right, calling him Antony instead of Anthony. The telegram, dated 12 September, was received at Ealing post office from Air Ministry, 73 Oxford Street, London, at 12.33 pm and duly sent round to the house. It read:

> 'Regret to inform you that your brother Squadron Leader Antony William Raw DFC AFC, 67624, is reported missing as the result of air operations on 11 September. Enquiries are being made through the International Red Cross Committee and any further information received will be communicated to you immediately. Should news of him reach you from any other source please advise this department. His wife is being informed. No information should be given to the press without consulting her.'

A handwritten letter from Wing Commander Donald Falconer quickly followed, sent directly to Agnes:

156 Squadron, Royal Air Force
Upwood, Huntingdonshire

12 Sep. 1944

'Dear Mrs Raw,

'It is with deep regret that I write to confirm the sad news which you have already received regarding your husband, Acting Squadron Leader A W Raw DFC AFC.

'His aircraft was engaged in an attack on Gelsenkirchen on 11 Sept, 1944, but as no message was received from his aircraft after leaving this country there is little that can be added to the bare statement reporting him as missing.

'I had the fullest confidence in your husband's ability and I am sure that he and his companions gave a very good account of themselves under whatever circumstances prevented them from bringing their aircraft back to this country. I can only hope that they were able to make a safe landing, either by parachute or in the aircraft itself.

'News of this nature however, reaches us only through the International Red Cross Committee, and normally takes up to six weeks to come through. My sympathy, and that of all members of my squadron, is with you in this anxious time of waiting.

'It is desired to explain that the request in the telegram notifying you of the casualty to your husband was included with the object of avoiding his chance of escape being prejudiced by undue publicity in case he is still at liberty. This is not to say that any information about him is available, but is a precaution adopted in case of all personnel reported missing.

'Any information received will be communicated to you immediately, and please do not hesitate to write to me if I can be of any service to you.'

This was followed by a more formal letter from the casualty section of the Air Ministry, in London's Oxford Street, four days later.

'Madam,

'I am commanded by the Air Council to express to you their great regret on learning that your husband, Acting Squadron Leader Antony William Raw DFC AFC RAF, is missing as the result of air operations on

11 Sept 1944, when a Lancaster aircraft in which he was captain set out to bomb Gelsenkirchen and failed to return.

'This does not necessarily mean that he is killed or wounded, and if he is a prisoner of war he should be able to communicate with you in due course. Meanwhile, enquiries are being made through the International Red Cross Committee and as soon as any definite news is received you will be at once informed.

'If any information regarding your husband is received by you from any source you are requested to be kind enough to communicate it immediately to the Air Ministry.

'The Air Council desire me to convey to you their sympathy in your present anxiety.

I am, Madam,
Your obedient servant,
J A Smith.'

Agnes now returned to London, residing at 40 Gordon Road, Ealing. In late October 1944 she wrote to Michael Raw:

'Dear Mike,

'Many thanks for your letter which, as you so rightly said, came as a great surprise!! Nevertheless, a very welcome one.

'So you are feeling bored this term – obviously a bad case of "lack of work". I can suggest a remedy, Mike, but I don't think I will, or it might encourage you to slack off work more than ever!

'I'm glad you like the photo of Tony. I like the other one much better now I've got used to it. I've heard no news yet, Mike, and I'm getting very, very eager. It is six weeks now, but apparently it takes between two and three months before one hears from prisoners these days. Gosh, Mike, I do hope he's OK. Life's simply awful without his funny ways. Do you still feel very sure?

'Yes, Paula walks all over the house now, and is a perfect menace and a public nuisance! She has discovered my dressing table drawers and is forever diving into them and producing all my powder, etc. Nothing stops her making a bee-line there and throwing everything out. What a life!

'They've sent Tony's things along, and his clarinet is there, safe and sound. It's quite sad to see it looking so dull and lifeless. He used to keep it so shiny. Ah! Something for you to do on your next leave. Whizz-oh! Keep you busy!

'I think you had better put some trumpet hours in now you're not so busy! Old Tony will want to hear "Indian Summer" when he returns. Or do you think he'll be so dashed busy playing himself that he won't have time for anyone else. I think so somehow.

'We went to tea to Ma Fenton's the other day, and whilst there we found that Paula had disappeared. After numerous searches, Mavis found her at the very top of the house. She had climbed three flights, very silently and very 'nippily'. She's not the slightest bit afraid of anything. Must take after her wonderful mother!

'Well, I think I've gassed enough, perhaps too much. Anyway, all the best old boy, be good – no cider, no nothing!!

Much love, Agnes'

In the December issue of the Wellington school magazine there appeared under the heading of 'Old Boys Notes' where over recent years the passing in battle of many former Wellington boys are recorded, the following. Errors had crept in, but the entry read:

'Squadron Leader Anthony William Raw DFC AFC ('31-39) is missing from a raid on Berlin [sic]. Tony had been reading law before the war, when, like his brothers, he joined the Royal Air Force. He took part in a very large number of operations, until finally, he was appointed instructor to operational instructors. For his high gallantry in active service as an instructor he was awarded the Air Force Cross in the New Year Honours this year. It was only this last summer that he came to see us; the same unspoilt, charming fellow we had known at school, grown not to the fullness of stature of proper manhood. He told us quietly of a little of his work and his anxious urge to return to operations, despite the inhibitions of his superior authorities. In the end they took heed of his importunate volunteering and once more Tony was on operations as a Pathfinder. From a raid over the heart of Germany in September he did not return. Our prayers and thoughts are with his mother, his brother and his wife. John – Peter – Tony. It is tragic grief. Wellington is proud in its sorrow – and humbly grateful.'

Another Air Ministry telegram, received at Ealing post office on 12 December, three months after the first shattering telegram had been received – still addressed to Mr P E Raw at Mount Park Crescent:

> '11/12/44. Deeply regret to advise you that according to information received through the International Red Cross Committee, your brother A/S/L Antony William Raw DFC AFC is believed to have lost his life as the result of air operations on 11/9/44. The Air Council express their profound sympathy. His wife has been informed.'

Thus any hope by Agnes and the rest of the family, that Tony may have survived, either as a prisoner or an evader, were dashed with sudden finality. Agnes had lost a loving husband, Paula a father she would not remember or live to know, and Mike, the third of his four brothers. For Irene Raw, her emotional life had been slowly collapsing. Her husband and now three of her four sons had been taken away. If her men-folk had shown courage, she was showing it too – in abundance.

One supposes that the grieving family could be forgiven for not writing to Air Ministry in order to correct their records over Tony's male next of kin as it must have appeared in their files. And if they had done so, it must have been equally galling to receive more letters addressed to a dead son about another dead son. Air Ministry, Oxford Street, wrote on 10 April 1945:

> 'Sir,
>
> 'With reference to the telegram from this department of 11 December 1944, I am directed to inform you that no further information regarding the reported death of your brother, Acting Squadron Leader A W Raw DFC AFC, has been received. In view, however, of the report from the International Red Cross Committee and of the lapse of time, action has now been taken to presume, for official purposes, that he lost his life on 11 September 1944.
>
> 'I am to express sympathy of the department with you in your great loss and to assure you that should any additional details be received at a later date you will be duly notified.'

Another Air Ministry letter addressed to Peter, dated 3 July 1945 – the European war now at an end – confirmed that he was buried in grave number two in the south left row four in the East Military Cemetery, Gladbeck, Germany.

Post-war, the bodies of Tony and his crew were all moved and reinterred at the Reichswald Forest War Cemetery, grave thirty. D. 1. They do not lie alone.

Bruce Cole

We complete this chapter with some words on the close family friend, Bruce Cole, known especially to Tony Raw, and later Mike.

Robert Bruce Cole had been born in Quetta, India, on Armistice Day, 1919. His father was Lieutenant-Colonel R F Cole MBE DCM. Although to the Raw family he was always Bruce, in some RAF circles he was known as Bob. On attempting to join the RAF in 1940 he was put on 'deferred service' until August when he was inducted at a receiving centre in Babbacombe. From there he travelled a not unfamiliar route to many embryo pilots: ITW, EFTS – although this was in Rhodesia – 25 EFTS – 20 SFTS, Salisbury, then to a pilot pool in Egypt until finally he was posted to his first operational unit, 250 Squadron in Palestine.

With 250 he was sent to Alexandria next, then into the Western Desert in June 1941, then Libya until, as mentioned earlier in this book, he was shot down by JG27 on 5 December, ending up in hospital. It was not until March that he recovered, then after some sick leave he was with 'X' Flight at Abadan near Basra, Iraq, before returning to 250 Squadron in Egypt in November 1942.

He remained with 250 throughout the desert campaign and throughout 1943, seeing action over Libya, Tunisia, Malta, Sicily and finally Italy. In 1943 he was awarded the Distinguished Flying Cross having completed two tours with his squadron. He had been wounded again in March 1943 over Tunisia, but was back within a month. Much of the squadron's work was undertaken as fighter-bombers, flying American P40 Tomahawk fighters but in air combat he had been credited with four Me109s damaged.

In early 1944 he was back in England, and sent to the Fighter Leader School at Milfield, from where he and Tony had managed to meet up on occasion. He continued to fly at Milfield at the time of the Normandy invasion, working on Air Support Development, then 3 TEU (Technical Exercise Unit) at Chedworth, Gloucestershire, in September, 83 Group's support unit at RAF Thorney Island 'til October. When he was finally back on operations, he went to 274 Squadron in Holland, on 14 October, as a flight commander, flying Tempest V fighters.

On 5 December he had an encounter with a German Me262 jet north of Rheine but he was only able to claim a damaged. Another damaged claim, this time over a FW190 on 23 January 1945, heralded his move to 3 Squadron, also in Holland, but this time as commanding officer. These Tempest squadrons were exceptionally busy during the last weeks of the war, not only trying to keep the air clear of enemy aircraft, but also attacking ground targets, mostly transport and enemy airfields.

During those last weeks he destroyed one enemy aircraft on the ground, a FW190 in the air, and probably destroyed a Me109 in air combat. He received a Bar to his DFC. His citation recorded not only his combat claims but also that in attacking ground targets he had personally destroyed or damaged forty-eight loco-motives, thirty-two trucks, twelve other road vehicles, and five canal barges. On one such raid he and his number two attacked a German airfield but his Tempest was badly hit by ground fire and he was wounded in the face and arm. Both his DFC awards were 'Immediate'.

Although the war ended in May, Bruce continued to command 3 Squadron until April 1947, at which time he was posted to the Central Flying School, and later to the RAF Staff College at Cranwell, as a flying instructor. He remained there until March 1952. In 1953-54 he was attached to the US Air Force in Florida, and was highly praised by the Americans for his work there. So much so that he was given four letters of commendation, each signed by Brigadier General Edward P Mechling, commander of the HQ Air Force Armament Centre, Air Research Development Command, Eglin Air Force Base, Florida.

The first one, dated 13 July 1953:

'1. I wish to extend my appreciation to you for doing a superior job of test flying since your assignment to this Command. Although having been here only a short time, you have demonstrated exemplary drive and competence in the accomplishment of your duties.

'The Royal Air Force should indeed be proud that it has officers of your ability to rely upon in these difficult and trying times.'

Then on 22 October 1953:

'The recent conference on Compressor-Stall, held at the Air Force Arma-ment Center, was highly successful. The conclusions and recommendations of the conferees will, I am certain, lend in many ways to the furtherance of the capabilities of the center. In addition, the air force as a whole will receive the fruits of your many efforts to provide a solution to this problem.

I am well aware of the many long hours of work you accomplished to insure the success of this conference, and I will want to assure you that your efforts did not go unnoticed.

It is with personal knowledge of your untiring efforts in pursuing this project to gain test information with which could be the basis for such discussions, that I take great pleasure in expressing to you my sincere appreciation.'

On 21 July came a letter that was a result of an emergency in the air:

'I wish to take this opportunity to commend you for the exceptional judgement and flying ability displayed in an emergency situation occasioned by engine failure in an F-86D aircraft on 15 July 1954.

'Your correct and timely actions not only saved the aircraft and prevented possible damage to ground installations, but, more important, it conclusively proved to the younger pilots of this organisation that by remaining calm and thinking logically while under pressure, difficult situations can be overcome in a routine manner.

'The skilfully executed "dead stick" landing of a high performance, swept wing aircraft reflects most favourably on you as an individual and on the entire Royal Air Force. It is indeed a pleasure to have an officer of your caliber and ability serving with the United States Air Force.'

(A copy of this letter went to the British Joint Services Mission (AF Staff), in Washington, DC.)

Brigadier Mechling's final letter, undated, relates:

'I desire to commend you for your outstanding performance as a test pilot during the compressor stall investigation conducted by the Air Force Armament Center during the period June 1953 to June 1954.

'Your exceptional flying skill and willingness to place personal safety second to the requirements of the mission, which were amply demonstrated during the course of this important test program, are characteristic of the high standard of performance we have observed during your tour of duty with the Air Force Armament Center. The information obtained from this test as contributed to the effectiveness of air armament in this country and in your own. You may take justifiable pride in your significant part in this program.

'I am referring this commendation to your superiors and recommending that it be included in your official service records.'

Bruce Cole's last command was the tactics branch of the All-Weather Wing of the Central Flying School at West Raynham. His peacetime rewards were the King's Commendation for Valuable Service in the Air, *London Gazette* 2 January 1950, followed by the Air Force Cross, in the New Year Honours List on 1 January 1951, and a Bar to this on 1 January 1955, no doubt the latter reflecting his work in America.

Bruce had started to write to young Michael Raw during the war. In fact, one letter that survives is from Bruce while he was with 250 Squadron in the desert, and is dated 3 May 1943:

'Dear Mike, I have just had your letter which was dated 31 March; it had taken nearly a month to arrive.

'I expect you are quite a "blood" at swimming now. How fast can you swim the hundred now? We don't get much swimming except when we are near the sea, but then it is wizard! We can do a lot of surfing too. I was pleased to hear you were in the ATC [Air Training Corps]. How do you like it?

'I'm afraid that I shall not be able to come home until I have finished my second tour of "ops". I have been in hospital and I have just come back to my squadron. I was shot in the knee doing some ground strafing. We do quite a lot of this work.

'I have not had any mail from your mother, and I am wondering if there were some letters from her on a mail plane which crashed and burned everything up. There are some very pretty French girls where I am now. You should see them Mike!

'Please write again as it's wizard to have letters from home, and they don't, or shouldn't, take long to arrive. All the best of luck, Bruce.'

Once back in the UK, he often stayed with Mrs Raw at Mount Park Crescent, Ealing. From here he wrote to Mike on 11 October 1944, saying he was at Thorney Island, Hampshire, but about to go over to Holland, and confirming he was now flying Tempests. On the last day of October he wrote again, this time his address being 274 Squadron, BLA:

'I expect you know by now what I'm flying and where I am, etc. [He had told him in the previous letter, but now his correspondence would be read by the censors.] In spite of the ropy weather we have been having we've been quite busy, and I haven't been able to get out and see much, which is a pity as there is much to be seen.

'When do your holidays start – let me know as soon as you can and I will try and get my leave about then. It's pretty cold out here. We've managed to get a building to live in which is an extremely good thing but dawn readiness is a nasty bleak business.

'Must close now as they're threatening to put out the lights.'

After the war, Bruce had also exchanged letters with Mike when the youngster was thinking about a career. It appears at one stage he was thinking of joining the Indian army, but Bruce was pleased when Mike decided against that plan of action. It seemed only natural that Mike would consider the RAF, what with his three brothers and Bruce all being pilots. What his mother must have thought when this came up one can only imagine.

But consider it he did, and in the end he joined. One imagines Bruce may well have helped, but only a few years later, Bruce too had been killed. By the end of 1955, Wing Commander Bruce Cole DFC & Bar, AFC & Bar, was an extremely experienced pilot. At thirty-seven years of age, he had over 3,500 flying hours in his log books. But this would count for nothing.

On 16 January 1956 he and another experienced pilot, Squadron Leader Peter Needham AFC, aged thirty-two and with some 2,600 flying hours to his name, took off from RAF West Raynham, Lincolnshire, in an English Electric Canberra PR7 (tail number WT529) on a routine flight, but had to return soon afterwards to have a minor electrical fault rectified. This done they took off again and were seen to be flying straight and level at about 4,000 feet. People on the ground then saw the Canberra enter a dive at forty-five degrees, which increased to the near vertical. Without pulling out, and with both men being totally aware during those last few seconds that there was no escape from the inevitable, the aircraft smashed into the ground. Cole and Needham died instantly. The accident was thought to have been caused by a runaway trim motor leading to a sudden and uncontrollable nose down change in trim. It was a sad and tragic loss.

Bruce was so close to the Raw family that another flying death must have hit both Michael and Mrs Raw hard. Mrs Raw died the following year, aged sixty-four.

Not surprisingly his American friends in Florida were quick to send a signal once the news had reached them.

From: COMAFAC ARDC EGLIN AFS FLA
To: COMDT CENTRAL FIGHTER ESTABLISHMENT RAF WEST
RAYNHAM NORFOLK ENG

'It was with a deep sense of personal loss that we at the Air Force Armament Center learned of the untimely death of Wing Commander Robert Bruce Cole. This brilliant young officer made truly significant contributions to the mission of this center and his keen analytical mind was responsible for major accomplishments in the field of armament testing. Please convey to his family our warmest sympathy.

Major General Edward P Mechling.'

The commandant of CFE, Air Commodore John Grandy DSO, acknowledged this message and sent a copy to Bruce's family. Grandy also wrote the following to Bruce's mother:

'Dear Mrs Cole,

'I write with regard to the tragic death of your son, Wing Commander Robert Bruce Cole DFC AFC, which, as you know, occurred in a flying accident last Monday morning. His death brings to an untimely end a magnificent and outstanding career and both the Royal Air Force and the country have suffered a great loss.

'Your son and Squadron Leader P Needham AFC, one of his staff officers and a friend of his, took off from here at about 12.30 that morning in a Canberra aircraft for an hour's practice flying. The aircraft crashed some eleven minutes later in a field outside the village of Sudbrook, near Cranwell in Lincolnshire. I have of course, been to the scene of the accident and there is no doubt whatsoever that both your son and Squadron Leader Needham were killed instantly.

'Bruce Cole was an exceptional officer. I am glad that I am able to tell you with all sincerity that in some twenty-five years service I have rarely met an officer with such high ideals or strong sense of purpose. Professionally his ability and aeronautical knowledge were far above those of most of his fellows and in his work at the Central Fighter Establishment the contribution he made towards our studies in connection with the air defence of this country was quite outstanding. Most popular, he was held in high regard and affection not only by all of us here but by a very wide circle of friends in the Royal Air Force and the United States Air Force with whom he recently served with such distinction.

'As I expect he will have told you, he and I, with a team of several others from West Raynham, recently undertook a tour of Australia and the East, which included visits to the Royal Australian Air Force in Australia and our own air force in Singapore and Aden. On this tour Bruce was my right-hand man and on many occasions, particularly in Australia, senior officers and others, who had met Bruce for the first time and listened to his lectures and views, remarked on his brilliance and congratulated me on my good fortune in having a man of his calibre in my team. He was a magnificent ambassador for the RAF and for our country at all times and on this tour in particular he shone in this field of our activities. He loved the flying, the work and adventure of it all and, further, he was very happy at this time having become engaged to be married. We had several talks about this together and he made it quite clear to me that inwardly he was very content.

'Since his death I have already received many communications from those in the service and aircraft industry who knew him and they all stress what a great gap this tragic accident has caused. I myself feel deeply that I have lost an inspiring friend and fellow officer who can never be replaced. You will be very proud of your son because those of his calibre rarely walk through this life. I have today sent to *The Times* a few words as an obituary notice which I hope they will publish.

'Wing Commander Harvey will be writing from here to Mr K H Cole, regarding the various administrative arrangements connected with the winding up of Bruce's estate.

In great sympathy,
Yours sincerely,
John Grandy.'

Chapter Ten

MICHAEL

When Commander Raw died in June 1932, baby Michael was just four years old, so he recalled little of his father. Although christened Robert Michael, he was only ever referred to as Michael, or Mike (sometimes Mick), born on 20 April 1928.

Like his elder brothers, Michael began his education at nearby Hillsborough School and then went to Wellington, in 1938 at the age of ten. Michael would prove as prolific a letter writer as his brothers. Letters in Britain, even during the war years, could be almost guaranteed delivery the next day. And in those days there was often two, if not three postal deliveries each day. Like letters from John, Peter and Tony, Michael's were often concerning the daily, mundane, routines of life, but they all give us an insight into the lives of three loving sons. They were ever mindful that their mother struggled on as a widow, doing her best for six children, and trying to be there for them all. Although early missives are unfortunately undated, they began soon after Michael's arrival at Wellington School. A very early letter, written in pencil, came from the Alfred Yarrow Home & Hospital for Children at Broadstairs.[1] Exactly why Michael was there is not known, but he sent off a quaint letter to his mother. On the face of it, it seems this might well have been the first she heard that he had been sent to hospital! His early writing and spelling have a certain charm as handwritten by Michael:

'Dear Mummy, will you come and see me. I was sick so I am in ded. I have deen to the deach. I am in Norman Ward. Three other doys are in ded too. I do like it here. Love from Michael.'

[1] Yarrow Home had been set up by Alfred Fernandez Yarrow, a millionaire ship builder of torpedo boats and destroyers! Perhaps Mrs Raw had some connection with this home. It was used as a convalescent home for fifty boys and fifty girls recovering from ailments. It was set in over ten acres on Ramsgate Road.

Obviously he was not sure of words beginning with the letter b!

Another letter almost turned into a diary as did several of his missives. His spelling is not of the best, but he was still only ten years old:

16 May 1938

'I hope you are better now. Mrs Russell says that when I put Mrs Raw Esq [on envelopes] it is wrong, so what shall I put? Tell Pat that [when swimming] she must be able to dive, if not I will beat her hands down, tell her that. When I come home there must be 4½d under the front door mat so I can get some Nestlé milk [chocolate]. I must have baked potatoes for dinner and fish cakes for tea. Penalty is £5.

'I had two letters today, one from Nannie [sic] and the other from Trixie, but not one from John. A boy had a birthday today but I was not in his party. Goodbye for today.

'Well here I am again. I went out in the car up to the moneyment [sic] and cawt [sic] some lizards with Reg. I fell in the marshy ground and [went through] my knee in my black long trousers. I had a gym vest from Mr Russell and used that. I hope that you read my bad spelling. I was nearly ded [sic] when I finished the mile. I don't know what place Tony came in. I was second from the last, so don't know who won it. I don't no [sic] who won the cup [either]. I had to sing to Mr Clarke to get in the choir.

'I don't have much prep. Mr Russell and Mr Hughes take us the most. I saw Sheila on Saturday at the sports and on Sunday. The name of her best friend is Stopfis. I have done a lot of drawing. Will you thank Nanny for the picture and for her letter, and Trixie? Mr Russell hasn't given us any sweets yet. I have been playing cricket for the first time this term. Well, goodbye 'til tomorrow.

'It is Wednesday now. When you write to John tell him to write to me and Peter. I played a proper game of cricket today. I don't know where to go on Sunday. I got my comic this morning at lunch time.

'It is Friday today, if you want to no [sic]. Tony is getting nasty, so is Pritchard. They throw knives at you. I must put a stop to it. I tell the boys stories every night in the doormatre [sic] about crooks. I don't know how to spell it. Can I play tennis, if I can, will you send me my racket? It is light so won't cost much only about £3, that is all. Thank Pat for the letter she sent and Nanny and Trixie and yourself. Well, goodbye for today.

'It is Saturday today. Ask Peter if he wants these stamps, if he doesn't give them to Pat. My neck is very sore because of these collars. I don't know what to write about, there is not much news today. I played cricket this afternoon but I don't know who won. I got three runs. We can go for walks or to the baths. I would go to the baths any old day. Goodbye for today.

'It is Sunday today. I have just been to chapel. I am enclosing a card that shows what we are doing. I think Tony is sending one too. Here is a present for you, some stamps. If you don't want them give them to Pat. Well, goodbye.'

[Note: the moneyment was of course the monument to Lord Wellington, that could be seen on the top of a hill from the school.]

The letters got better, although again the next few letters are undated, although they must have been around July 1938, for his mother had her tonsils out on 1 July:

'Saturday. How is your throat, is it very sore? As soon as you get this letter, begin to pack my chess board, the one you gave me for Christmas, and send it to me. How is Pat, getting on at school? Is that horrible teacher still there, the one that taught the first form? On Friday I won a race at the Meade King Cup under 11s.

'It is Sunday today and I am going swimming this afternoon. Where did you have your tonsils out, in the hospital by Doctor Richards? Mrs Marshall sent me some home-made sweets. I will give Pat some sums to tell her to do, so tell her to send them back.'

His next letters (undated) again suffered from poor spelling:

'Dear Mummy, I am very sorry that you can't come down to the sports. On jym [sic] days we all had some races and I oune [sic] all of them. Will you thank Pat for her letter that she sent me? I will wright [sic] you every Wednesday and you must wright back. I thought I had chicken pox but it was [just] heet [sic] bumps.

'How is Peter, Pat, Trixie, Nanny? I wish it was the swimming sports now, don't you? Is Peter coming down for them? Last Sunday I went up to the monement [sic] and cawt [sic] seven lizards and a viper. I don't like the look of it much, it will bight [sic] me. I played cricket with Stopfis

– funny name! Well, goodbye, With lots of love, Michael.

'P.S. Pat's spelling is bad. She puts lots, losts and lorts.'

No doubt this P.S. caused his mother to smile!

In all of Michael's letters he asked the writer to send him questions. As he never refers to answers, one must assume he merely answers them for his self amusement and edification, as if he is trying to test and improve himself.

13 June 1938

'I had fire practis [sic] on Sunday when we were in bed and we came down the fire escape into the playground in our byjamers [sic]. Tony went shooting today, up by the .... I can not spell it but it is something to do with the Duke of Wellington. I must go for my bath now. Goodbye.

'It is Tuesday today. I will be going to Pat Russell's birthday and will have strawberries and cream. Thank you for your letter. I am very glad that we are going to Selsea [sic] for a holiday. I am going to take the boat that I have got here and Tony's [toy] yacht. I don't know how old Pat will be tomorrow.

'It is Wednesday today. I had a nice time at Pat's birthday. We had strawberries and pineapple and cream, and cake, and nice strawberry jam. We had a game of cricket today against the up school boys. We oune esely [sic] by about fifty runs. I have taken up climbing trees. It is good fun and can jump from tree to tree.

'It is Thursday today. All the scouts went away today and they did all the cooking; each boy did his own. When you come down to the swimming sports will you bring me some cocernut [sic] please? I had a big lump on my nose today and it went off bang and it bled like anything.'

There are no surviving letters until one dated 5 October 1940, again from Wellington School by which time the war was more than a year old. His spelling, however, has improved:

'Dear Mummy, I hope you are very well, I am. Please mum, will you send me my geometry box? I haven't got one here and if I buy one it costs 1/4d [a sum that bears no relation to today's 7 pence. Ed.], and also it might get bombed. It can't get up and walk to the air-raid shelter. If you send it wrap it up and pad it, so much that it won't be damaged in the post. If you don't send it, store it somewhere down in the air-raid shelter and take it with you to Evesham. Please send it. I have not been fined yet. Peter wrote to me the other day and sent me 2/6d [22½p] and showed me some German money. Here it is if you like to see it, send it [back] in your next letter.

'The first part of this week just about the whole school was having a conker fight. We picked sides and made barricades and then just threw as hard and as accurate as we could. Mr Snow caught us and we got forty lines each; this is what they were. "I must not throw chestnuts about." The next punishment was two pages of dictation that we got for talking after lights out. We grow walnuts in the avenue garden and Mr Snow let us climb the tree and get them down, and for the last two days we have had some for dinner. I will finish this letter on Sunday.

'Sunday. Last night entertainment was the best we have had for a lecture. It was "Mr "X" on secret war work. Mr "X" turned out to be Mr Price. He told us of his experiences in the last war. He was in the Royal Naval Flying Corps, and he told us all the names of the planes that he flew. He told us all about P-boats. And once he bombed and sank a submarine and bubbles came to the top, and oil. Although he did not take any photographs of it so the Admiralty said that it [only] may have sunk. Once a very brave German submarine commander, who was being chased by our ships, because he had run right into the middle of a convoy and sank warships, but he never sunk unarmed merchant ships. Well, one day he sunk an innocent fishing boat just off Selsey Bill. He thought it was a minesweeper, so when he found out that it wasn't he came up to the top and rescued all the fishermen, then he crept into the shore and landed them, but just when he was waving to the last one, an English searchlight caught him and he was blown to bits. And they say, on 3 August, at half past twelve to one o'clock at night, a grey thing comes up to the shore and you see nine men get out and swim ashore, and then you see the commander waving and then you see a flash of an explosion and it all disappears. Do you believe it? I must go and see one day.

'Another of his experiences was when he was asked by a destroyer (he was in an aeroplane) to show them where a German submarine was. Mr Price signalled that he was going to try and bomb it, but it was much too

deep so the destroyer came along and tried to sink it but he couldn't and
an hour went by and he still couldn't sink it so about five P-boats and these
destroyers came and they all tried to sink it and after all that the Admiralty
said it was believed sunk. When he was going back to his base he flew over
Bournemouth and became terribly low and hopped over all the piers and
got into trouble for it. He had also landed a spy in Germany. Love Michael.'

Michael made several attempts at keeping diaries but often appears to lose interest
after a few weeks. However, in early 1943 he made a number of interesting comments:

18 Jan	Helped mum put [air raid] shelter up in kitchen. An alert sounded at 7.55 pm for twenty minutes.
25 Jan	Back to school.
10 Feb	Letter from mum saying there was something in a telegram about Peter. He had bust five more trains and one barge.
16 Feb	Peter's squadron mentioned in *Telegraph*.
20 Feb	Tony, Agnes and 'Tiger' came to school and took me out to lunch in Taunton. Tony gave me a silver pencil and £1.
25 Feb	Scarlet fever in school. Joined ATC (Air Training Corps).
29 Mar	[I was] Confirmed today by the Bishop of Korea.

There is a huge gap in the letters at this point. In fact the next letter in the collection is to Mike from his mother, and dated 2 February 1943, Mike approaching
his fifteenth birthday. After some routine comments about clothes and a missing
wallet, she continued:

'Tony and Agnes have been here over the weekend, and Tony goes to
Hullavington, near Bath, today. He says he will write to you from there
and also intends to try and see you at school, but not on a Sunday as he
does not want to read the lesson!

'We celebrated his birthday yesterday evening as he does not think
he can get home for the 9th, but darling, you try and write to him for that
day, don't forget. He had a writing case from me we found at one of the
army and navy stores. Such a lovely one in a leather case. I am also trying
to get him a pen. Trixie gave him a rug and Peter gave him £3.10/-. He
bought a dozen table knives with this for when he has a home. I also gave

him a tie pin of Daddy's and the watch I always carried in my bag from John. Tony always wanted this and we could not find a new one.

'Glad you are going to confirmation classes. It has been simply awful weather here and it's a wonder the poplars did not come down. Peter was ill with tummy trouble again yesterday and so went to bed. Oh, yes, he has been busting some more trains, quite exciting as he arrived back with soot all over one wing from the explosion from the engine. It was on the front page of the *Telegraph* but did not give his name. In one paper it said he came from Ealing and before the war he was an insurance clerk.

'I have found your music and C-Ration coupons. I see you have forty-four. I expect we shall need them next term for shirts etc. I can't find your rugger socks, I feel sure I packed them.

'Well, darling old boy, I must finish now. I miss you very much.'

Michael had saved hard and bought Tony an initialled silver brandy hip-flask, which cost £2, for his birthday.

8 February 1943

'My darling Mike, thank you for your letter. I am glad you found your wallet. You will be pleased to hear that Pete has been on the war-path again, he shot up five engines and a barge yesterday and flew through telegraph pole wires. He phoned us last night and told us about it. One of his friends is missing.

'As you know Tony has gone to Hullavington. He is trying to get rooms for Agnes and then, on his day off will try to come and see you. They get one day off a week. Peter brought his dog Pluto [seen in the photo section on his Typhoon] home the other day, he is simply beautiful.'

The next letter was written on Tuesday 9 March 1943, from his mother to Michael:

'You seem to be changing your character from a lazy old thing who never would walk to an energetic young man. I am glad, you will certainly feel much better for it.

'It is tomorrow night Peter is boxing. Yes I will let you know what happens, there was a report in the *Standard & Star* last night about Peter and the boxing, said he was from Wellington School. I have not managed to secure a paper, Mr Keddie read it out to me on the 'phone and said he was sending it to Stuart to put on the [notice] board, so perhaps he will let you have it afterwards. In the meantime, I will try to get another copy. I enclose another piece about the squadron and goat! Keep a lookout in the papers this week as Pete says reporters have taken his photo with the goat.

'I have just received the papers about scarlet fever. I hope you keep free of it dear, with plenty of exercise I should think you will not get it.

'I enclose a letter for you to write a nice long newsy letter card to Bruce, he would like it. I have put his address in pencil so you can write it again in ink.

'Pat said she was coming home again for the day but she hasn't been. Stanley came for the day on Sunday and oh boy does he look tough! Quite the commando! He is tons bigger. I think you should send old Pete a telegram of good luck if you receive this in time, until 4 pm and then I am afraid I don't know his address at Stanmore, where Mavis is.

'I have got a very funny old man digging in the garden today. Doesn't look much good but we will wait and see.'

His mother's next letter was dated 16 March, mainly concerning Peter:

'I forgot to enclose the cutting last week but will remember today. Last night's evening news had another little bit about Pete so I will enclose that too. Last night a reporter from the *Daily Mail* rang me up and wanted to know all about Pete, his swimming, boxing and exploits in the RAF. Of course, as usual my memory left me at the critical moment and I could hardly tell him anything. He asked me about Mavis, Tony, Agnes and Daddy; what he wanted it for I don't know as it was not in this morning. Pat is here until tomorrow. She seems very merry and bright. Tony and Agnes went back yesterday. He had finished his course and passed out with, "above average, excellent for piloting and instructing", the only one to get it for both. He gets his proper leave next week I believe.

'Lots and lots of love my darling and millions of kisses. From your loving Mother.

'P.S. I forgot to tell you – Pete won his boxing match on points. He was rather disappointed in the fight as the man would not fight properly and kept covering up. He has a nice little silver cup.'

There is another long gap in surviving letters, the next one dated 9 November 1943. Mike must have injured himself for she begins:

'How is your toe? Have you played rugger yet? Just fancy, I wrote to Bruce for Xmas about three weeks ago, to make sure I should be in time, and if you please, I have had an answer already! I suppose I must write again. He is in Italy but not at a very nice spot. He says they shoot rabbits and ducks to pass the time.

'Tony came home yesterday, he is very pleased with himself now he had taken over the station band! This afternoon he has gone up to town to buy a new clarinet – they played at the station dance one night, and you can imagine old Tony letting forth with all his might.

'We have sirens nearly every night now, it is a nuisance. David [Trixie's son] sleeps in the shelter every night – he hates the noise of the sirens, calls it the "Ding-Dong". You will see a great change in Anthony when you come home. He is getting so big, he laughs and makes sweet little "coos" – he is most like you.

'Well, how to you think the war is going? It seems much better to me. I expect the Germans will give in before Xmas!!!'

The next letter is dated 7 February 1944 and mentions Bruce Cole again:

'You will be surprised to hear old Bruce rang up yesterday and we hope he is coming to see us today. He has three weeks leave, so I think I will leave this letter open so I can tell you all his news.

'The ducks have been laying every day. We had seven eggs yesterday and so I am putting some down now. Pete is pleased, by the way, and hasn't gone yet [to his new posting], it was cancelled and he is waiting until he can go to a station with the planes he wants – Hawker's insist upon it. Pat likes her job [at a hospital for convalescent children in Woking] very much, she seems to be pleasing the matron.'

Later:

'Bruce came and he looks very well but thinner. He was very glad to be home in England. He bought us lots of perfume, powder and lipstick,

and wants to take us to the theatre. Of course, Pete has organised all sorts
of things for him and I believe they are going up to see Tony tomorrow.
Bruce said something about having a watch for you but it was a bit vague
so I would not count on it if I were you.

'He is going to stay here for a few nights so perhaps you should write
to him and say how glad you are that he is home. He had three narrow
squeaks: once shot all down one side and another time in the knee and
only just made the beach with his plane when his engine failed. Another
time he started running, thinking he had landed where the Germans were
but to his delight found the Americans had just moved in. He has shot
down four Stukas.'[2]

In February 1944, Michael was just two months short of his sixteenth birthday,
and it was time for him to start seriously to consider his future. Although he still
had two more years to go before he would leave Wellington, they would be crucial
years during which time his career path would need to be mapped out. On 10
February, his headmaster, Mr A J Pirie, wrote to his mother with all this in mind:

'Michael and I talked yesterday, partly about his work and partly about
possible futures, I think that he sees the way to get on now with his work
and to ensure getting a certificate.

'As to his future, we discussed no end of things together. He rather
now seems to be favouring the air force instead of the navy, but although
I didn't tell him, I feel no small sympathy with his mother and the
prospect of Michael going into the air force as well. Of course, by the
time Michael is old enough, we don't know whether Cranwell will be
started again or what the conditions of entry will be. I told Michael he
was not to worry one little bit about deciding as to the future; that as he
got older his horizons would broaden and he would gradually see what
he wanted to do. This is indeed the case. Quite possibly, by next September even, he will be considerably clearer in his own mind.

---

[2] Unsure where this comment came from as Bruce had, in North Africa, been credited
with damaging four Me109 fighters, rather than four Ju87 Stukas. This had been over
a couple of days in November 1941 flying with 250 Squadron, and probably Mrs Raw
mistook the type of enemy aeroplane.

'We also talked about many other things, and I do want to assure you, if any assurance is needed, that Michael is really an exceptionally sound young fellow. His young character is of really sterling quality, and he will make a very fine man when he grows up. There is something remarkably nice about him.

'I just want to add that little bit more about him, because I do want you to feel that you need have no misgivings or anxieties about him in any way. And please don't answer this letter because there is nothing to reply.'

Whether she replied we don't know, but it was a nice letter to receive. How anxious she must have been concerning the possibility of Michael joining the RAF is not known either. True she had lost one son, and knew perfectly well that her other two were facing abnormal dangers, but she would still have let Michael follow a path he chose. No doubt that view changed dramatically during that same year, as first Peter and then Tony, gave their lives for their country.

In Mrs Raw's 1945 diary she made several notes. Mostly, of course, followed her daily routine of cleaning, washing, and so on, but others are of interest to our story:

7 Jan	Mavis's twenty-third birthday. The following babies came to tea – Pat, Harry, Ida, Agnes, Anjela, Christine, Maureen Paula, Trixie, Anthony and David. [She calls all the sons and daughter-in-laws 'babies'.]
2 Apr	No V1 rockets [this week].
20 Apr	Mike's seventeenth birthday.
29 Apr	Germans in Italy surrender.
2 May	Hitler dead.
4 May	Germans in north-west surrender to General Monty.
8 May	London going mad with rejoicing millions on streets.
4 Jul	Heard where Tony is buried, Grave II, Row 4, East Military Hospital, Gladback, Germany.
9 Jul	Mike made prefect and got his colours.
10 Jul	Bruce came after being decorated by the King.
14 Aug	Peace at last, Japs surrender.
16 Aug	VJ Day.

Irene Raw knew it was time for things to change, and with the war at an end, she could at least stop that thought in the back of her mind that Mike might have to join the services. Michael still had some time to go before Wellington would release him into the world. On 7 May 1945, his mother had written to him:

'What a great day this is – Germany has surrendered and if only our dear ones were coming home, it would be one of the happiest days in my life, but now I suppose we must try and rejoice in the knowledge that others will be spared to return home.

'The Germans certainly are going through hell today I should think; what a punishment having to surrender must be. We are waiting for Mr Churchill to announce the victory this evening.

'Bruce has been here the past week, and this weekend he went home and is coming back to take us to "Strike a New Note" tomorrow. He has seen this show and liked it so much he is going again, so it is most strange, we shall be going to see it on VE Day and I expect the crowds will be enormous. I am wondering if we shall be able to get home again! I wish you were here. I should not be surprised to see Pat back home tomorrow.

'The weather today has been very hot, so we sat in the nice clean loggia and had tea. Thank you for clearing it out on your last visit. How is the swimming progressing – have you been in the baths yet? Bruce is so funny – every time they rave about the different parts surrendering, he looked most worried and said, "Here, I shall be out of a job!" He bought me 100 cigarettes and Trixie a fur hat, from a German factory where they were making them to use while fighting the Russians next winter!!

'I see a big flag has just popped out from a window over the road – oh, dear, I wish they would give you a week's holiday. Beamont is back I see[3], Stalag Luft III[4] has been liberated so perhaps Tony Hibell and Gus will be home soon.'

---

[3] Wing Commander R P Beamont DSO DFC had been shot down over Germany on 12 October 1944 leading a Tempest wing and remained a prisoner of war until May 1945.
[4] Stalag Luft III was the famous British prisoner of war camp, well known for the so-called 'Great Escape' in March 1944, which resulted in fifty of the escaping prisoners being shot on the orders of Adolf Hitler.

Life gradually got back to normal, although nobody doubted things could ever be the same after five years of war. Yet survivors of every conflict need to progress their lives in some direction or other. Michael carried on with schooling, enjoying cricket but was also suffering on and off with hay fever, which needed treatment from time to time.

Mrs Raw wrote to Michael on 24 September 1945:

'I do miss you old boy and am longing for your [next] letter. I enclose a pair of old gloves I have made into mittens, I hope they will be all right. What sort of a journey did you have? We went up to town after we left you and had a good time. My friend was on peak form and we had a good dinner at a Spanish place. I think you have been there. It poured with rain but lots of nice things to eat and drink compensated.

'Bruce has gone home until the 27th. John came on Saturday morning and I have heard went to the dance and made great headway with the Hickman girl! Congratulations on winning the 100 yards, that means you are the county champion of Somerset does it not? I knew you could do it.'

Michael seems now to have changed his mind about the RAF. It will be remembered that he had mentioned to Bruce Cole that he was considering the Indian army. This idea came up again at the start of 1946, and the new headmaster at Wellington (J M Bankes-Williams), wrote to Mrs Raw on 26 January:

'It is becoming urgent that we should try and settle something about Michael's immediate future. As he will tell you in his letter, he had an interview with Captain Pullein-Thompson of the Public Schools Employment Bureau, who is a first-class man on careers, and as a result he has made the following suggestions:

'Michael should apply for a cadetship in the Indian army. This involves his being enlisted into the Queens, doing four months training at Maidstone as a cadet and being then posted to one of the cadet colleges in India. He is then given an emergency commission in the British Army, but is seconded to the Indian army. When he is twenty he goes before a board which decides whether he can be offered a permanent commission in the British Army from which he would be seconded to the Indian army.

He could then decide whether he wants to make the army his career or not. The points that seem to matter to me are these:

- Michael will in any case have to do some form of military service.
- That military service, or at least part of it, will have to be spent abroad.
- This is the only method by which the whole of his service can be spent in the right surround.
- He will be quite free to choose whether he wants to continue as a regular officer or not.

'I have been worried at the fact that Michael is uncertain about his future, he simply has not found the kind of career that interests him yet. But there is no question whatever that he would make a first-class regimental officer. He seems very worried as to how you will react to the suggestion. He does not say much, but it is quite obvious what he feels, and I think that the whole thing hangs on the fact that he will have to serve and that part of his service will certainly be abroad.

'If he is to take this course we shall have to apply at once, and I have therefore asked him to send up the form to you to be completed, and re-turned to me with a birth certificate, if you can bring yourself to agree.

'I think you know what my opinion of Michael is, and there is no doubt whatever that as an officer he would command the loyalty, respect and admiration of his men.

'I hope perhaps you will be coming down to Wellington before very long. Incidentally, it would be possible to withdraw Michael's application if we should find an alternative which appealed to him more before the course starts next October.'

This of course, prompted a heartfelt and revealing reply from Mrs Raw, when she received Michael's next letter about the Indian army which the headmaster had referred to. It was dated 19 January:

'You were quite right dear, your letter and contents gave me an awful shock and has upset me more than you could possibly understand. I love you so very much and the thought of not seeing you many more times during my life gives me the feeling that I have already lost another son. This will be so of course, if you really have made up your mind to join the Indian army, but putting my feelings aside, which I have always tried to do where the happiness of any children have been concerned, I am wondering if Captain Pullein-Thompson told you all the snags of following this career. India is a horrible climate, heat, diseases, mosquitoes, etc, and if you marry, which I hope later on you will and have children, this will mean terrible upsets and heartbreaks, as your children will have to be parted from you like Agnes, Mavis and Molly were from their parents, because of the unsuitable climate, and your wife could be torn between staying with you or joining with them. I can imagine you will think me silly for mentioning a thing that seems so far away in the future but believe me, darling, it will come and that was one of the reasons Peter finally decided he would be better not to think of India.

'The pay is good we know, but many things cost so much more out there and if you remained a bachelor this would be all right, but believe me with a family the services are not good, that is why your father studied law, we were unable to contemplate paying for a good education for our children without help. Perhaps you do not mind cutting yourself off from all of us but to me it is heartbreaking, you do not get leave for years and years. I do not know about this for certain but I believe it is about every five or seven years. Oh, Mike, I had so looked forward to having you somewhere near in the future, it would make me feel so safe.

'I have filled in the forms, as I feel that whatever I say will make no difference, knowing you as I do. I can only pray that when you are twenty and have to decide, you will either find another job or remain in the British Army. I cannot understand why you suddenly have decided on the army, your letter does not sound very convincing. I think Captain Pullein-Thompson drew a very attractive picture of wonderful sport and pay, etc. Every one here thinks you are dotty to contemplate such a thing.

'I am enclosing your birth certificate, I wonder if they keep it? Mr Williams wrote me a very helpful letter but I think the whole thing has been decided too quickly. You should have had time to talk things over with different people.

'I am glad to hear you have had good skating, afraid it is all finished now, it is quite mild here today and raining.

'Lots of love darling and remember I love you so very much and that if you really feel this is your vocation in life I shall understand.'

While this letter sounds selfish, we must remember that this is a mother who had already lost a husband in 1932, and three sons during a devastating war, and with the thought of the fourth boy living half way around the world she was understandably hurting.

However, whether her words melted Michael's heart or helped him to change his mind when perhaps not totally made up, the Indian army did not secure him. By the time we read the next letter from Wellington's headmaster, a new career had been chosen. He was now going to join the Royal Air Force.

There is no doubt this decision eased Mrs Raw's mind about time and distance, but having lost John, Peter and Tony in the RAF, one can imagine that military flying might not have been a more favourable choice to her:

10 May 1946

'Dear Mrs Raw,
    'As I expect Michael has told you, Cranwell is reopening in October, and the first course will consist of sixty boys who will be nominated and selected by the Air Ministry. I know that Michael is really keen on starting his career through Cranwell. He seemed a bit exercised as to whether it would be essential for him to remain in the RAF permanently, but I have no doubt that he would have the chance of getting out of it if he found it unpleasant after four or five years commissioned service. The alternative seems to be a rather indefinite period of service in the ranks of the RAF during which time he might make a certain number of useful contacts, but the decision as to his future would still be in the air. I am afraid I can't hold out any certain hope of his getting his Higher Certificate. As far as the costs of Cranwell are concerned, the whole thing is free, and he would at any rate get training while there, which could not help being valuable if he afterwards went into some branch of the air service in general. He always comes back to flying, or something connected with it when we are considering his future. Nominations have to be in before the end of this month, and I should very much like to know what your wishes are in the matter. Personally I would advise you to let him have the chance, although I do honestly understand the difficulties.
    'I don't think I need to tell you again what I think of Michael. I hope we shall see you down here for commemoration.'

His mother's next letter to Mike was dated a week later, 17 May. She began with hoping a treatment for his recurring hay fever would overcome his problem and also urging that now he had more or less decided on the RAF, he would buckle down in his final school exams – and give every one a surprise! She then continued:

'Bruce came on Wednesday for the evening, he was at Manston for a rehearsal for V-day parade. He is to lead the only three squadrons of Tempests coming from Germany and is extremely pleased with himself. He is back in Germany now but is coming for another rehearsal next week and he may come and see me again. You must write to him dear, I couldn't understand why you did not answer his letter. His address is still – 3(F) Squadron RAF, 123 Wing, BAFO, BOAR.

'He thinks the Cranwell idea the best of all and the only way to get in the RAF now. He will be here when you are so will be seeing you.

'My next news will surprise you. I had a lovely letter from Mona [John's widow] saying she is going to be married. Her letter is so sweet she is so afraid she would be hurting me but I have replied wishing her happiness and putting her mind at rest on that score. He is an army chap from Aberdeen named Bert Hall and is presently stationed at Belfast. It gave me a queer feeling when I read her letter, a sort of sadness, but I knew some day some lucky chap would want her, she is such a darling.'

When she next wrote, in early July 1946, Irene Raw said she had been on a visit to the school and was very proud to learn that Michael had been made school captain, and that he apparently was doing very well with his exams. She also wrote to say she was thinking of moving to a smaller house, as Mount Park Crescent and its garden was simply too big for her now. That same month Michael left Wellington.

Michael's achievements while at Wellington School are recorded thus:

Rugby, 1st XV	Librarian
Junior Cup Winner 1938	Captain of the Shooting Team
Captain of the School (Captain of the Light Blues)	School Certificate July-Dec 1944

Chapter Eleven

FLYING

In the summer of 1946, Michael, together with all the other hopefuls, applied to join the RAF via Cranwell. Not all got through, but in a table of results for a special competition to enter via a permanent commission, there were ten passes in Group 1, and forty-two passes in Group 2. The name Raw, R M, appeared in Group 2, so Mike was in.

Things soon began to happen. It was not long before he left Wellington School and was sent to RAF Cranwell to begin his training. His official joining date was 7 January, 1947. When he wrote home on 8 January, he gave his address as: 607026 Cadet R M Raw, B Flight, D Squadron, 47 Entry, Apprentices Wing, East Camp, RAF Cranwell, Lincs.

'My Dear Ma,

'As you can see I arrived here yesterday quite safely, at about 6.30 after a very cold journey. The LNER Company do not seem to provide any heating in their trains. Prissy may have told you that I only just managed to catch the train at King's Cross, there was not even time enough for me to get a ticket, although that did not really matter as I had the railway warrant.

'I must apologise for this very untidy writing, the reason is that I'm resting the pad on my knee and sitting on a none-too steady iron bed. We do not get much spare time here and I have already been twice interrupted while trying to write this letter. I started it this morning and the time is now 6.30 pm.

'Before I go any farther I must thank you for my very long holiday. At times, I know I have been exceedingly troublesome for you, and at these times have appeared not to have any affection for you, but believe me I have a very great affection for you and love you very much indeed, although I seldom show it. I hope that you will forgive me.

'There are forty of us in this particular entry and we all live and sleep in the same room, so as you can imagine it's a pretty big one. We have not started work yet as we have not been issued with uniforms etc, but we have been to quite a number of lectures about our two-and-a-half years course. We get our uniforms tomorrow morning and in the afternoon at 3 pm we are to be inoculated and vaccinated – that'll be fun!!

'I have just been interrupted in my letter writing again, this time the corporal has just taught us how to make our beds the air force way. Also the sergeant wanted to see me because I hadn't filled a form in properly. He was a little annoyed.

'They are very house proud here ('they' being the sgts & cpls) and we are not allowed to let our shoes or boots touch the highly polished lino floor and to prevent this we are provided with little square pieces of cloth on which to stand. When we walk we keep our feet on the cloth and carefully slide our feet along thus taking one step. There is quite an art to it. The first time we saw each other doing it we thought it rather amusing but we are used to the sight now.

'I have been interrupted again, this time the cpl taught us how to fold up our blankets and put them on our biscuits (small quarter mattresses). Then we all had to practise it.

'The time is now 9 pm and I will have to be getting ready for bed in a moment. We go to bed very early here, we have to be in our pyjamas by 9.30 and in bed with lights out by 10.

'We are issued with pyjamas but no one wears them as they have to be very carefully folded with bits of cardboard in them (to make them stiff) by inspection time in the morning which is at 8 am. We get up at 6 am and have to sweep and dust out our bed space, put our blankets and biscuits in a neat pile, get all the lockers, beds and boxes in a straight line up the room. This is done by stretching a piece of string from one end of the room to the other, thus making a straight line. [Then] We have to wash and shave (this is quite a job as there are only six basins to forty blokes) and then have our breakfast. And it all has to be done in time for the inspection – everything has to be spotless, including buttons, etc.

'I am now in bed so the writing will be worse still. The weather has been terrible. I have not seen the sun yet. It is very misty and cold, the snow was quite deep but it has started to thaw, and there is slush every-where. We all had our photos taken this morning in a group, as I was in the front row I had to kneel in the snow – it had a pleasant cooling effect.

'We are staying in the same building as a lot of apprentices, and we are told not to talk or mix with them as we are going to be officers. We are not allowed to have anything to do with the other AC2s about the camp [either].

'Thursday. The time is 8.30 am and the sun has just come up. We have just finished inspection and are waiting to go to be sworn into the RAF. I am going into partnership with three other blokes to buy an elec-tric iron. We are all meant to have them as we have to iron our uniforms three times a week.

'If you ever see any fountain pens in the shops for goodness sake get me one. I have to walk round the camp with a bottle of ink as my pen won't fill. Don't get one unless it has a medium nib. There was one in Smiths the other day costing 18/4d, would you or Pat see if it is still there? Of course, if you find a medium nib Parker fountain pen get that as that is what I have been trying to get.

'The time is now 11.10 am and it is a very fine day. There are lots of aeroplanes taking off and landing. I am very sorry this is such a scrappy and disjointed letter but it is hard to write one at every odd five minutes.'

14 January 1947.

'My dear Ma,

'Thanks very much indeed for your letter which I received this morning. The moment when the mail comes into the barrack room is the most exciting one of the whole day.

'Before I go any further I must tell you my best piece of news. I get four days leave on Friday, 14th, which is in exactly four weeks time – pretty good eh? So I will be seeing you soon, Ma, and looking forward to it.

'We have now started our training properly and it is exceedingly stiff and toughening. We had PT for the first time today and the instructor told us that he was going to make things as inconvenient for us as pos-sible. The reason for this is to teach us to grin and bear it and in that way strengthen our characters. We are given two minutes in which to change into gym kit. You may think two minutes is plenty of time but when there are forty blokes all crowded into a dressing room which is no bigger than the nursery at home, it is very difficult indeed, and when we are late he gets fighting mad. When we are in the gym every thing has to be done as fast as possible, push everyone out of the way and fight for positions etc. It's a sort of survival of the fittest. In this way we are made tough. Many of our NCOs went down some ranks so that they could come to Cranwell to train us, it is meant to be quite an honour to train us, the Cranwell cadets. Even though the PT instructor swears and curses at us, he said to us today that everyone in the air force, except officers and Cranwell cadets, were vermin and scum dressed in blue.

'Tomorrow we have got organised swimming in the camp swimming pool, but as I have no bathing trunks I shall have to swim in the nude. This is a little tricky as WAAFs [Women's Auxiliary Air Force] are liable to wander in. I bet you guess what I'm going to ask you now – that's right – will you please send my trunks? There are one or two other things that I need as well. I know this will really annoy you and I'm sorry.

'The other things I need, of course, are my rugby clothes. If we are good enough we can get into the college team. There is a trial game next Saturday afternoon and the selectors will pick the team from that, so if you could please send them by then would you do so. I will write a list for you at the end of this letter.

'Wednesday 15 January. I was inoculated and vaccinated the other day by the MO. The chap in front of me in the line up, an enormous six foot, thirteen stone, red-headed Scot, had to be held up by the medical orderly while he was being struck – he went as white as a sheet and swayed all over the place. It made me a bit hot under the collar to watch him but when it came to my turn, all was OK.

'We have lessons in the workshops two or three times a week and we are learning to make things in metal so that when we are officers we can understand the difficulties of fitters and engineers, etc. It's very interesting and good fun. We also have machine-drawing lessons in which we learn to be draughtsmen. This is also fascinating. I have been issued with a geometry box just like the one I have at home and other drawing instruments as well. I have also got an enormous box of tools down at the workshops for metal work, and when I do my first navigation lesson I am to be issued with a watch. This will be welcome as mine has stopped, which means that I have to keep on asking others the time.

'You said that you wished you had a photo of me in my uniform. Well, if you buy the next few copies of the *London Illustrated News* you will find my picture in one of them. The photographer from that magazine came down here yesterday and took quite a number of pictures while we were in the college and also in a group outside and while we were wandering. He took one of those other chaps and myself looking at King Edward VIII's uniform which was presented to the college.

'Talking of pictures, there is a painting of Captain von Richthofen, the famous German air ace of WW1 and another German ace, but the funny thing about it is that Hermann Göring presented the two paintings to the college.

'We have not been out of camp yet but there is a chance that we may be able to get out next Saturday afternoon and evening. I shall be playing rugger in the afternoon but in the evening I will be able to go into Sleaford and perhaps go to the flicks or buy a meal somewhere.

'The food here is not bad, we get quantity but not quality. When I first came I got very hungry in between meals as there is such a long break in between. Breakfast is at 7 am, lunch at 12.45 and tea is at 5.45, and after that we sometimes are allowed to go to the NAAFI for about half an hour and it is possible to get something to eat there.

'I must tell you what I was issued with when I received my first uniform, it was just like Christmas and quite exciting. We have five very good vests, two pairs of sirtex pants, four pairs of socks, one very good pair of shoes, three shirts with six collars, a tie, and of course our two uniforms and overalls etc. One pair of boots and a pair of Wellington boots. The sports kit is not too good, two pairs of gym shorts and a pair of gym shoes.

'Well I think I had better stop now and get on with my cleaning, so here is the list of things needed:
- two pairs of rugby shorts (one blue, one white)
- two rugby shirts (one blue and one Wellington or Ealing)
- one pair of rugby boots
- one rugby cap

- two pairs of rugby socks (one Ealing, one Wellington)
- one sheet of sandpaper (it is in the kitchen drawer under the knife box)
- one set of knife, dessert spoon and fork
- one tin mug
- any brass cleaning brushes you can spare.

'PS – When I was in the swimming baths this afternoon, the instructor came up to me and said I was the first real swimmer he had seen here, and that he will want me for the college team in the summer.'

In the event, Mike's rugger kit duly arrived just as the Saturday game was cancelled. There was no reason given but everyone assumed it was because arms were sore following the mass vaccinations; some chaps had even been admitted to hospital with vaccine fever. However, Michael thanked his mother when he wrote on the Monday evening, 20 January 1947:

'I was hoping to finish this letter on Wednesday but I've just not had the time. There was an AOC's inspection on Saturday morning so we had been working hard preparing our room for it.

'We now get up at 5.30 am as the NCO in charge of us decided that we were not doing our work before breakfast well enough so we were to have more time. I find it very difficult to get up at that time and it isn't until about 5.50 that I finally manage to roll out. I often think of you at that time and wish that I was in bed at home. It is the worst time of the whole day here.

'This afternoon I had a bath for the first time since I've been here – that shocks you I bet! The problem is there are only three baths in the whole building and there are at least 300 chaps living in it. If you want a bath it means queuing for it and we haven't the time to do so, and then you can't be sure the water will still be hot. Today I rushed back from lunch and bagged one before anyone else got there.

'The soap ration is also a bit tricky. We get those bars of toilet soap for eight weeks, and as well as washing ourselves we have to scrub our wooden lockers once a week and our large trunks that are about three feet long, two feet wide and a foot deep. Also the white bands that go round our hats have to be kept clean, so you can see that it is quite hard, but I'm just managing.

'Last week the bottom of my tea mug was found to be dirty on inspection parade and so I got seven days fatigues and my weekend pass stopped. This was the second time this has happened to me. Luckily a few days later we all did exceptionally well on parade and so all those who had had their passes stopped had them restored. So on Saturday afternoon I went into Sleaford where there is a marvellous NAAFI [the Navy, Army and Air Force Institute, instigated by Lord Nuffield, providing a place service men could go to relax and have refreshments etc. Scores of these sprung up during the war all over the place]. You can get a very good meal there including trifles and chocolates, etc.

'Think of me next Thursday evening at about 7.30 pm for I shall be boxing. We have all got to box while the officers on the station watch us, the reason being is that they want to see if we can fight. All Cranwell cadets will have to do it in the future. Unfortunately I have put on a good deal of weight in the last few weeks, so that I have to fight an enormous great bloke. Still, it can't be helped. I'll have a good bash before he knocks me down! We are only having two rounds of one-and-a-half minutes each which will not be too bad – but long enough!

'We had a game of rugger last Wednesday, it was the best game I've played in since I left school. It was terrific. The officers turned out to watch and pick a college team. At half time they picked out a pack of forwards for the team and had them playing on the same side. I was chosen amongst them as wing forward. So I hope and should be chosen for the team. All rugger has been cancelled as the ground here is covered with snow.

'Yesterday we had to go out on the north airfield to learn bayonet fighting and it was bitterly cold. We were not allowed to wear gloves and our hands became very painful. There is always a freezing wind sweeping across this place just to make it more unpleasant for us.'

Michael then had a period in hospital for some reason, but he wrote on 23 February 1947:

'My Darling Ma,

'I am still in hospital but I've been up and about for the last two days and I'm going out tomorrow. It has been a most pleasant week in here. The weather has been bitterly cold outside and has snowed continually

– but not once have I been cold. The hospital has got central heating and is therefore beautifully warm.

'We have got a wireless in the ward which is a very good thing. Even though the BBC only broadcasts at certain times, I have managed to get American stations etc, in between the close downs. Unfortunately, it often goes wrong but we've got a flying officer in the ward who knows how to fix it.

'We do not go into the airmen's ward in the hospital when we are ill, but into the officers' ward, that's why there is a flying officer in here with us. The lack of fuel and the transport difficulties have caused some RAF stations to send most of their personnel on indefinite leave, but unfortunately there is not much chance of that happening to us. Even if Cranwell did get into that state, the cadets would remain.

'The CO came into see us the other day, and when we asked him what chances there were of our being sent on leave, he said that since Cranwell was the RAF we therefore would carry on regardless. Our CO is a good bloke, he is only twenty-three. The other day he asked one of our chaps what his age was, and when he told him, he said, "Good lad, you're nearly as old as I am." Some of our blokes are twenty-one.

'Yesterday he came into the ward to see us again, entering the hospital on a pair of skis and he wore a woollen balaclava helmet. He looked damn funny.'

Michael's next letter home was on 8 March:

'The weather has been really terrible here for the past few weeks, I wonder if it's the same in London? It has snowed and snowed and snowed and everything has been covered by the accursed stuff. There is a steam train railway which runs all over the camp and part of the time crosses the north airfield. Well, the other day I was looking across the airfield and there were a lot of men digging the snow off the track, but all I could see was a line of heads and occasionally a shovel shovelling snow. It was most amusing.

'For the past few days the apprentices at the camp have been clearing the snow off the Cranwell to Sleaford road. Today a bus skidded off the road and went straight into the snow, and there it stuck until they could get something to come and pull it out. Actually all the ice and snow has started to thaw today, and consequently there is slush everywhere – the place is in an awful mess. Unfortunately it freezes in the night which means there will be ice on all the roads.

'At this very moment, I'm sitting in an armchair in the dance hall at the NAAFI Club in Sleaford, and as there is a dance in progress, I'm finding it exceedingly difficult to concentrate. It's a good thing that I'm unable to dance as it would be even harder to concentrate. They have got a really wizard band here, it is the swing sextet from the RAF Cranwell Band. It would be much better if I could go to the writing room, but it is filled up already.

'So Bruce has finally got a leave, has he? He seems pretty determined to chop up his handsome face. I must write to him when I get the time. There are tons of letters I must write, but they keep us so busy that there just isn't the time to do anything. I had to go without lunch today so that I could have a bath.

'We are having our end of term exams soon, which means that I had better make headway with my college work. Unfortunately, I missed quite a good deal while I was in hospital.

'Last Wednesday evening I went to the camp cinema, which was a great event, to see "Theirs is the Glory" (the film about Arnhem). And then on Thursday afternoon instead of going to the workshops as usual, we all had to go on parade and march to the camp cinema to see the same film, so I saw it two days running!'

During the summer of 1947 Michael began his flight training. There is not a lot of information on what he was doing, but in a letter during November, his mother does remark that he must be doing quite a lot flying. She had hoped he might be part of the celebrations for a royal wedding – presumably Princess Elizabeth and Prince Philip.

Meantime, Mrs Raw was actively trying to sell 10 Mount Park Crescent. She was asking £6,000 and a young couple of newlyweds were negotiating with the estate agent and the purchasers had gradually increased their offer from £5,250, to £5,600, until they finally agreed the asking price. Not that she was over anxious to move, but knew she had to get a smaller house soon. In the event she did sell and managed to buy a house at 28 Delamere Road, by Ealing Common, in 1948.

Another surviving letter from Mike is dated 29 May 1948, this time he shows his address on Cranwell-headed paper, and marked by 'A' Squadron. He began with saying he hoped she had enjoyed a recent holiday and commiserated with her struggling to find a new house in which to live:

'My Darling Ma,

'Just after I'd written to you last week I was idly looking through my drawer when, behold, I pulled out my post office savings book and out fell my clothing coupon book, so all is OK and under control now.

'It doesn't seem as though I've been back here a couple of weeks but I shall be coming home the weekend after next, on 12 June, for my half-term break; isn't it wizard? Time really flies in this place.

'By far the most important news I have for you this week is that on Friday, 28 May I completed my first solo flight in a Harvard IIB. I can now fly the advanced trainer and when I've finished with it I go on to such aircraft as Spitfires or Mosquitoes, etc. Unfortunately that won't be until I've left the college, although there was a rumour that we would have them in our last two terms – but you know what rumours are like.

'My first solo on Harvards was nearly as amusing as the one on Tiger Moths. I'll tell you all about it sometime. I became very industrious the other day and wrote to Pat, and to a friend, but haven't received a reply [from either] yet. Bit slack, aren't they?

'I've been doing quite an amount of swimming again this week, even though the weather had become considerably cooler. Next Saturday is the big match of the season against Sandhurst. I think one of my friends, called David Lloyd, who lives in Ealing, will be swimming for them.

'I hope to go to Germany next leave, for a week. I shall give my name in to go and then hope it's picked out of the hat. The visit will be from the end of term 'til 5 August, which is about a week. I will then return to Cranwell, collect my kit and go home before I leave for France.'

Cadet Raw passed all his ground examinations and came thirty-third out of the thirty-seven cadets that still remained with 47 Entry. Then on 25 July 1949 he received the good news from the Air Ministry that he had been appointed to a permanent commission in the general duties branch of the Royal Air Force as a pilot with the rank of pilot officer, with effect from 27 July. He had successfully followed his brothers into the commissioned ranks of their chosen service.

He also had another feather in his cap, having captained the college swimming team in 1949. A report on the activities of this team was written up by one of the team members, Cadet M G Skipp:

'Under the guidance of Flight Lieutenant White and the captaincy of R M Raw, the team has practised hard and long and, in consequence, enjoyed a very successful season. Six matches have been swum and, of these, five were won and the other drawn. The most outstanding achievement was that of beating the RMA Sandhurst by twenty-nine points to twenty-four, after a ding-dong struggle, in which first one team and then the other gained the lead, and the issue was in doubt until the very end.'

Results:
'v' The Station, won 44½ - 36½
'v' RMA Sandhurst, won 29-24
'v' Stowe School, won 33-10
'v' Charterhouse, won 26-12
'v' Oundle School, drew 24-24

At the end of the swimming season, the following members were awarded colours: R M Raw, M E Walsh, H E Clements, with half-colours going to D Parratt and J B Lightfoot. Michael had also excelled in rugby and cricket.

The college graduation day occurred on 27 July 1949, the reviewing officer being no less a personage than Marshal of the Royal Air Force, Lord Trenchard GCB GCVO DSO DCL LL.D. Amongst others, 47 Entry marched onto the parade ground under a lowering sky, that, it was said, to have: '...threatened to distract the attention of the more exotically hatted section of the audience.' The King's Colour was carried at the head of Michael's entry, by fellow entrant, Flight Cadet Corporal R B A George.

Lord Trenchard, at the end of his speech, concluded with: "Believe in yourselves; believe in the service. Each one of you must do his utmost in his particular job and make that efficient. Without that you can do nothing, with that you can do everything." That evening there was a graduation ball for cadets and their guests. The presence of some thirty-five pilot officers in very new uniforms was very apparent.

The very next day, 28 July 1949, Michael was posted to 204 Advanced Flying School at RAF Brize Norton, Oxfordshire, equipped with DH Mosquito T3 and

T6 machines – the training versions of this versatile aircraft. He would be trained as a night-fighter pilot. He also had a period at RAF Leeming where he teamed-up with his navigator/radar crewman.

We can now skip ahead to 1950. By this time Michael had met and courted his future wife, Maureen Butler. (They were married on 16 August 1952 and would have five children, daughters Elizabeth and Sarah, and sons Robert, Bruce and Peter. An address in Lammas Park Road, Ealing, seems to be where they first resided, although later, with Michael often away, Maureen moved in with Michael's mother in Delamere Road.)

With his training complete Michael's first operational posting was to 85 Squadron, based at West Malling, on 14 March 1950. He arrived from RAF Leeming, together with his crewman, Sergeant Betts. Betts was designated as a number two, which meant he was responsible for navigation and radar operations. Their commanding officer was Squadron Leader J R Gardner. The squadron had been flying De Havilland Mosquito NF36 aircraft when they arrived, having gained fame as a night-fighter squadron since 1941. 85 Squadron's history ran from the spring of 1918 when it had been a single-seater fighter unit in France with SE5 machines. Disbanded in 1919 it had been reformed in 1938 as a day-fighter unit flying Gloster Gladiator biplanes, but quickly moved over to Hawker Hurricanes. It had fought in France 1939-40, then during the Battle of Britain, before being selected for the night-fighter role, which it had carried out with much success flying various marks of Mosquito, both in defending Britain, and on night offensive actions over France and Germany. It had moved to West Malling to convert to jets, actually the Gloster Meteor NF11.

The Gloster Meteor had been the RAF's first operational jet aeroplane, 616 Squadron being the first to take it into action during 1944. It had a brief appearance that summer against the German V1 rocket bombs and in the last weeks of the war it operated on the continent. However, it came into its own immediately post-war and became initially the main stay of the RAF's jet fighter force. Many variants were produced, including a two-seat trainer, photographic reconnaissance and of course night fighters. This had a two-man crew, with a navigator/radar operator sitting behind the pilot operating the airborne interception radar.

During his tour with 85 Squadron, Michael became rather an expert at night-fighter tactics and progressed well. He and Sergeant Betts were quite a team and often 'scored' well on night exercises, tasked with intercepting other aircraft by radar and then carrying out a mock attack. The night-fighter fraternity used a phrase when they returned and had managed to pick up and intercept another aircraft in the darkness. The radar screen showed a line which was disturbed after a contact was made. This was referred to as 'having your weapon bent' so of course, this became an amusing phrase amongst aircrew. Michael and Sergeant Betts often returned having had their 'weapons bent'. There was also a change of CO, Gardner leaving in July to be attached to the United States Marine Corps in the USA. His place was taken, in September, by Squadron Leader W A Griffiths DFC.

Virtually all peacetime flying is a constant mix of training, exercises and evaluations, but there has always been room for inter-squadron rivalry. While at this distance one cannot tell how the following signal came into being, it is nice to know that this rivalry continued. Michael obviously knew all about it and felt obliged to keep it amongst his papers:

From: - NOT SO Sprog Section, 11 FG/A Squadron, RAF WUNDORF, BAOR 5.
To: -   SLIGHTLY MORE SPROG Section, 85 NF Squadron, RAF WEST MALLING
Date: 20 June, 1951.
Ref: Air/Adm/Org/4739218/1694737/57/

FINGER

In respect of your communication dated 4 July, 1950 Ref. AIR/ADM/ORG/4739217/1694736/56/?, which my staff have been studying for the past eleven months. The following points have come to light.

You are a BUM.

You are perhaps an even bigger BUM than I thought possible.

Your almost complete illiteracy is amply displayed by your having to type your communication.

Get some promotion exams in chum.

Yours Insincerely,
(signature) FLG OFF
(11 FG/A SQDN)

PS. I am forced to send you a copy of the original letter in case your mind has not been able to cope satisfactorily.

Michael ended his tour with 85 Squadron in June 1952. Before moving to another operational squadron, he was for a period at 228 Operational Conversion Unit at RAF Leeming, Yorkshire, the former Bomber Command base in WW2. This was equipped with Meteor NF11s but not long after he joined it, the OCU moved to RAF Coltishall.

Michael's mother wrote in October 1952 about a local war memorial in Ealing, upon which the names of local people who had died in the war had been inscribed. When she visited it she noticed they had missed out adding the letters 'DFC' after Peter's name. At St Peter's Church, on Armistice Day, a service, arranged just for relatives, was held in a small side chapel. Mrs Raw mentioned the missing reference to Peter's gallantry award to the vicar who promised to have it added. Mrs Raw wrote to Michael saying that Peter was probably laughing about it. She had laid a laurel wreath at the memorial and noted that is was still there at the end of November.

Michael was honoured with the award of the Air Force Cross, the announcement appearing in the *London Gazette* in the New Year's Honours List, on 1 January 1955. Another name on the same page of that supplement, was that of Acting Wing Commander Robert Bruce Cole DFC AFC. The AFC is a decoration given for exceptional valour, courage and devotion to duty whilst flying, though not in active operations against an enemy. Brother Tony's award of the AFC had been for instructing. In Michael's case the award was for 'outstanding work in connection with night-fighter training'.

This would mean a visit to Buckingham Palace to receive his award and this started to be arranged in February/March 1955. One letter of congratulations came from Squadron Leader J C Stewart DFC:

'Dear Mick,

'Heartiest congratulations on the award of your very well deserved decoration. It gave me the greatest pleasure to see your name prominently displayed in the New Year's Honours and to know it was so well earned is indeed gratifying.

'Anne joins me in wishing yourself and Maureen a "Happy and Prosperous New Year" and also my thanks to you for an excellent job of work done during the past year.

'Yours sincerely.
"The Boss"'

Meantime, Michael had also been posted – or had he? His mother wrote on 24 February 1955:

'I expect you were surprised and not at all pleased when you found you had been posted near Cambridge – what sort of station is it? Rather far from here too I should imagine. I wonder what they will think of Wing Commander G... cancelling it!

'I wonder when the investiture will be. I haven't been out to buy a new hat, so let's hope it is not until the end of March. When the vicar called round the other night he wanted to know all about your AFC. I told him all about the times I had been to the palace, he was most interested to learn I had been there during the reign of George V, then George VI and now, if I go, Queen Elizabeth. He thinks it is quite a record.'

On the face of it this seems quite the opposite from what Michael told his mother in a letter dated two days later, 26 February:

'To stop you skipping through this quickly to see if I'm posted, I'll tell you now that I'm not. Not even a rumour has reached me this week. We are becoming resigned to spending the rest of my air force career at Leeming. In only three-and-a-half months we'll have been here three long years. My sentence should be shortened for good behaviour like any other of Her Majesty's prisoners.

'I heard from the Central Chancery of the Orders of Knighthood yesterday. It was a most impressive envelope stamped with the words "Immediate" and "Lord Chamberlain, St James's Palace", and addressed to Flight Lieutenant Robert M Raw AFC, Royal Air Force. (I hope the Queen realises that my name is really Michael, not Robert.) Anyway, Brigadier I de la Bere, secretary of the above-mentioned chancery, informed me that the Queen will hold an Investiture at Buckingham Palace on Tuesday, 15 March 1955, at which my attendance is requested. He went on to say that two guests may accompany me to watch the ceremony and enclosed an application for tickets. I have returned the form already asking for tickets for you and Maureen. We must arrive at the palace between 10 and 10.30 am on the Tuesday.

'I have various suggestions for our arrangements on the actual day and you can choose the one which suits you most.

- Plan 1. Hire a car to take you, Maureen and me to the palace then to a restaurant for lunch before coming back home.

- Plan 2. Hire a car to take you, Maureen and me to the palace then return home to eat a chicken with wine which I would bring down with me.

- Plan 3. Get Stan to take you, Maureen and me to the palace then meet Trixie afterwards and lunch at a restaurant.

- Plan 4. Get Stan to take you, Maureen and me to the palace then meet Trix at home to eat two chickens or one goose with wine which I will bring down with me.

- Plan 5. Same as plan 4 but Harry, Pat, Ag and anyone else you'd like to invite, to join us as well and I'll provide more grub.

'You can juggle with these plans as you wish and perhaps you have better ideas. My reason for suggesting that we eat at home is that if, as you feared when I last saw you, you feel ill on the day and Trix takes your place, or you don't feel up to the restaurant after the ceremony; if that should happen then we can still be together and comfortable at home. Another reason is that Nan can join us, although there is no reason why she shouldn't meet us at a restaurant. Well that's all I have to say about 15 March this week. I'll await your reply with interest.

'The Italians gave us a very enjoyable cocktail party, Maureen had a great time dancing and flirting with one of them, it was meant to finish at eight but we couldn't get away 'til eleven. I had an awful headache next morning.

'That's all my news, mum so love from Maureen and me, we'll see you the Saturday before the 15th.'

In a letter to Mike from his mother dated 5 March, she wrote:

'I think Plan 4 is the best one – I suppose you have a copy so there is no need to repeat it, or is there? Yes, on second thoughts I will. Stan and Trixie go with us and afterwards to return here to eat two chickens or one goose with wine! You are a darling to think it all out so wonderfully for my benefit and I do appreciate it so much. Tell Maureen I managed to get to Ealing Broadway yesterday and bought a new hat and gloves. The hat is black and has a trimming of velvet and a lovely big white rose at the side to make it look festive. It cost the earth and is very good straw so will come in for best during the summer.

'Trixie met me in the Broadway and helped me choose the hat. The sun was shining and it was a lovely day, so we thought we would celebrate and went to Paul's and had a very good lunch.

'Pat's family have all been down with 'flu – Pat was in bed for some days and the baby too. I believe Harry took time off and Jenny, who was much better, went to her Granny Smith. I think we will ask Pat, Harry and Agnes to come down in the evening on the 15th, but will leave it up to you. I somehow feel I am in Agnes's bad books. As Stan is taking us to the palace I do not think Pat and Co will feel it strange that they come back to lunch with us.

'I wonder if the Lord Chamberlain told you whether the car would be allowed to take us right up to the entrance of the palace? I hope so. I am afraid the Queen will only know you as Robert, when they read your name out. I wonder if Bruce has been yet – rather funny if he is there too.'

The grand event took place on Tuesday, 15 March, and accompanied by his mother and wife, he duly received his AFC from the Queen, although a photograph in the *County Times* and *Gazette of Ealing* recorded his wife as Doreen instead of Maureen.

In May 1955, there was a rumour that Michael was going on a course to Germany, but he then wrote to his mother on 7 June, to say it had been cancelled:

'You'll have gathered that my course in Germany fell through, most disappointing. Two months flying American aircraft in the sun would have been a grand lark. Still, not to worry, perhaps I'll get another chance. They promised to keep my name in mind next time.

'On Whit Monday Maureen and I were given a ride to Redcar, a seaside town near Middlesbrough. The sun was shining brilliantly but the wind off the North Sea was so cold that I was unable to take off my coat let alone put on my bathing trunks. We took our lunch and had a picnic on the grass-covered dunes by the beach. During the afternoon we played miniature golf and on the way back stopped at a couple of country pubs, but the beer was not good and I for one had an upset tummy the next day.

'I have heard secretly on the grapevine at Group HQ that Flight Lieutenant Raw and Flight Sergeant Jones (my navigator) have been posted from Leeming. Unfortunately I couldn't find out where we were going so my friend is going to ask his friend tomorrow morning to find out for me. This means that I will probably receive a posting notice very shortly. Wouldn't that be grand?

'I am flying to a mess ball at West Raynham next Friday, Wing Commander G … is coming with me. They usually hold very good parties so we should enjoy ourselves. My uniform hasn't come back from Gieves yet so I am wondering if I dare wear my tails.

'Thursday. It's the Queen's birthday today so we have been given the day off. I was unable to finish this yesterday because they made it a full working day, whereas we normally call Wednesday afternoon, sports afternoon, and all go home. My friend's friend wasn't at home when he rang so I've not more news of the posting. I will now have to wait until Friday.

'As well as writing this letter I am listening to the Test Match [England v South Africa] commentary – England 146 for 1. Maureen has gone shopping at Ripon fourteen miles away so I've got the place to myself. She is getting me a winged collar because I found all mine were too dirty and I am thinking even more determinedly about wearing my tails at Raynham tomorrow.

'I must finish now, lots of things to do before I go out. Uniform to press, shoes to clean. I'll let you know about the posting when I have any news.'

The posting, when it finally came, was to another night-fighter unit, 29 Squadron, based at RAF Tangmere, Sussex. It was commanded by Squadron Leader E B Sismore DSO DFC, and like 85, was equipped with the Meteor NF11 night fighter. It had been the RAF's first jet night-fighter squadron and for some years it was to be the proving ground for tactics and development of the Meteor night-fighter types.

However, Michael's time with 29 only lasted until February 1956. Following a few months break, during which time he was based at RAF Hornchurch, Essex, he was head-hunted, as the following letter shows:

Imperial Defence College, Seaford House
37 Belgrave Square, SW1

23 November 1956

'Dear Raw,

'I have asked Fighter Command to set the machinery in motion to get you here as my P.A.

'The idea is for you to go as soon as convenient in order that you may get an idea of the job before I arrive.

'You might also seize the opportunity to get some aviation in. I start work on 1 January.

'I am very pleased about this, and I hope you are.

Yours sincerely,
Donald Evans.'

Air Commodore Donald Randell Evans CB DFC had been a product of RAF Cranwell and during WW2 commanded the Fighter Interception Unit (FIU), an outfit that tested night-fighter tactics and equipment. They were also part of Fighter Command's night-fighter force, and during air operations, Donald Evans had been awarded the DFC for night actions against German raiders. Later in the war he had overseen signals planning for the invasion of both Sicily and D-Day.

A group captain by 1949 he was director of operational requirements (B) at the Air Ministry, and would be at the Imperial Defence College at the start of 1957. Born in Richmond, Surrey in 1912, he had attended Wellington School, leaving for Cranwell in 1930. One would like to think the 'old boy network' was working well and the Raw boys had not been forgotten. Evans was made KBE in 1964, having been SASO at Fighter Command during 1957-58, followed by being commandant of the School of Land/Air Warfare, 1959-64 and then assistant chief of the defence staff 'til 1963. The following year he was AOC-in-C at HQ, Technical Training Command. He retired from the RAF in 1970 (air chief marshal) and died in 1975. There was a memorial service at St Clement Danes on 9 May, which Michael attended.

Michael officially left 29 Squadron in February 1956 and presumably completed his task at the IDC under Donald Evans. His next posting was to Elmendorf, Alaska, USA in September 1958. Seconded to the USAF, he flew with the 317th Fighter Interception Squadron (FIS) for a year, to August 1959. The 317th

Squadron were equipped with F-102 – Convair Delta Daggers. In the 1950s, these all-weather, delta-wing interceptor fighters equipped more than twenty-five USAF squadrons of America's Air Defense Command.

Michael's name appeared in the supplement to the *London Gazette* dated 1 January 1960, with his promotion from flight lieutenant to squadron leader. His next flying post was with 19 Squadron at RAF Leconfield, Yorkshire, commencing 4 July 1961 – as its commanding officer.

His new squadron was equipped with the ubiquitous Hawker Hunter F6, single-seat day fighter, so quite a change from two-seat night fighters. Obviously his experience on the American F-102 fighters had made a mark. The Hunter was a wonderfully sleek aeroplane and it saw long and faithful service with the RAF. It was powered by a Rolls-Royce Avon 203 turbojet that gave it a speed of over 700 mph (1,130 km/h), a ceiling of 51,500 feet (15,700 m) and a range of 1,900 miles (3,085 km). Its armament consisted of four 30 mm cannon and it could carry externally 2,000 lbs (907 kg) of bombs.

For the vast majority of fighter squadron commanders, commanding a squadron was the pinnacle of their flying days, and for Michael it was no different. Despite the enforced paperwork and the responsibility of scores of air and ground crew, it was the job to have. While the RAF system of command and control was finally honed, probably leading a fast jet squadron was the final experience of personal control of one's element. Those rising above to further high rank inevitably had to deal with politics in addition to their other duties.

In early September 1961, Michael took the squadron on detachment to RAF Skrydstrup, in Denmark for a NATO exercise called 'Checkmate'. This exercise was put in place to examine the defence and flexibility of NATO forces. 19 Squadron's role was to test their low-level interception tactics. Unfortunately, on the 12th Flying Officer D M Nicholls was killed during a low-level patrol mission when he was seen to roll over and hit the ground.

Everything in RAF squadrons in peacetime was constant practice. In October, 19 Squadron managed twenty-one operational turn-rounds, in order to give the ground crews practice in re-fuelling and re-arming aircraft as quickly as possible in as near an operational scenario as could be arranged. It also gave the pilots the chance to fire their guns in the air. Next came exercise 'Halyard' where the squadron were able to practise high-level interceptions and use cine-gun cameras in competition.

Michael had the honour of welcoming Her Majesty the Queen Mother to the base at Leconfield on 23 October, where she spent the afternoon. Several of the officers, NCOs and airmen were presented to Her Majesty when she visited the squadron coffee bar.

In October 1962 the squadron changed its equipment, starting with the first arrival of an English Electric Lightning T4, with another arriving by November. In December Michael and his flight commanders had been able to convert a number of pilots to the new aeroplane and 19 Squadron became the first RAF unit to be designated to be equipped with the Lightning F2, along with 92 Squadron, which also re-equipped with this type, and became the Leconfield Wing. Only forty-four of the F2 variant were built. Training on the new machine continued into the new year and by February 1963 most of the pilots were ready for operational conversion and the squadron now had twelve Lightning F2s on strength. By the end of June the squadron was declared partially operational.

Michael did not see the squadron become fully operational as his tour as CO came to an end on 24 July, at which time his replacement, Squadron Leader W F Page took over.

In 1965 Michael had an assignment to Norway with NATO and he had also seen service in Alaska and Germany during his time before his final posting in 1974. This final posting was one that most pilots can only dream of – to fly Spitfires with the Battle of Britain Memorial Flight (BBMF) at RAF Coltishall, Norfolk, and from RAF Coningsby, Lincolnshire, whence the flight re-located in January 1976. He often flew Spitfire P7350, a genuine former Battle of Britain machine. This Mark IIa Spitfire had been built at Castle Bromwich and had entered RAF service in August 1940, serving with 266 and 603 Squadrons. Towards the end of October 1940, she was involved in an air battle with Messerschmitt 109 fighters and being hit had force-landed. Rebuilt, she was flying again within three weeks at 37 Maintenance Unit.

Back in service P7350 went on to fly with 616 and 64 Squadrons, then with the Central Gunnery School, 57 Operational Training Unit and finally with 39 Maintenance Unit. After being sold she was with the museum at RAF Colerne until 1967 at which time she was refurbished, restored to airworthiness and given the civil register G-AWIJ so she could take part in the famous Battle of Britain film. After filming had ended she was presented to the BBMF. Since being with the Flight, being the oldest airworthy Spitfire IIa in the world, she had carried various markings representing famous squadrons or pilots.

By 1975 Michael was a flight commander with the BBMF as well as flying in various displays all over the country. Whilst flying Spitfire P7350 and also Hurricane IIc LF363[1] during these displays, he often took on board post office first day covers, which he and other famous pilots signed. They were sold later to raise money for RAF charity. Finally, in March 1976, he was given command of the BBMF, and his last flight occurred on 29 September of that year. He retired from the RAF on 28 January 1977.

After a career of thirty years with the RAF he undertook a complete change of scene and became involved in the road haulage business. Sadly, Michael Raw died early following a long illness, on 16 August 1986, aged fifty-eight.

This story has been about four brothers all of whom gave valiant service to the Royal Air Force, three in war, one in peace. The first three gave their lives for the cause of freedom from Nazi domination, leaving those who follow to carry on the traditions and courage of their native land. We must not forget their father Frederick, who equally gave gallant service with the Royal Navy in WW1. Frederick's premature death at least spared him the knowledge of the cruel fate of his three eldest boys. Sadly, their mother was left alone to cope with the certain death of a son, and to receive the equally dreadful telegrams marked 'missing in action' of two more.

We have read of a loving and devoted family, a testament to a period in British history when standards and morals were high, duty paramount, and courage unflinching. It is a story to cherish.

---

[1] Hurricane (LF363) was also used in films: Angels One Five; Reach for the Sky; One That Got Away; Battle of Britain.

APPENDICES

This story is centred around numerous letters from four pilot brothers to their mother, and her replies. The following few have been selected to give a flavour of the three eldest boys' writings during WW2, and a few official letters received.

Appendix A

John's letter to his mother dated 26 June 1940 during his training, and missing his sister's wedding.

Still don't
know.
26 6-40.

My darling Mother.
I'm so sorry I couldn't get home for the wedding. It was all I could do to get away to send a telegram, as a matter of fact when I came back I was late for a parade. We've done nothing much all the week except clean out the lato. etc., I polished all the brass, We're being posted on Monday, so they are going hell for leather to get us fully equipt. I'll send you a wire as soon as I know where we are, then you can send me all my letters. I hope there's quite a pile from Mona by now. How did the wedding go?

Who gave Trixie away? Peter? Was Uncle Jaylas there? Was there enough drink? Did it rain? Let me know all about it because I do wish I could have been there.
We were all enoculated & vaxinated the other day. Quite a lot of them passed out but it did not effect me at all. My arm just felt as if some one had hit it.
Has nanny got her teeth yet?
I'm sending home my clothes, will you please wash the pants and vests, the socks & the handkerchiefs & send them back to me. The keys belong to this case, my big case & my trunk. Will you please look after them

for me. Will you please see if my pilots log book is in the wardrobe or any where else. I'm not certain if I bought it from Ireland with me - if I did, It might be in the dining room desk. It's a small blue book with PILOTS LOG BOOK on the cover.
How was Peter, were his eyes any better. I suppose he got the goggles alright It looks as if we'll get very little leave if any, they're cut the course from 6 months to three. The weather is terrible here, I hope its better with you. Oh, you can keep the coloured silk handkerchiefs at home, I don't want them here.
Cheerio for the moment.
Lots of love
John.

Appendix B

John's letter from RAF Sealand, 12 November 1940, not long after his wedding to Mona. He is awaiting another posting and asking about brother Tony.

Appendix C

By April 1941 John is with a Hurricane squadron in Northern Ireland.

Appendix D

John's last letter home, 29 April 1941, soon after his arrival at the Central Flying School to become an instructor. He was killed the following evening.

Appendix E

Peter's letter of 9 July 1941 during his early flight training, wherein he tells his mother about flying the Tiger Moth.

Appendix F

More flying at RAF Sealand in August 1941, and his visit to his Uncle Arthur.

Telegrams- Aeronautics, Chester.
Telephone- Connah's Quay 390.

OFFICERS MESS,
ROYAL AIR FORCE,
SEALAND,
Nr CHESTER.

11·8·41.

My darling Mother,

I am so sorry I haven't written before, but I must say I have some excuse as I have been flying until 9 P.M. each evening last week and Saturday evening I flew to Manchester & stayed with Uncle Douglas until Sunday evening when I flew back just before dark. I averaged five hours flying each day last week, besides having lectures for half of each day.

I did enjoy myself at Uncle's but I can't stand that women Aunty Sandy, she hen pecks poor Uncle Arthur all the time &

I think he is pretty scared of her. He seems to spend her time criticizing other people and thinks she knows everything. She looks for scandal. She wanted to know if the story of it was wife of the officer, who flew over me, that he was going to stay with.

When I arrived on Saturday evening we all went to the local hop and Uncle Douglas & I had a job dancing with them all. There were finger of one session of fancy dancing and Aunty Sandy made such an exhibition of herself that they gave her the booby prize. "an onion." When we got back, Uncle and I had a good drink together. He dug out all his saved bottles of wines including sherry & port. He did enjoy himself telling me all about the home guard and how the army of to-day really needed the old soldiers. He

wants my khaki shorts when I change into blue. On Sunday morning I went for a swim with two of the girls. Uncle and Robin watched. In the afternoon we went down to sand pits and did some shooting (Robin Uncle & I) Uncle has tons of guns and ammunition so we had some good fun.

I am well ahead with my flying as I have completed fifty hours. I have my exams over next week and so if I get leave I should be home on about the 20th August.

If you have time would you keep an eye open for a christening present for Butch from me. I do hope you are keeping well & fit. Please write soon. Then & tons of love Peter.

Appendix G

Peter was flying from RAF Manston with 609 Squadron when he wrote on 19 November 1942, and typically he does not worry his mother about operations, calming her by saying things are pretty boring.

ROYAL AIR FORCE,
MANSTON, KENT.
19.11.42.

My darling Mother,

thank you so much for your letter. I'm so glad to hear you were enjoying your stay at Evenham. It will have made quite a change for you. I do expect Mar has told you, I am due home for leave on Monday tea time. I would very much like to stay with you for a change, but if I take it, it can't be did on account of the dogs.

The station here isn't so bad after all, but a little too far from home. We are very comfortable and there are plenty of flicks to see in Margate. Our work is very boring and very safe. I do hope you are keeping well Mum — will see you soon. — I will really make an effort to chop some logs this time.

Tons & tons of love
from Pete.

Appendix H

Still at Manston when he wrote on 6 April 1943, he tells his mother things are pretty quiet (apart from operating over France at night shooting up trains). His main concern is that one of his dogs had gone missing. He also mentions that Captain Orde had made a sketch of him.

ROYAL AIR FORCE.
MANSTON, KENT.
6.4.43.

My dear Mother,

I do hope you enjoyed your stay at Wellington. I should think it is quite some time since you were last there. How is Mike getting along? I don't suppose you saw George.

Things have been very quiet here just lately, old Jerry seems to have given up his reprisal raids following our bombers' night attacks.

We have had some very fine weather the last few days and it has been so hot I have been walking about in shirt sleeves, but to-day there is a gale blowing and it is darker.

I don't know if Mavis has told you but I am afraid Pluto wandered whilst I was last home on leave and I have not seen him since – I have told the police and searched everywhere without any results. I feel very sad about it as I liked him so much.

My portrait was drawn yesterday by Capt. Orde. It will not be my property as it is being done for Air Commodore Peake who was the first C.O. of our Squadron, but I think I will be able to get a photographed copy. I think Mavis [will] be going to see it at Capt Ord's in town, you can go

and see it with her if you like. Well Mum, I hope to get some time off soon just to pop home for a night, so I hope to be seeing you.

I do hope you are keeping well and please give my love to Trixie & David & tons & tons of love to you with a big hug from Pete.

207

Appendix I

The recommendation for Peter's award of the DFC, submitted by S/L R P Beamont, and counter-signed by G/C A G Adnams, the station commander, A/Cdr Hugh Saunders, AOC 11 Group, and finally approved by the C-in-C Fighter Command, AM Trafford Leigh-Mallory, on 29 April 1943.

RECOMMENDATION FOR HONOURS & AWARDS.

Christian Names :- PETER, EDWARD.   Surname :- RAW.

Rank :- P/O.   Present Decorations :- NIL.

Number :- 119259.   Command :- FIGHTER.   Group :- NO. 11 (F).

Unit :- No. 609 WR. Squadron. MANSTON.   Nationality :- BRITISH.

If R.A.F. - Whether R.A.F. or R...F.V.R. :- R.A.F.V.R.

Particulars of meritorious service for which the recommendation is made, including date and place.

P/O. Raw is a pilot of exceptional courage and ability, and is always eager to hunt and engage the enemy. During a period of three months he has attacked and immobilized 17 locomotives, 11 by day and 6 by night, during offensive operations over France and Belgium. Recently he has taken part in two attacks on enemy shipping, and in the face of intense Flak has severely damaged two and scored hits on two more enemy motor minesweepers. He has also damaged a FW. 190 raider.

Recognition Recommended.... Distinguished Flying Cross.

Appointment held (or Trade). Section Leader of "A" Flight.

Date.... 7/4/43.

R P Beaumont

Squadron Leader, Commanding,
No. 609 WR. Squadron, A.A.F.

COVERING REMARKS BY STATION COMMANDER.   P/O. Raw has displayed the offensive spirit to a very marked degree. He has taken advantage of every opportunity to seek out and attack the enemy.   I strongly support the recommendation of his Squadron Commander.

Date.. 9.4.43   Commanding, R.A.F., Station,
W/C.   MANSTON, KENT.

COVERING REMARKS BY SECTOR COMMANDER (IN THE CASE OF FLYING AWARDS).

Commanding, R...F., Station,

Date.............

COVERING REMARKS BY THE AIR OFFICER COMMANDING.

Recommended for the immediate Award of the D.F.C. J Saunders Arc

Commanding, No. 11 Group.

Date. 18/4/43

COVERING REMARKS BY THE AIR OFFICER COMMANDING-IN-CHIEF.

approved T Leigh-Mallory

Air Marshal,
Air Officer Commanding-in-Chief,
Commanding, Fighter Command.
ROYAL AIR FORCE.

Date. 29/4/43.

Appendix J

Peter's last letter home incorrectly dated 1 April 1944, from RAF Tangmere. Operating with 183 Squadron he was killed in action on 21 March.

[Handwritten letter on Officers' Mess, Royal Air Force, Tangmere, Sussex letterhead, dated 1.4.44]

P.S. Thank you so very much for all the lovely things you sent for me whilst I was on rest the other.

My dear Mother,

I am so very sorry to hear that Grandma is ill and you had to go to Wareham. I do hope everything is O.K. now.

I enclose a present of some sweets, which I know you will like. I expect Nan would like a packet of barley sugar and Trixie would like some so you give as you think fit. I find it very easy to get sweets and things here, so I am buying all I can.

I do hope the chickens & ducks are carrying on the good work and not giving you too much trouble.

I am kept terribly busy here looking after my flight, and I am enjoying every moment of it. I have a nice bedroom all to myself and we are exceptionally well fed. For supper we have soup, fish, meat savoury or sweet and cheese & coffee. There is a camp flick house just near the men and they change the films every two days.

I have managed to organise my leave for the 12th March which is in a few days so I will be seeing you.

Look after yourself
Tons & tons of love
To you everyone
Pete.

Appendix K

The Air Ministry letter of 21 April 1949 confirming the location of Peter's grave just over five years after his loss.

EFS
Tel. No. Edgware 2361
~~ABBEY 0411, Ext.~~

P.414980/44/S.14 Cas.C.6.

AIR MINISTRY,
~~WHITEHALL,~~
~~LONDON, S.W.1.~~

London Road,
Stanmore,
Middlesex.

21 APR 1949

Dear Mrs. Raw,

I hesitate to refer, after so long an interval, to the loss in action of your son, Flight Lieutenant P.E.Raw, D.F.C. but I feel sure you will wish to know the result of investigations undertaken by the Royal Air Force Missing Research and Enquiry Service in Holland.

These investigations show that his aircraft crashed near Virlingsbeek and that he was recovered from the wreckage by the Germans and buried in Grave 14, Plot KK, of Eindhoven (Woensel) Cemetery.

We have therefore arranged for this grave to be registered with the Imperial War Graves Commission who will ensure that it is properly cared for for all time.

I am sorry that, owing to the formidable task of our search teams, it has not been possible to let you have this information earlier, but I do hope this news, belated as it is, will afford you a measure of comfort in your sad loss.

Yours sincerely,

Rowley

Mrs. I. Raw,
10, Mount Park Crescent,
Ealing,
London, W.5.

Appendix L

Tony's letter of 16 February 1941 upon his arrival at RAF Cranwell.

L.A.C. Raw. 1287513.
No 22. Course
Cadets Mess
R.A.F College
Cranwell.
Lincolnshire.
16/2/41.

Dear Mother,

just a note to let you know I have arrived and what it is like.

It is a terrific place miles & miles of it.

When I arrived with some other chaps all togged up as you saw me leave home they sent us to the wrong place twice before they showed us to the actual college, so we walked miles with all our stuff before we came to the right place, were we annoyed.

But I am glad to be here it is marvellous, I have a room with my friend, we have a basin (hot & cold water) chest of draws, wardrobe & writing desk, one arm chair and one writing chair. A batman cleans our boots, & buttons and presses our trousers. We dine in a beautiful dining hall and have excellent food there is a bathroom outside my door. So I am quite satisfied. We have a swimming bath & two cinemas in the camp.

I think we work until 7 o'clock at night, but we can't have everything can we? I have not been up in an Oxford yet, I shall tomorrow, I looked over the cockpit today it looks very complicated we are told our weight exam is to be in 8 weeks. Has Trixie got settled in her flat yet! I hope so. It looks as if I shall

more or less stay in camp always as we finish so late and Sleaford is six miles away, but I believe we get some week-ends, if now an again so I shall be able to come home for a couple of days sometimes I hope.

I think thats about all my news for the present.

With love

from Tony.

Appendix M

By July 1941 Tony is at RAF Upper Heyford on the last lap of his flight training.
Note the reference to a meal at an Indian restaurant at such an early date.

R.A.F. STATION,
UPPER HEYFORD,
OXFORD.

TELEPHONE: BICESTER 197.

8th July 1941.

Dear Mother,

I hope you are keeping well. I had a marvelous time this last weekend. I was lucky enough not to be on night flying on Saturday night (although Tony Hibell was) and on Sunday night when I was supposed to be on night flying, it was cancelled.

So I was able to be off for Saturday afternoon and evening and also Sunday afternoon and evening. I had to fly on Sunday morning. We spent nearly all our time on the river, the weather was beautiful. We had supper in an Indian restaurant called the "Taj Mahal", and eat curry. Boy was I full. Peter was looking very well, was he not?

TELEPHONE: BICESTER 197.

and then had some lunch, as I was night flying last night, I have only 12 hours more night flying to do in this flight, so I hope with a bit of luck to get home some time next weekend.

I went for a little flip over to Evesham in a Hampden yesterday afternoon. I circled uncle's house a few times and picked out grandma's house but I did not see anyone. I was rather high at about 15,000 ft.

How are Butch & Mrs Butch getting on well I hope. I hope the nurse has learnt to drive Daff by now.

I am going into Bicester tonight to get the tickets of health once to...

I expect he is very pleased to start flying. I was going to try and get a flip in a Hampden (as I forgot to tell you I went solo in a Hampden the other day) but it could not be arranged. It was a lucky thing on Sunday morning because I was supposed to be flying and practising right circuits and landings on the aerodrome. I thought of going to Evesham and shooting up Ellie at Evesham, but I resisted the temptation. However Peter said someone came over very low in a Hampden and zoomed about so he waved to him, he said he was sure it was me. Well on Monday morning myself and five others who were flying on Sunday morning were interrogated by the flying commander to find who was low flying over Evesham on Sunday morning because he had been reported. I was alleged that I had not gone over there. The chap was not caught. I have just had a rice also and a...

I hope this beautiful weather keeps up for when I get my next leave in a month's time. I really will get my week or more, there is no danger of being called back like Ellie was. My wrist is quite better now it has healed up nicely.

Well grandma has much. Tony will have to be finishing now.

With love

from

Tony.

Appendix N

When writing this letter in January 1942, Tony is in the middle of his tour of night operations, but says little about it to his mother. He is far too concerned with her accepting that he and Agnes want to marry.

ROYAL AIR FORCE STATION,
NORTH LUFFENHAM,
OAKHAM,
RUTLAND.

17.1.42.
Friday evening.

My darling Mother,

thank you so much for your letter. Yes, as you say being a Flight Lieutenant has made things very busy for me and to tell you the truth I am a bit lost at the moment and seem to do nothing but work all the time from morning till night, but I will get used to it and have it buttoned up soon. Things are really worse than they should be because I am really doing the work of the Squadron Leader's work because he is detached.

I thought I was coming up to see you today because we had the day off (at least everybody else did) but I was suddenly told (just as I thought I had finished) that I was officer in charge of night flying. I have just got a rest and am spending it writing to you.

I have been thinking this over for the last month or so Mum and feel I must tell you, I want to get married to Agnes. I can see your face now Mum, I expect you will say oh! becoming a flirt has gone to his head but I can promise you I had been thinking about it for a long time before I ever heard of promotion, this has only made things easier for me but I have no doubt have begged your permission sooner or later white still a flo.

Honestly Mum it is the one thing that will make me really truly happy; I sometimes think that I just can't go on nipping up to London every now and again and then having to leave wondering if I will ever see her again; you may think that sounds absurd but I have been in enough jams now to know how bad it is, and I feel I want to take my happiness while I still have the chance.

I am young I ● know, very young, but I have plenty of responsibilities now, worthy of twice my age and I will show you that I can tackle them. It is not a thing that I am rushing into, I have thought it out for a long while and know my mind perfectly. Agnes and I suit each

other perfectly and we would be very very happy together, I have never been more certain of anything before.

I can't really see why there should be such a fuss about it, having a wife is a responsibility, a great responsibility I know, I am not forgetting that for one moment, but I am certain that I can manage and will never regret having a wife to look after.

I think that you urge me to wait a bit longer, say a year or so, but I feel I just can't wait that long it seems an age and anything may have happened by that time.

I have talked it over with Agnes and she says that nothing would make her happier but she does not want to urge me on in the least bit; she says she wants me to do just what I feel is right and will not encourage me and yet will not discourage me, she will marry me at any time I wish.

I have written to Peter and told him all about it but I have not had a reply yet; I don't know what he will have to say.

I hope this is not too much of a shock to you Mummy, I wanted to get home to talk it out with you (as I well at the first opportunity) but it is difficult to get home when I want to now; If you refuse me permission I shall be unhappy and I know I shall never be happy until I am married in the meantime or till the war is finished and lets me lead a normal normal life, and even if the war were to finish I would still want to marry her now, how ever young we are.

Well good night Mother darling I am going to bed now, I am hoping for a favourable answer soon. All my love to you

Tony.

Give my love to Trixie.
Love Tony.

Appendix O

Tony's letter of 15 February 1942. He mentions briefly that he had been involved on the attack upon the German battleships in the English Channel three days earlier – and saving up for his forthcoming marriage.

Appendix P

Tony's last letter to his mother dated 30 August 1944. He mentions he is unlikely to get his leave for another fortnight, but he was killed in action on 11 September, before his leave came along.

The Officers mess.
R.A.F.
Upwood.
Ramsey.
Huntingdon.
30/8/44.

My Dearest Mother,
    I received a letter from you which was forwarded from Ossington, it was written about a month ago.
    As you will see I have moved to another aerodrome, it is only across the road from the other place about four miles away.
    It looks as if I shall not be getting my leave for another fortnight some where about the 20th September I think. I am still not sure though. If it that is so I wonder if Mike could go back to school a bit late. When do the results of his school out come out. Bruce flew down to town the other day and gave Pat a bit of a fright at about Park I think. I whistled down the next evening to see him (it quite easy to get to town from here but I arrived late and had to catch an early train back so I stayed in town with Bruce. Keep it under your hat because I had just come back from seeing Agnes and she would take a dim view. I phoned Eve

from Ossington the other day. She is moving into the digs next door to hers as the woman she is with is going into hospital. She is hoping to live near them soon. The trunk call system is terrible here. I have not been able to get one through since I have been here.
    Well I hope all is well at Evesham.
    I hope I shall be able to see you soon. Maybe the war will finish before my leave but I doubt it. The doodle bugs might though.
    Tons of love to all at Evesham. Toe.

Appendix Q

The telegram reporting Tony's loss dated 12 September 1944. Cruelly it was addressed to his already dead brother Peter, who was still noted as his next of kin.

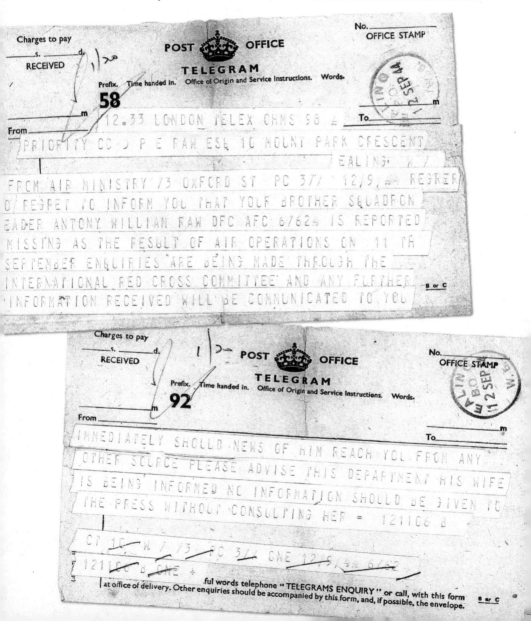

Appendix R

Another telegram three months later – again to Peter – dashes hope that Tony might have survived.

POST OFFICE TELEGRAM

14 ... 9.20 LONDON TELEX PTY CC
OF YTDAY 80

PRIORITYCC P E RAW ESQ 10 MOUNT PARK CRESCENT
EALING W 5 =

FROM AIR MINISTRY 77 OXFORD ST W 1 PC 231
11/12/44 DEPLY REGRET TO ADVISE YOU THAT ACCORDING
TO INFORMATION RECEIVED THROUGH THE INTERNATIONAL

POST OFFICE TELEGRAM

P. E. Raw 10, Mount Park Cres W.5

RED CROSS COMMITTEE YOUR BROTHER A/S/L ANTONY
WILLIAM RAW DFC AFC IS BELIEVED TO HAVE LOST HIS
LIFE AS THE RESULT OF AIR OPERATIONS ON 11/9/44
STOP THE AIR COUNCIL EXPRESS THEIR PROFOUND
SYMPATHY STOP HIS WIFE HAS BEEN INFORMED STOP
UNDER SECRETARY OF STATE STOP + 1818 A +

Appendix S

Even by 10 April 1945 Air Ministry was still writing to Peter, this letter presuming Tony's death on 11 September 1944.

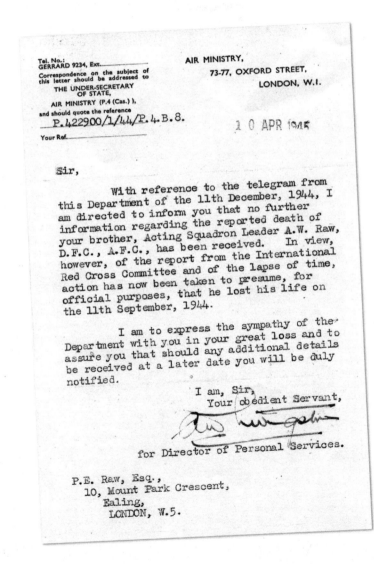

Tel. No.:
GERRARD 9234, Ext.

Correspondence on the subject of this letter should be addressed to

THE UNDER-SECRETARY
OF STATE,

AIR MINISTRY (P.4 (Cas.)),

and should quote the reference

P.422900/1/44/P.4.B.8.

Your Ref.

AIR MINISTRY,
73-77, OXFORD STREET,
LONDON, W.I.

1 0 APR 1945

Sir,

    With reference to the telegram from this Department of the 11th December, 1944, I am directed to inform you that no further information regarding the reported death of your brother, Acting Squadron Leader A.W. Raw, D.F.C., A.F.C., has been received. In view, however, of the report from the International Red Cross Committee and of the lapse of time, action has now been taken to presume, for official purposes, that he lost his life on the 11th September, 1944.

    I am to express the sympathy of the Department with you in your great loss and to assure you that should any additional details be received at a later date you will be duly notified.

            I am, Sir,
            Your obedient Servant,

           for Director of Personal Services.

P.E. Raw, Esq.,
   10, Mount Park Crescent,
     Ealing,
     LONDON, W.5.

Appendix T

Three months later Tony's death was confirmed with his place of burial – still addressed to Peter.

Tel. No. :
GERRARD 9234, Ext._____

F C Rawdee.

Correspondence on the subject of
this letter should be addressed to
THE UNDER SECRETARY
OF STATE,
AIR MINISTRY [P.4 (Cas.)],
and should quote the reference

P.422900/1/44/P.4.B.4.

Your Ref._____

AIR MINISTRY
73-77 OXFORD STREET
LONDON, W.1

3 July, 1945.

Sir,

I am directed to refer to a telegram despatched to you from this Department dated 11th December, 1944, and to inform you with regret that a further report has now been received from the International Red Cross Committee, Geneva, which unhappily confirms that your brother, Acting Squadron Leader Antony William Raw, D.F.C., A.F.C., Royal Air Force, lost his life on the 11th September, 1944, and adds that he was buried in Grave No.2 in the south left Row 4 in the East Military Cemetery, Gladbeck, Germany.

In conveying this information, I am again to express the deep sympathy of the Department with you in your bereavement.

I am, Sir,
Your obedient Servant,

[signature]

for Director of Personal Services.

P.E.Raw, Esq.,
10, Mount Park Crescent,
Ealing,
W.5.

Appendix U

Four years later, in May 1949, Peter is again written to by Air Ministry. This letter informs the family that Tony's remains had been moved to the British Military Cemetery at Reichswald Forest, NW Germany.

BNT

Tel. No.   Edgware 2361
ABBEY 3171, Ext...............

Ref: P.422900/44/S.14.Cas/M.R.2.

AIR MINISTRY, (Casualty Branch)
WHITEHALL,
LONDON, S.W.1.
London Road,
Stanmore,
Middlesex.

1 3 MAY 1949

Dear Mr. Raw,

I am writing to let you know that a report has been received from the Royal Air Force Missing Research and Enquiry Service, stating that your brother, Squadron Leader A.W. Raw, D.F.C., A.F.C., has been moved to the British Military Cemetery at Reichswald Forest, situated three miles South West of Cleve, North West Germany, where he now rests in Grave 1, Row D, Plot 35

This reburial is in accordance with the policy agreed upon by His Majesty's and the Commonwealth Governments, that our fallen should be transferred to specially selected military cemeteries where the graves will be maintained, for all time, by the Imperial War Graves Commission.

A photograph of the cross marking the grave should reach you shortly.

Yours sincerely,

JKRawley

P.E. Raw, Esq.,
10, Mount Park Crescent,
Ealing,
W.5.

Appendix V

The Ministry of Pensions' letter to Mrs Raw dated 9 December 1948 confirming that it was now possible to issue her with Memorial Scrolls to commemorate her late sons.

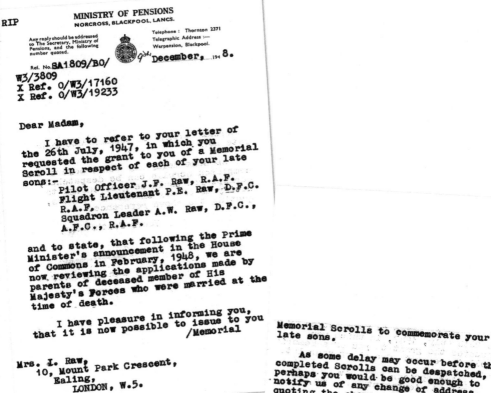

RIP

MINISTRY OF PENSIONS
NORCROSS, BLACKPOOL, LANCS.

Any reply should be addressed to The Secretary, Ministry of Pensions, and the following number quoted.

Telephone : Thornton 2371
Telegraphic Address :—
Warpension, Blackpool.

Ref. No. SA1809/BO/ ....9th December, ...194 8.

W3/3809
X Ref. O/W3/17160
X Ref. O/W3/19233

Dear Madam,

I have to refer to your letter of the 26th July, 1947, in which you requested the grant to you of a Memorial Scroll in respect of each of your late sons:-
Pilot Officer J.F. Raw, R.A.F.
Flight Lieutenant P.E. Raw, D.F.C. R.A.F,
Squadron Leader A.W. Raw, D.F.C., A.F.C., R.A.F.

and to state, that following the Prime Minister's announcement in the House of Commons in February, 1948, we are now reviewing the applications made by parents of deceased member of His Majesty's Forces who were married at the time of death.

I have pleasure in informing you, that it is now possible to issue to you /Memorial

Mrs. I. Raw,
10, Mount Park Crescent,
Ealing,
LONDON, W.5.

Memorial Scrolls to commemorate your late sons.

As some delay may occur before the completed Scrolls can be despatched, perhaps you would be good enough to notify us of any change of address, quoting the above reference.

Yours faithfully,

I Thompson.

for Secretary.

INDEX

Adnams, GC A G 83
Amor, PO H D F 64
Astbury, FO J G 61
Atkinson, FL J A 60, 61, 62, 66-69, 74, 82, 139

Baillie, Paul 6
Baldwin, FL J RT 64, 69
Balfour, H H 24
Baness, Sgt J H H 123, 127
Bankes-Williams, J M 173
Barker, WO W T 75
Barnard, Mr & Mrs C 11
Barrett, GC J F T 112
Barte, Oblt W 119fn
Baxter, Sgt 108
Beamont, WC R P 6, 63, 64, 71, 72, 76-8, 82, 85, 86, 88, 147-8, 172, 208
Beck family, 44, 51, 54, 55, 57, 118
Beck, Molly van der, 57
Bell, Dave 6
Bennett, Alycia 6
Bere, Brig I de la 192
Betts, Sgt 189, 190
Black, Geo 80
Blake, J D 36
Blanco, Adj A 71, 76

Boulting, PO J 63
Broad, Hubert 88
Brooks, PO A & Mrs M 146
Bucklebury, Peggy 22, 46

Cameron, FO M 72, 76
Carrie, Sgt W G 117, 120
Chandler, Sue 6
Chapman, L 101
Clarke, Mrs 101
Clements, H E 188
Cobb, Sgt H 117, 120
Cole, K H 160
Cole, SL R B 8, 36, 106, 126, 142, 144, 149, 154-160, 169-70, 171, 172, 173, 177, 186, 189, 191
Cole, Lt-Col R F 154
Cole, Mrs 159
Corner, W 19
Cribbin, 106

Dancklefsen, T 22
Darley, SL H S 59
Davies, John 9
Day, Graham 6
de Broke, GC Lord W 67
de Goat, WC W 77, 86, 87

de Moulin, FO C 78
de Saxce, Sgt-Ch A C 67
De Selys, FL J 61, 67, 72
Denny, P F 100
Dopere, PO R 62
Douglas, ACM Sholto 59
Dring, SL W 90
Drummond, J F 20
Dundas, FS Lord 130

Ebben, J 95
Epsley, Richard 6
Erskine-Hill, David 6
Evans, AC D R 196
Evans, FO G 65, 72, 74, 76

Falconer, WC D B 145, 149
Fejfar, FL S 9
Fenton, S G D 26, 29, 40, 103fn, 138, 193
Flash, Martin 6
Foster, Richard 9
Fredericks, J B 93, 95
Frost, B 19

Gardner, SL J R 189, 190
George, Cpl R B A 188
Gibbs, Anna 6
Gilbert, PO H 60, 66